75 CLASSIC RIDES
WASHINGTON

Mike McQuaide

75 CLASSIC RIDES
WASHINGTON
THE BEST ROAD BIKING ROUTES

THE MOUNTAINEERS BOOKS

THE MOUNTAINEERS BOOKS
is the nonprofit publishing arm of The Mountaineers, an organization founded in 1906 and dedicated to the exploration, preservation, and enjoyment of outdoor and wilderness areas.

1001 SW Klickitat Way, Suite 201, Seattle, WA 98134

© 2012 by Mike McQuaide

First edition, 2012

Manufactured in China
Distributed in the United Kingdom by Cordee, www.cordee.co

Copy Editor: Joan Gregory
Cover, Book Design, and Layout: Heidi Smets, heidismets.com
Layout: Heidi Smets, heidismets.com
Cartographer: Pease Press Cartography
Photographer: All photographs by the author unless otherwise noted.

Cover photograph: *The upper reaches of the Mount Baker Highway*
Frontispiece: *Mount Shuksan and the road to Artist Point*

Library of Congress Cataloging-in-Publication Data
McQuaide, Mike.
    75 classic rides, Washington : the best road biking routes / Mike McQuaide. — 1st ed.
        p.   cm.
    Includes index.   4870 5171   6/12
    ISBN 978-1-59485-506-1 (ppb)
1. Cycling—Washington (State)—Guidebooks. 2. Washington (State)—Guidebooks. I. Title. II. Title: Seventy-five classic rides, Washington.
    GV1045.5.W2M47 2012
    796.609797—dc23
                        2012002266

ISBN (paperback): 978-1-59485-506-1
ISBN (e-book): 978-1-59485-507-8

CONTENTS

LEGEND

- →- -	Featured Route	■	Building/Point of Interest
⋯→⋯	Route on Bike Path	▲	Campground
S	Start/Finish	ⵊ	Picnic
F	Finish	▲	Peak
↱	Turnaround Point	) (	Pass
═⟨5⟩═	Interstate Highway	▬	Dam
═⟨395⟩═	US Highway	⚏	Bridge
═⟨542⟩═	State Highway	⇒)(⇐	Tunnel
= =·123·= =	Forest Road		Park
═══════	Secondary Road	⌐ ¬	Boundary
=======	Unpaved Road		Water
- - - - -	Other Bike Path		

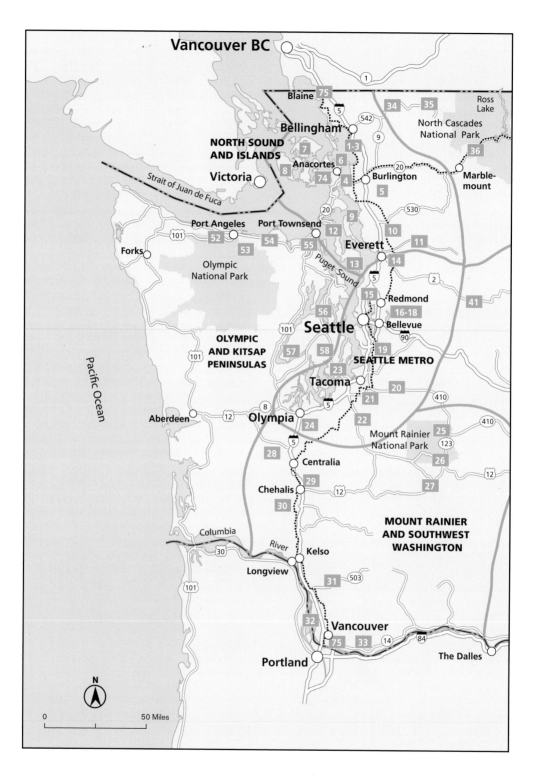

Vancouver BC

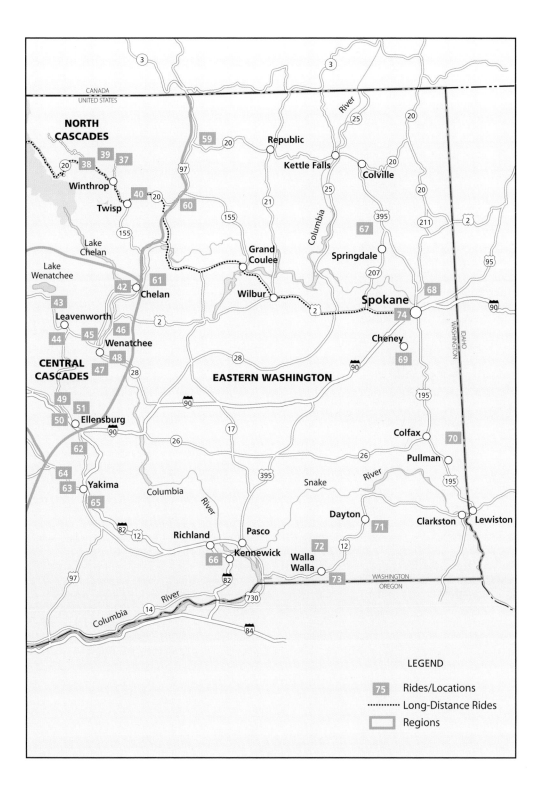

CANADA
UNITED STATES

NORTH CASCADES

3

3

(20)

(25)

(20)

59
20

Republic

Kettle Falls

River

Colville

(20)

(20)

38
39
37

(20)

Winthrop

40
(20)

Twisp

(155)

60

(97)

(21)

(25)

(395)

(20)

(211)

2

Lake Chelan

(155)

(155)

67

(95)

Lake Wenatchee

Grand Coulee

Springdale

Columbia

(207)

42
61

Chelan

Wilbur

2

68

(90)

43

2

Spokane
74

Leavenworth

(28)

Cheney

IDAHO
WASHINGTON

44
45
46

Wenatchee

69

48

CENTRAL CASCADES

47

(28)

EASTERN WASHINGTON

(90)

(195)

49
51

(90)

50
Ellensburg

(90)

(17)

Colfax

70

62

(26)

(26)

Pullman

(195)

64

63

Yakima

Columbia

River

(395)

Snake

River

65

82
(12)

Richland

Pasco

Dayton

71

Clarkston

Lewiston

66

82

Kennewick

Walla Walla

72

(12)

73

WASHINGTON
OREGON

(97)

Columbia

River

14

84

730

LEGEND

75   Rides/Locations

.... Long-Distance Rides

☐   Regions

9

RIDES AT-A-GLANCE

NO.	RIDE	DIFFICULTY RATING	DISTANCE (IN MILES)	ELEVATION GAIN (IN FEET)	TIME (IN HOURS)	POINTS OF INTEREST
1	Tour de Whatcom	Strenuous	106.8	2860	5 to 8	Small towns, Mount Baker views, farmland, Birch Bay
2	Colony Road Loop	Moderate	36	1875	2 to 3	Chuckanut Dr., island views, Lake Samish
3	Samish Island–Bow Hill Loop	Moderate	56	2535	3 to 4.5	Chuckanut Dr., water views, Lake Samish
4	Skagit (Mostly) Flats	Easy	51.2	1240	2.5 to 4	Water views, La Conner, no hills
5	Big Lake–SR 530–Darrington Loop	Strenuous	104.4	3535	5.5 to 8	Small towns, rural roads, Skagit River
6	Fidalgo Island–Mount Erie Leg Shredder	Strenuous	50.6	3460	3 to 5	Water views, Mount Erie, Anacortes Community Forest Lands
7	Orcas Island 50-Miler	Strenuous	50.7	5850	3.5 to 6	Mount Constitution, Moran State Park, farmland, artsy town
8	San Juan Island Crisscross	Strenuous	53.9	3880	3 to 5	Historical parks, water views, artsy town, whales
9	Camano Island Loop	Moderate	40.8	2675	2 to 3.5	Artsy island riding, state parks
10	Arlington–La Conner–Stanwood Loop	Moderate	62.1	1245	3 to 5.5	Flatland riding, La Conner, island views
11	Granite Falls–Barlow Pass (Mountain Loop Highway)	Moderate	61.6	3270	3 to 5.5	Mountain views, forested riding, mining history
12	Tour de North Whidbey	Strenuous	59.7	4015	3.5 to 6	Coastal riding, rolling hills, Coupeville
13	South Whidbey Island	Strenuous	54.9	4100	3 to 5	Coastal riding, rolling hills, Langley
14	Snohomish–Granite Falls–Monroe Loop	Moderate	47.6	1630	2.5 to 4	Centennial Trail, rural riding, Lake Roesiger
15	Kenmore–Sultan Loop	Strenuous	69.7	2950	3.5 to 6	Paved trail, rural riding, Snoqualmie and Skykomish rivers
16	Super Torture Metric Century	Very Strenuous	58.2	6250	4 to 7	Urban riding, hills galore, city sights
17	Marymoor–Monroe–Snohomish Loop	Moderate	51.4	1935	2.5 to 4	Small towns, Snoqualmie Valley, farmland
18	Flying Wheels 42-Miler	Moderate	42	2120	2 to 3.5	Marymoor Park, Snoqualmie River valley, farmland

NO.	RIDE	DIFFICULTY RATING	DISTANCE (IN MILES)	ELEVATION GAIN (IN FEET)	TIME (IN HOURS)	POINTS OF INTEREST
19	Renton–Black Diamond	Moderate	43.2	1895	2 to 3.5	Cedar River Trail, rolling countryside, Black Diamond Bakery
20	Enumclaw–Ravensdale	Moderate	41.1	1575	2 to 3.5	Farmland, Flaming Geyser State Park, bakery
21	Sumner–Carbonado–Orting	Strenuous	69.7	3430	3.5 to 6	Small towns, Mount Rainier views, Carbon River canyon
22	Orting–Eatonville (Daffodil Metric Century)	Strenuous	61.9	2735	3 to 5.5	Mount Rainier views, small towns, rural riding
23	Gig Harbor–Port Orchard Loop	Strenuous	56.1	3620	3 to 5	Artsy town, rural riding, water views
24	Olympia–Rochester–Rainier	Strenuous	66.2	1930	3 to 6	Small towns, rural roads, paved trails
25	Sunrise–Cayuse–Chinook	Very Strenuous	54.4	5850	4 to 7	Two big climbs, Mount Rainier views
26	Paradise from Stevens Canyon	Strenuous	42.3	4950	3 to 5	Paradise, Mount Rainier National Park, Grove of the Patriarchs
27	Packwood–Paradise–Stevens Canyon Loop	Very Strenuous	78.2	6030	4.5 to 7	Longmire, Paradise, Mount Rainier National Park
28	Rochester–Route 6 (Adna) Loop	Moderate	46.7	1470	2.5 to 4	Rural riding, farmland, small towns
29	Centralia–Rainier–Littlerock Loop	Strenuous	66.9	1620	3 to 6	Flatland prairie, rural riding, small towns, paved trail
30	Adna (Chehalis)–Vader Loop	Moderate	48.3	1800	2.5 to 4	Rural riding, farmland, small towns, world's largest egg
31	North Clark County–Tumtum Mountain	Very Strenuous	73.9	6025	4 to 7	Small towns, Tumtum Mountain, national forest
32	Ride Around Clark County	Strenuous	65	3010	3 to 6	Urban and rural riding, farmland, Columbia River views
33	Washougal and East, Hillz 'n' More	Very Strenuous	63.5	5225	3.5 to 6	Hills, urban and rural riding, Columbia River views
34	Everson to Mount Baker	Very Strenuous	99	7210	5.5 to 8	Artist Point, Nooksack River, national forest
35	Mount Baker Hill Climb	Strenuous	47.8	4850	3 to 4.5	Artist Point, national forest, Nooksack Falls
36	Newhalem to Winthrop (one-way)	Very Strenuous	73	6425	4.5 to 7	Washington Pass, North Cascades scenery, Methow Valley
37	Winthrop to Andrews Creek and Back	Moderate	46.8	2260	2.5 to 4	National forest riding, Chewuch River

NO.	RIDE	DIFFICULTY RATING	DISTANCE (IN MILES)	ELEVATION GAIN (IN FEET)	TIME (IN HOURS)	POINTS OF INTEREST
38	Winthrop to Washington Pass via Mazama	Strenuous	61	4750	3.5 to 5	Methow River, forest riding, Washington Pass
39	Winthrop to Falls Creek	Strenuous	44.5	3920	2.5 to 4	National forest road riding, Chewuch River, mountain views
40	Tour de Okanogan	Very Strenuous	103.8	6060	5 to 9	Loup Loup Pass, Columbia and Methow rivers
41	Skykomish to Leavenworth (one-way)	Strenuous	51	4215	2.5 to 5	Stevens Pass, Western Washington becomes Eastern Washington, Wenatchee River
42	Chelan–McNeil Canyon	Strenuous	40.4	4100	3 to 5	Steep climb to Waterville Plateau, Lake Chelan, Columbia River
43	Leavenworth–Plain Loop	Moderate	38.4	1490	2 to 3.5	Wenatchee River, Icicle Ridge views, forest riding
44	Icicle Road	Easy	28	1945	1.5 to 3	Icicle Creek, Alpine Lakes Wilderness, Wenatchee River
45	Wenatchee–Leavenworth 'n' Back	Moderate	46.3	3000	2.5 to 4	Orchard riding, Wenatchee River, behind-the-scenes view of Leavenworth
46	Wenatchee–Chelan–Wenatchee	Very Strenuous	101.4	4440	5 to 9	Columbia River, Lincoln Rock, orchards, Lake Chelan
47	Joe Miller Road–Wenatchee Heights Loop	Strenuous	26.2	2960	2 to 3.5	Steep climb, Columbia River, orchards, Wenatchee Heights
48	Badger Mountain–Waterville Loop	Strenuous	50	4700	3 to 5.5	Waterville Plateau, Wenatchee Valley views, Columbia River
49	Ellensburg to Leavenworth (Blewett Pass) (one-way)	Strenuous	57.6	3570	3 to 5	Kittitas Valley views, wind turbines, Blewett Pass
50	Manastash Metric Century	Moderate	63.4	2225	3.5 to 6	Yakima, Cle Elum, Manastash Ridge views
51	Lion Rock Climb	Strenuous	44.8	4350	3 to 4.5	Steep climb, national forest road riding, Kittitas Valley views
52	Port Angeles–Lake Crescent–Joyce Loop	Moderate	42.3	3555	2 to 3.5	Lake Crescent, Olympic National Park, Strait of Juan de Fuca
53	Hurricane Ridge	Very Strenuous	37.6	5100	2.5 to 4	Washington's biggest climb, stunning views
54	Sequim–Spit Loop	Easy	33.3	1425	1.5 to 3	Dungeness Spit, Sequim rain shadow, water views
55	Port T to Fort F	Moderate	47	2600	2.5 to 4	Port Townsend, water views, historic fort
56	Silverdale–Port Gamble–East Bremerton	Moderate	51	3270	2.5 to 4	Port Gamble, Poulsbo, water views

NO.	RIDE	DIFFICULTY RATING	DISTANCE (IN MILES)	ELEVATION GAIN (IN FEET)	TIME (IN HOURS)	POINTS OF INTEREST
57	Belfair State Park–Tahuya–Seabeck Loop	Strenuous	64.7	3260	3.5 to 6	Rural riding, water and mountain views, Tahuya State Forest
58	Burly Burley–Key Peninsula Route	Moderate	48.8	3185	2.5 to 4	Rural roads, forests, small towns, water views
59	Tonasket–Oroville–Palmer Lake Loop	Very Strenuous	79.5	5925	4.5 to 8	Okanogan highlands, Similkameen River, small towns, orchards
60	Omak Lake–Nespelem Loop	Very Strenuous	79.2	5275	4.5 to 8	Omak Lake, Colville Indian Reservation, Columbia River, Disautel Pass
61	Chelan–Bridgeport–Mansfield	Very Strenuous	93.4	4220	5.5 to 9	Columbia River riding, small towns, Waterville Plateau
62	Yakima Canyon	Moderate	45.5	2110	2 to 3.5	Yakima Canyon gorge, wildlife, recreational sites
63	Naches Heights–Wenas Lake	Moderate	46.5	2490	2.5 to 4	Orchard and vineyard riding, Naches River, Wenas Valley views
64	Yakima–Whistlin' Jack	Strenuous	72.8	2650	3.5 to 5.5	Naches and Yakima rivers, Wenatchee National Forest
65	Konnowac Pass Loop	Easy	28.5	885	1.5 to 3	Orchard riding, Union Gap, Yakima Valley views
66	Kennewick–Clodfelter Road Loop	Moderate	45.9	2375	2.5 to 4	Columbia River, wheat fields, Horse Heaven Hills
67	Springdale–Hunters–Chewelah Loop	Very Strenuous	81.7	5235	4.5 to 8	Camas Valley, Roosevelt Lake, forests, small towns
68	Mount Spokane	Strenuous	55.7	4740	3 to 6	Big climb, stunning views, forested mountain road
69	Cheney–Rock Lake Loop	Strenuous	76.1	3160	4 to 6.5	Forests, farmland, the Palouse, wildlife refuge
70	Palouse to Steptoe Butte	Strenuous	64.4	3275	3 to 5.5	Steptoe Butte State park, rural riding, the Palouse
71	Dayton–Bluewood Ski Area	Moderate	43.4	3320	2.5 to 4	Forested mountain road, Blue Mountains
72	Walla Walla–Middle Waitsburg Loop	Moderate	40.6	2550	2 to 3.5	Rolling hills, wheat fields, Waitsburg
73	Kooskooskie–Cottonwood Ride	Moderate	38.7	1780	2 to 3	Blue Mountains, forested mountain road, wheat fields
74	Anacortes to Spokane (one-way)	Very Strenuous	331.6	18,650	3 to 6+ days	North Cascades, Columbia River, Eastern Washington, Grand Coulee Dam, Spokane
75	Blaine to Vancouver (one-way)	Very Strenuous	329.7	10,830	3 to 6+ days	Water and mountain views, Seattle metro area

ACKNOWLEDGMENTS

A huge shout-out of thanks, gratitude, and appreciation to the numerous bike clubs, bike shops, and cycling-obsessed individuals who helped me tremendously, by offering route suggestions and/or their camaraderie and good cheer. Space won't allow me to mention all of them here...but what the heck, I'll give it a try anyway. Here goes!

John Clark and Scott Young (the Titanium Cowboys), Kathleen McQuaide and dog Roy, Brian Cantwell at the *Seattle Times*, Paul Haskins and Alaine Borgias at *Adventures NW Magazine*, Charlie Heggem, Steve Noble, Tammy Bennett, Glenn Gervais, Daryl Smith, Erik DeRoche, Steven VanderStaay, Ryan Rickerts, Mark Rhode, Jim Clevenger, Chris Behee, Bob Stanton, Sue Duffy, Tracy Erbeck, Mark Peterson, Rick Schranck, Joe Schretenthaler, Tom Meloy, David Longdon, Carol Noble-Potts, Mark Clausen, Corrina Marote, G. Todd Williams, Scott Rittscher, Luke Britton, Jim Kelly, Christopher Fast, Justin Yeager, Karla Segale, Lap Lai, Mike Sirott, Andy Kindig, Jake Maedke, Carla Andringa, Mark Thomas, Craig Langley, Ray Pope, Geoff Swarts, Kimberley Brittain, Charlie Naismith, Narayan Krishnamoorthy, and Jeff Beilfuss.

Also, Joe Brown and Julie Muyllaert at Methow Cycle and Sport; the folks at Kulshan Cycles, Fanatik Bike Co., Fairhaven Bike and Ski, Jack's Bicycle Center, Revolution Cycles, Mount Baker Bicycle Club, Vancouver Bicycle Club, Spokane Rocket Velo Cycling Club, Cascade Bicycle Club, Cascade's High Performance Cycling Team, Port Townsend Bicycle Association, Tri-City Bicycle Club, Seattle International Randonneurs, Skagit Bicycle Club, B.I.K.E.S. Club of Snohomish County.

Thanks too to the fine folks at The Mountaineers Books for helping make this book a reality.

Lastly, a special note of thanks and love to Jen and Baker McQuaide for putting up with the countless hours I spent away from home, crisscrossing this grand Evergreen State.

With your purchase of this book, you also get access to our easy-to-use, downloadable cue sheets:

» Go to our website: www.mountaineersbooks.org/75ClassicWashington.
» Download a complete set of mileage cue sheets for all 75 rides in this book.
» When you open the document on your computer, enter the code "WARideQ" when prompted.

It's our way of thanking you for supporting The Mountaineers Books and our mission of outdoor recreation and conservation.

Artist Point, at the end of the Mount Baker Highway >

INTRODUCTION

The trite, hackneyed sentiment expressed in the worn-out sentence "(Noun) offers something for everyone" is unoriginal and almost always a lie.

Except for here.

I can honestly say that road cycling in Washington State offers something for everyone. Truly.

For riders who love hills and riders who hate hills; riders who love paved urban pathways and riders who want to feel as though they are in the middle of nowhere; riders who love steep, endless climbs into mountains and onto high plateaus and riders who love roller-coaster ups and downs along rivers, lakes, and Puget Sound. Yes, my friends, road cycling in Washington offers something for everyone.

This book is for adventurous cyclists who love all types of riding. Folks who mount their trusty two-wheeled steeds anticipating an exciting, perhaps challenging, ride that explores all that an area's terrain has to offer. Riders who, when they dismount their bikes at the end of a ride, want to feel as though they've been somewhere, seen something amazing and, if they're a bit worn out after having done so, all the better.

Being fast, skinny, and/or the owner of a mega-expensive, micro-weight bike is not a requirement for enjoying the routes in this book. But a passion for cycling is, and for immersing oneself in some truly spectacular settings throughout Washington State.

Now, about the routes. When compiling my list, I contacted dozens of cycling clubs, bike shops, and skinny-tire-obsessed folks like myself seeking input on Washington classic road rides. And boy, did they come through! I was looking for fun, oft-challenging routes mostly in the 40- to 80-mile range. I particularly wanted to include an area's signature physical features—a renowned climb like Lion Rock or Badger Mountain, a cool

stretch along the Columbia River or past Grand Coulee Dam, or through the wheat fields of the Palouse. Many route descriptions include a "Variations" feature for shortening or lengthening the rides, or for avoiding a particularly steep hill.

SAFETY

Yes, bikes are subject to the same laws as cars—ride on the right side of the road, stop at stop signs, yield when signs say yield, and so on—but here's something I've noticed. Cars are much bigger than bikes, they don't always see bikes, and truth be told, some drivers aren't too happy about cyclists when they do see them. So follow all laws, use proper hand signals when turning, always wear bright colors even if you ride during the day only, and wear flashing lights if you're likely to be riding at dusk, dawn, or at night. I always carry a cell phone and wear an identification bracelet as well. Always ride defensively. I think it's great for riders to know their rights and privileges, but it's not realistic to assume that drivers know what those are, let alone follow and respect them. It is up to you to keep yourself safe.

Here are some smart tips that hopefully are common sense.

» Always wear a helmet. According to the National Highway Traffic Safety Administration, helmets are effective in preventing 85 percent of head and brain injuries; they're also required in King County and Seattle and in many places throughout Washington State.
» Make sure your bike is safe to ride—tires inflated to recommended air pressure, brakes in proper working order, chain lubricated. Make sure there aren't spokes that appear loose and that, in general, nothing is

loose or rattles. Fix or tighten what you can yourself, otherwise use this as an opportunity to establish a relationship with your local bike shop and to learn a few things about how to fix your bike.

» If you're going to ride when it's dark, make sure you have adequate lighting to ensure that you can be seen—use flashing headlights and taillights. (In fact, for night riding, Washington State law requires a white front light that's visible for 500 feet and a red rear reflector that's visible for up to 600 feet.) Wear bright clothing and/or reflective gear such as arm or leg bands.

» Always ride with traffic, never against it.

» Follow all traffic signals, signs, roadway markings, and the like.

» Yield to pedestrians.

» When riding alongside parked cars, be on the watch for opening doors; ride far enough out that an open door can't hit you.

» Communicate with drivers by making eye contact at intersections; use hand signals when turning and stopping. Don't ride erratically.

» As much as you can, be aware of what is going on behind you. Helmet- and eyeglass-mounted mirrors are recommended.

» Use hand signals when turning, slowing, or stopping. Very simply, extend your right hand to the right when turning right, extend your left hand to the left when turning left. When slowing, extend your left hand down with palm facing back toward traffic.

» When approaching railroad tracks, try to cross them at as close to a 90-degree angle as you can in order to avoid catching a tire.

Just north of Winthrop, some equine cycling fans jostle to get a better view of passing riders.

Riders getting high at Mount Rainier National Park (David Longdon)

» When riding on urban trails such as the Burke-Gilman (in Seattle), remember that cyclists must yield to pedestrians. Use a bell or your voice to signal to pedestrians and other riders when passing.

Some final thoughts: Although the overwhelming majority of riders I know and see are respectful and law-abiding, there are those who do bonehead things such as taking up whole lanes by riding three abreast or cruising through red lights. Behavior like this gives all of us a black eye and only serves to foment the vitriol that a certain segment of the population already has toward us.

I try to ride like a bike ambassador, someone who disproves the notion that all riders are chuckleheads. I obey signs and traffic lights. If I'm on a winding road and I can see that it's clear ahead but know the car behind me can't see, I give them the all-clear sign to pass when it's appropriate. And when I do so, I almost always get a wave of appreciation (as opposed to a middle-finger salute). Hopefully, my riding behavior earns a few checkmarks in the pro-cycling column for all us two-wheelers. My hope is that if we as cyclists ride respectfully, drivers will drive respectfully.

THE BIKE

First off, you'll need a bike in good working order. If you haven't ridden yours for a while, take it to your local bike shop for a tune-up. As for the bike itself, the options (and price ranges) are limitless. So are the opinions. There's been a definite move toward carbon as the material of choice, but just as there are music lovers who are still vinyl devotees, there are those who swear that only steel is real. Then there's titanium, aluminum, aluminum (or steel) and carbon mix—that is, an aluminum (or steel) frame with carbon fork. These days, most bikes have at least a carbon fork. Carbon is strong, lightweight, and renowned for its vibration-damping abilities. An entire frame of the stuff offers a dreamy ride, wrote this all-carbon advocate.

Recent years have also seen a movement toward compact cranks. That is, the chainrings are smaller—with 34 and 50 teeth as opposed to what used to be the standard 39 and 53—which helps when climbing hills and mostly does away with the need for a triple-chainring crank. There are more options now for rear cassettes, too, which helps when it comes to climbing. SRAM recently came out with its Apex group, which offers a 32-tooth cog. Combine that with a 34-tooth chainring and the near 1-to-1 ratio should enable one to climb up the side of the Space Needle.

When choosing a bike, test ride a bunch. Get a feel for what's comfortable. More and more manufacturers are offering bikes in what they call the plush or endurance category. These boast the same material and components as more race-focused bikes but have a more relaxed geometry. That is, the rider sits a little more upright, which some find more comfortable on longer rides. These bikes might have beefed-up forks or seat stays for more road-vibration damping as well.

Be sure the bike fits you too. Sure, bargains can be found online, but if you're relatively new to cycling (or getting back into it after time away), try to work with your local shop. They'll ensure you get a bike that fits and most will even custom fit it to your body once you've purchased it. I've heard too many stories of folks who couldn't pass up a killer deal online for a bike that was just a little too big and who ended up injured and thus unable to ride.

THE RIDER

Here are some items that you either need or that make cycling a whole lot more enjoyable.

» An ANSI- or similar agency-approved helmet.
» Padded bike shorts make longer rides more comfortable and thus the cycling experience more enjoyable.
» A good seat goes a long way in the comfort department as well.
» Clipless pedals improve your pedaling efficiency while conserving energy and, like good bike shorts, improve the whole ride experience as well. Compared to riding with the old-school strap-and-toe clips, they're like legalized doping.
» More than likely, your bike comes with a water bottle cage or two so be sure to fill your bottles up before you head out.
» Bike gloves help absorb road chatter as well as protect your palms in case of a fall.
» Cycling jersey with pockets in the back for carrying gear.
» Wraparound sunglasses.
» Arm warmers, leg warmers, depending on temperature and personal preference.
» Lightweight compact rain jacket or vest that you can stick in your back pocket.
» Energy bars or some kind of compact food item that fits in a pocket or seat pack.
» Extra tube, mini-pump or CO_2 inflator, tire levers, and a bike-specific multi-tool that enables you to make minor repairs. Before heading out, be sure you know how to use these tools and to do basic repairs, such as fixing a flat tire. Many bike clubs and shops (such as REI) offer basic (and advanced) repair classes, always a good idea.
» A seat pack (or similar) to carry necessary gear.
» Sunscreen.
» Cell phone.

This sign near La Conner captures what it's like to ride at the front of a pack.

HOW TO USE THIS BOOK

I have given you 75 classic road routes that offer something for everyone. Pick one, or ten, or twenty. Venture out. Explore. Challenge yourself. Challenge your friends. But in all cases, have fun!

If you're just starting out or are returning to cycling after some time away, it's a good idea to ride with other people. Hook up with a club or stop in at your local bike shop and ask about regular group rides. Many places have weekend or midweek group rides that usually follow the same route. Seattle's Cascade Bicycle Club offers organized group rides every day of the week somewhere in the Puget Sound area. These are great for camaraderie, learning how to ride in a pack, and for

building your speed and endurance.

Many of these rides have turnaround spots along the way, so you can ease into them. Perhaps try to make it 15 miles your first time. After you feel comfortable with that, extend your ride to 20 miles, or try that big hill you've always avoided. As with most things, building endurance and gaining confidence in your bike-handling and hill-climbing skills takes time, patience, and consistent effort. But it sure it feels good and it's a huge confidence boost when you see progress.

ORGANIZATION

The rides in this book are organized into seven regions: North Sound and Islands, Seattle

Metro, Mount Rainier and Southwest Washington, North Cascades, Central Cascades, Olympic and Kitsap Peninsulas, and Eastern Washington. Two cross-state descriptions provide the general outline for rides across Washington. For details for the west–east route, refer to the North Sound and Islands, North Cascades, and Eastern Washington sections. For north-to-south details, see North Sound and Islands, Seattle Metro, and Mount Rainier and Southwest Washington, disregarding the Mount Rainier part.

RIDE DESCRIPTIONS

Each ride description includes an information block that summarizes the particulars of the route: its difficulty level, ride time, distance, and elevation gain. After that are a description of the road/riding conditions, driving directions to the starting point, a detailed route description (including, in some cases, route variations), mileage log, route map, and elevation profile.

A route's **difficulty** is, of course, subjective. What one rider may find lovely and easy, another might find arduous and miserable. Basically, however, the rating takes into account two things: distance and elevation gain.

Easy rides are those on the short side— fewer than 40 miles. Although they may include some climbing, it won't be relentless

Moderate rides are mostly in the 40- to 60-mile range. These routes include some climbing, but nothing that will turn non-climbers into noncyclists. Scenic 50-milers through the Skagit Flats are examples of moderate rides.

Strenuous rides are either in the 60- to 80-plus mile range, or are rides that target a region's signature climb and/or hilly area. Climbing to Artist Point on Mount Baker or to Mount Rainier's Paradise Lodge from the east side might be shorter than 50 miles, but these rides will include sustained climbs that

are 10 and 13 miles long respectively. That earns a "Strenuous" rating in my book.

Very Strenuous are strenuous rides on steroids. They're long. They're hilly. Often they also showcase several of an area's signature climbs. Along with a number of one-day rides rated "very strenuous," this book includes two multi-day cross-state routes—a north-to-south route and a west-to-east route—which both definitely qualify as very strenuous.

Like difficulty, a route's ride **time** is subjective. In general, I estimated riding time anywhere between 10 and 20 miles per hour—fully anticipating that some people will react with "Are you crazy—there's no way anyone could ride this route that fast!?!" and others will respond with "Are you crazy—there's no way anyone would ride this route that slow!?!"

Distance and **elevation gain** were measured using a combination of GPS-based bike computer and its corresponding website. Maps and elevation profiles were generated using the same tools.

A NOTE ABOUT SAFETY

Safety is an important concern in all outdoor activities. No guidebook can alert you to every hazard or anticipate the limitations of every reader. Therefore, the descriptions of roads, trails, routes, and natural features in this book are not representations that a particular place or excursion will be safe for your party. When you follow any of the routes described in this book, you assume responsibility for your own safety. Under normal conditions, such excursions require the usual attention to traffic, road and trail conditions, weather, terrain, the capabilities of your party, and other factors. Keeping informed on current conditions and exercising common sense are the keys to a safe, enjoyable outing.

—*The Mountaineers Books*

NORTH SOUND AND ISLANDS

Among the routes you'll find here are ones that roll through rural Whatcom County and the popular Skagit Flats. Island routes too, which, along with their scenic beauty and winding, low-traveled roads, offer punchy, roller-coaster hills. You'll find smaller, bike-friendly cities such as Bellingham as well as quaint historic enclaves that offer plenty of opps for café stops.

1 TOUR DE WHATCOM

Difficulty	Strenuous
Time	5 to 8 hours
Distance	106.8 miles
Elevation Gain	2860 feet

ROAD CONDITIONS: Mix of rural country roads with low traffic and in-town riding on bike lanes. A couple stretches of state highway have the potential for high-speed traffic, but there are ample road shoulders.

GETTING THERE: From I-5, take exit 250 in Bellingham and head west on Old Fairhaven Pkwy. (SR 11) for 1.4 miles into Fairhaven, Bellingham's southside neighborhood. Turn right on 12th St. and in 0.1 mile, left onto Harris Ave. Continue for two blocks to 10th St. and turn right. The Village Green, an open space used for gatherings, fairs, and outdoor movies, is on the right. Free on-street parking is available throughout Fairhaven.

This is the century route (plus a little more) for the Tour de Whatcom, a popular charity ride held annually in late July. It's aptly named, for along with passing through just about every incorporated city and census-designated burg in the county, it serves as a sampler of many of

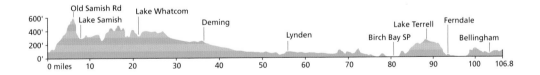

< *With snowy Mount Baker reflected in Padilla Bay, a bald eagle keeps watch over the March Point shoreline.*

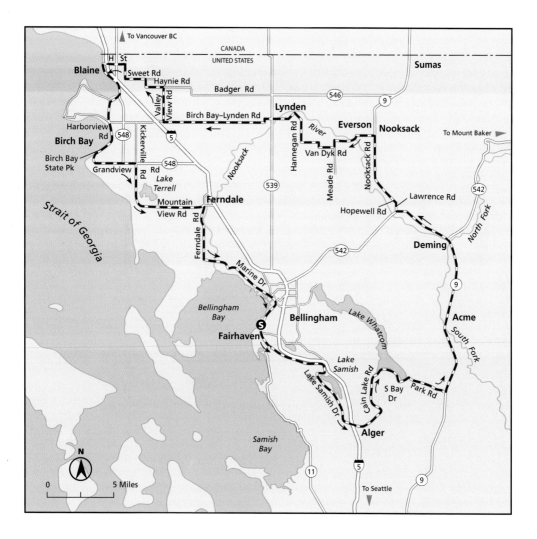

the county's rich natural wonders. Stunning Cascade and Mount Baker views, far-reaching pastureland and berry fields, and the northern Puget Sound shoreline are just some of what you'll see on this ride. It's also surprisingly flat and is a terrific route on which to try for your fastest century.

From Bellingham's Fairhaven district, head south via Chuckanut Drive for about a mile before turning left onto Old Samish Road. Following the lower flank of Chuckanut Mountain, the road rolls and climbs a bit—the most climbing of the route—for about 4 miles before topping out at the route's high point (a whopping 560 feet!), above the Lake Samish basin. Following a fun descent and half the lakeside loop, the route heads south for a quick foray into northern Skagit County. Though light on traffic, the roads are a little rougher and more chip-sealy here. Foray done, the route heads north and back into Whatcom County for a few more lakes—Cain, Reed, and the southern reaches of Lake Whatcom, the county's main water supply.

Leaving the big lake behind, head east via Park Road for 3 miles to State Route 9. Turn left and (wind willing) begin the fast section of the route. Now heading north, the next 10-plus miles of State Route 9 are flat, glass-smooth with a nice wide shoulder, and, given that it runs smack down the middle of a valley floor with a couple of foothills on either side, almost always the recipient of a killer tailwind from the south. Some of the route's best views are along this section. Mount Baker peeks over the foothills and Alps-like Twin Sisters to the east, and along with passing through rich pasture- and farmland, the middle 30 miles roughly follow the Nooksack River.

After heading west for 4 miles on the high-traffic Mount Baker Highway (State Route 542)—ample shoulder but watch for rumble strips and general roadside detritus—

regain State Route 9 and resume your north-trending, tailwind-aided breakaway for almost 7 miles to Nooksack. Though State Route 9 isn't quite as smooth nor the shoulder quite as wide, the traffic volume is much lower here. You need to watch out for tractor tire dirt clods as much as anything out here.

At Nooksack, a small town of under a thousand, turn left and begin heading due west, first passing through slightly less tiny Everson, then Lynden, and eventually Blaine at the northwest corner of the contiguous United States. Along the way, it's about 25 miles of mostly scenic rural roads through berry fields and farmland with little tree cover. If the wind is from the west, you'll know it. Besides Bellingham, Lynden, which

A winter group ride passes through Birch Bay State Park.

you pass through at the 55-mile mark, is the biggest town on the route and offers numerous places to stop for drinks, eats, and restrooms.

Once in Blaine, turn left and head south along the eastern rim of Drayton Harbor and enjoy views across the water to Semiahmoo Spit and White Rock, BC, beyond. Count the great blue herons, which crisscross the skies here by the dozens or hang out on rocks and pilings out on the mudflats. Just south, after a quick 1.5-mile inland jaunt, do the same thing at Birch Bay, home to Birch Bay State Park (restrooms available).

From here it's a series of perpendicular county roads—one heading south, followed by one east, and so on—including a fun fast descent into Ferndale, where once again, you meet up with the Nooksack River. In fact, you follow the Nooksack for 5 miles before it hands you off to Bellingham Bay, which you follow for about the last 6 miles of the route, through downtown Bellingham and back into Fairhaven.

MILEAGE LOG

0.0	From Fairhaven, roll onto 12th St. heading south.
0.5	Left onto Chuckanut Dr. (SR 11).
1.7	Left onto Old Samish Rd.
6.2	Right onto Lake Samish Dr.
7.0	Bear right onto N. Lake Samish Dr.
7.9	Cross bridge; road becomes W. Lake Samish Dr.
9.2	Bear left, still on W. Lake Samish Dr.
10.8	Continue through four-way intersection; road becomes Lake Samish Rd.
13.3	Continue through intersection; road becomes Alger–Cain Lake Rd.
16.1	Road becomes Cain Lake Rd.
18.2	Right onto Lake Whatcom Blvd. (Also called S. Bay Dr.)
21.8	Right onto Park Rd.
24.7	Left onto SR 9.
36.0	Left onto SR 542 (Mount Baker Hwy.).
40.6	Right onto Lawrence Rd. (SR 9).
43.8	Left onto Hopewell Rd. (still SR 9).
44.4	Right onto Nooksack Rd. (still SR 9).
47.0	Left onto SR 544 (Main St.) in Nooksack; follow west through Everson.
48.1	Bear left and cross Nooksack River via Everson Rd. (still SR 544).
48.8	Right onto Meade Ave. (Becomes Nolte Rd.)
50.6	Right onto Van Dyk Rd.
51.7	Right onto Holz Rd.
52.0	Left onto Van Dyk Rd.
53.4	Right onto Hannegan Rd.
55.6	Left onto Front St.
57.4	Through Guide Meridian intersection; road becomes Tromp Rd.
58.2	Right onto Birch Bay–Lynden Rd.
65.6	Right onto Valley View Rd.
68.0	Left onto Haynie Rd.
69.4	Right onto Stadvold Rd.
69.8	Bear left onto Sweet Rd.

71.6	Right onto Odell Rd.
72.5	Left onto H St.
73.8	Left onto Peace Portal Dr. in Blaine.
75.6	Right onto Bell Rd. (Becomes Blaine Rd.)
76.4	Right onto Drayton Harbor Rd.
77.4	Left on Harborview Rd.
78.9	Left onto Birch Bay Dr.
80.1	Right at intersection; continue on Birch Bay Dr.
80.9	Enter Birch Bay State Park.
82.1	Bear left out of park onto Point Whitehorn Rd.
82.7	Left onto Grandview Rd.
85.7	Right onto Kickerville Rd.
87.8	Left onto Rainbow Rd.
88.8	Bear left onto Mountain View Rd. (Becomes Main St. in Ferndale.)
93.7	Right onto 1st Ave.
93.9	Left onto Cherry St.
94.0	Right onto Front Ave. (Ferndale Rd.)
97.7	Left onto Marine Dr. (Becomes County Ln., then Bancroft Rd.)
99.9	Left onto Marine Dr. (In Bellingham, becomes Eldridge Ave., then W. Holly St.)
104.0	Right onto Bay St.
104.1	Left onto W. Chestnut St.
104.4	Right onto N. State St. (Becomes Boulevard St., S. State St. and 11th St.)
106.7	Right onto Mill Ave.
106.8	Finish at starting point in Fairhaven.

2 COLONY ROAD LOOP

Difficulty	Moderate
Time	2 to 3 hours
Distance	36 miles
Elevation Gain	1875 feet

ROAD CONDITIONS: Bike lanes within Bellingham city limits; narrow shoulder on Chuckanut Drive; chip-seal surface in Skagit County can be a little chattery.

GETTING THERE: From I-5, take exit 253 in Bellingham and follow Lakeway Dr. west into downtown Bellingham. In 0.3 mile, Lakeway becomes E. Holly. Follow for 0.4 mile to Railroad Ave. and turn left. On-street parking is available here and/or a block ahead at the Market Square Depot (except Saturdays during the farmers market).

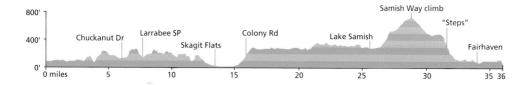

800'
400'
0'

Chuckanut Dr

Larrabee SP

Skagit Flats

Colony Rd

Lake Samish

Samish Way climb

"Steps"

Fairhaven

0 miles   5   10   15   20   25   30   35 36

Truly a favorite among Northwest Washington riders, this route boasts renowned Chuckanut Drive, one of the state's grandest roadways. Stunning views of the San Juan Islands and Olympic peaks are on offer as well as close-ups of Chuckanut Mountain, which rises nearly 2000 feet right out of the waters of northern Puget Sound. Add to this the 1890s old town vibe of Bellingham's Fairhaven district, some fun rolling hills past a couple of lakes, one challenging but not devastating hill, and you've got the makings of a truly nice, variety-is-the-spice-of-life ride.

Begin by heading south along State Street/Boulevard Street toward Fairhaven. The sparkling waters on your right are Bellingham Bay, with Lummi Island in the foreground and Orcas Island peeking over just beyond. A pleasant gravel trail parallels this section to your right (waterside) and eventually meets up with this route a couple miles south in Fairhaven. If you're concerned that your skinny road tires might not survive that surface, stick to the street, which offers a bike lane.

Speeding down Chuckanut Drive across the fast Skagit flatlands

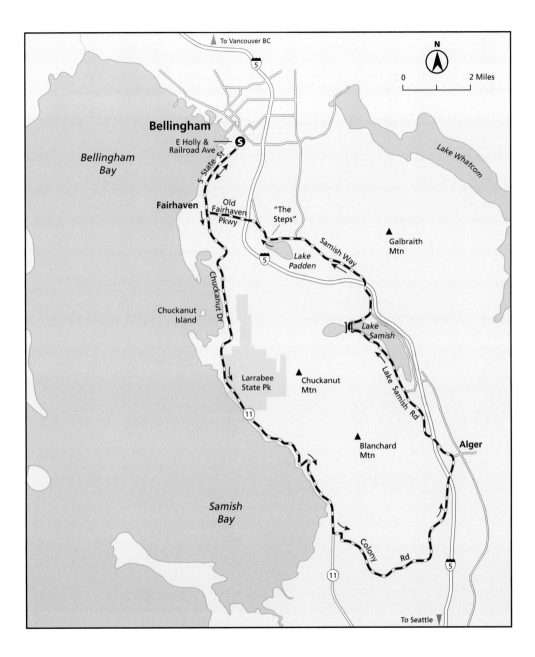

South through Fairhaven, continue straight (with a slight slant to the left at a well-signed intersection) and voila!—you're on Chuckanut Drive. For the next 11 miles, the rolling, up-and-down, cliff-hanging roadway snakes its way along the lower flanks of Chuckanut Mountain. Thankfully, the road is smooth, but because it is so scenic, it can get crowded with cars (and motorcycles), especially on nice weather weekends. The optimal times to ride this stretch are weekdays or early weekend mornings. And while most of this stretch is plenty wide, there are a couple narrow spots farther south where it will be best to keep 'er moving and get through as quickly as possible.

Along with passing Larrabee State Park (Washington's first state park) and a couple high-end eateries worth a return visit when you're not so spandex-clad, Chuckanut Drive offers several pullouts where you can enjoy the spectacular vista.

Once past Chuckanut Mountain, the road immediately flattens out. You can thank the Skagit River floodplain for that. But you only get to enjoy it for a mile or so because soon enough the route leaves Chuckanut Drive and heads inland, up Colony Road, which climbs gradually for the next 5 miles. A true country road, the surface is a bit chip-sealy and can be rough. But, as is usually the case when roads get chip-seal choppy, traffic is sparse. Still, watch for tractors and other farm equipment in this rural patch of Skagit County.

Shortly after crossing under Interstate 5, the route passes a service station-espresso-mini-mart offering replenishment as well as restrooms. Soon you'll reach the rolling 6-mile loop around Lake Samish, a popular swimming, boating, and water-skiing hole. This route does about two-thirds of the loop before heading up and out of the Lake Samish basin on the route's one sustained climb. You'll gain 460 feet over the next 3.5 miles with the first half of the climb being the toughest.

From here, it's mostly all downhill—some of it steep, especially a section known as "The Steps," just past Lake Padden Park—for the next 4 miles back to Fairhaven. Continue north again on Boulevard and State streets to complete the route in downtown Bellingham.

MILEAGE LOG

0.0	From downtown Bellingham, head south on Railroad Ave. Left onto E. Maple St.
0.1	Right onto N. State St. (Becomes Boulevard St., S. State St., 11th St., 12th St.)
2.7	Left onto Chuckanut Dr. (SR 11).
13.9	Left onto Colony Rd.
20.5	Left onto Lake Samish Rd.
23.0	Continue through intersection with Lake Samish Dr.; road becomes W. Lake Samish Dr.
25.3	Cross bridge; road becomes N. Lake Samish Dr.
26.4	Bear left at intersection; road becomes Lake Samish Dr.
27.4	Cross over I-5; road becomes Samish Wy.
30.6	Left onto Wilkin St. (just past Lake Padden Park entrance).
31.1	Right onto 40th St.
31.2	Left onto Broad St.
31.3	Right onto 38th St.
31.4	Left onto Harrison St.
31.5	Right onto 37th St.
31.6	Left onto South Ave.
31.7	Right onto 36th St.
31.8	Left onto Connelly Ave. (Becomes Old Fairhaven Pkwy.)
33.3	Right onto 12th St. (Becomes 11th St., S. State St., Boulevard St., N. State St.)
35.5	Bear right onto N. Forest St.
35.9	Left onto E. Maple St.
36.0	Right onto Railroad Ave. where you started.

3 SAMISH ISLAND–BOW HILL LOOP

Difficulty	Moderate
Time	3 to 4½ hours
Distance	56 miles
Elevation Gain	2535 feet

ROAD CONDITIONS: Bike lanes within Bellingham city limits, narrow shoulder on Chuckanut Dr., Skagit County chip seal can be a little chattery.

GETTING THERE: From I-5, take exit 253 in Bellingham and follow Lakeway Dr. west into downtown Bellingham. In 0.3 mile, Lakeway becomes E. Holly. Follow for 0.4 mile to Railroad Ave. and turn left. On-street parking is available here and/or a block ahead at the Market Square Depot (except Saturdays during the farmers market).

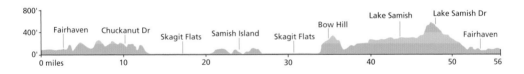

Because of its flat and lightly traveled roads, with their long straightaways and terrific views to the surrounding mountains, the Skagit Valley is a popular destination for cyclists. This route gives you a taste of the valley—along with a visit to off-the-beaten-path Samish Island—before heading inland to the rolling country roads along the Whatcom-Skagit border.

From downtown Bellingham, roll south along Bellingham Bay via State Street/Boulevard Street into and through Fairhaven, Bellingham's charming southside neighborhood. Just south, bear left onto Chuckanut Drive, a scenic 11-mile roller coaster that winds along the lower, wooded, western flank of Chuckanut Mountain. A lot of stunning island, water, eagle 'n' heron, and kite-boarder views here, but keep your eyes on the road, tough as that may be. Throughout, the road shoul-

der isn't very wide and in a couple places, it's downright nonexistent; get through those sections quickly. Luckily, several pullouts afford opportunities to stop and bask in the stunning island and water views.

Just past the Chuckanut Manor, a popular restaurant and bed-and-breakfast, pop out of the trees and after crossing the Samish River bridge, enter the northern reaches of the Skagit Flats. You'll know it because it's, well, flat. Pancake flat and just a smidge above sea level. Get into time trial mode here or, if there's a stiff wind from the south, tuck in behind another rider and let her do the work. After 2 miles heading due south, turn right and make your way toward the tiny Skagit enclave of Edison (pop. 133) and boyhood home of Edward R. Murrow. There's a terrific bakery here and some cute antique shops—it's sort of an abbreviated version of La Conner—as well as a fun

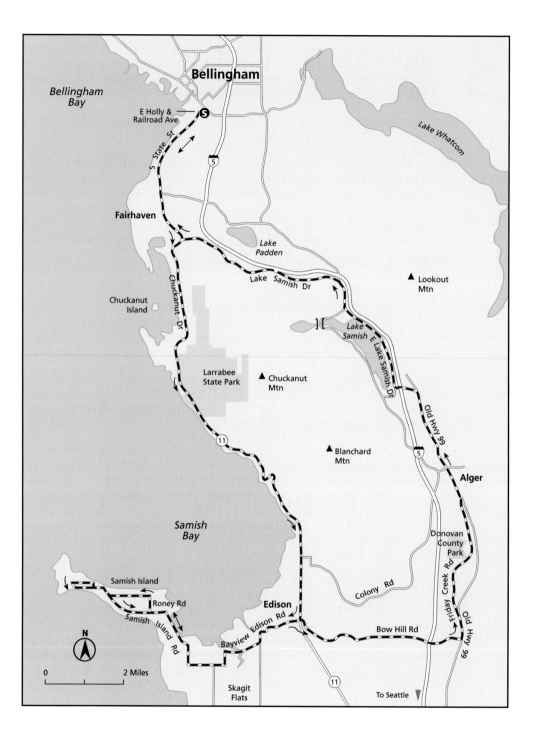

Bellingham Bay

Bellingham

E Holly &
Railroad Ave

Lake Whatcom

S State St

Fairhaven

Lake Padden

Lake Samish Dr

Lookout Mtn

Chuckanut Dr

Chuckanut Island

Lake Samish

E Lake Samish Dr

Larrabee State Park

Chuckanut Mtn

Old Hwy 99

11

Blanchard Mtn

5

Alger

Samish Bay

Donovan County Park

Samish Island

Roney Rd

Samish Island Rd

Colony Rd

Edison

Friday Creek Rd

Old Hwy 99

N

Bayview Edison Rd

Bow Hill Rd

0   2 Miles

Skagit Flats

11

To Seattle

S-curve that makes you feel as though you're going much faster than you really are.

Continue trending west, then south, then west some more toward the West 90, so named because of the abrupt 90-degree turn. It's a popular bird-watching spot—everything from eagles to harriers to herons to snowy owls draw birders here by the thousands during the winter months. The Fish and Wildlife parking lot with porta-potty makes it a handy stop for cyclists. Following the turn north, you soon approach the wooded gem that is Samish Island, which is more islandish than true island. (It's been connected to the mainland since dikes were built in the 1930s.) There's a quiet, unhurried pace up here along with 6 miles of rolling hills, a sort of figure eight that takes in just about the entire 4-square-mile island.

After Samish Island, return the way you came, through Edison and back to Chuckanut Drive. This time go straight on Bow Hill Road and soon approach the quad stinger known as Bow Hill, a 14 percent uptick that's thankfully fairly short (about a half mile).

Just ahead, cross under Interstate 5—a convenience store on the right offers cold drinks and munchies; the casino on the left the opportunity to lose money—and descend steeply down to Old Highway 99 where you turn left. And left again just ahead onto Friday Creek Road, a truly pleasant (save for the chip-seal surface) shaded foray along a creek

of the same name. This segment shows up on the route of the Skagit Bicycle Club's Spring Classic, which stages a rest stop at Donovan County Park, about three-quarters of a mile ahead on the left. Restrooms available.

Continue north to tiny Alger where you bear left back onto Old Highway 99 and make for Lake Samish. The road doesn't have much of a shoulder, but thankfully, with Interstate 5 paralleling it not much more than a stone's throw away, it doesn't have a lot of traffic. Just ahead bear left as 99 becomes Nulle Road, crosses back under the freeway, and cozies up along Lake Samish. For this route, turn right onto E. Lake Samish Drive, which follows the scenic lake for about 2.5 miles before climbing out of the basin. (A variation is to add a few miles by continuing straight and turning right onto W. Lake Samish Drive; together they form a loop around the lake.)

It's a mile-long climb, not too terrible, especially since this route cuts the climb in half by turning left onto Old Samish Road. From there, it's a zooming, mostly downhill and flat 5 miles back into Fairhaven. The only exception is the right-hand turn back onto Chuckanut Drive, which greets you with a steep half mile pitch. From there, retrace your pedal strokes back to where you started.

Note: Segments of this route appear on both the Mount Baker Bicycle Club's Chuckanut Century and the Skagit Bicycle Club's Spring Classic.

MILEAGE LOG

0.0	From downtown Bellingham, head south on Railroad Ave.; quick left onto E. Maple St.
0.1	Right onto N. State St. (Becomes Boulevard St., S. State St., 11th St., 12th St.)
2.7	Left onto Chuckanut Dr. (SR 11).
15.6	Right onto Bow Hill Rd. (Becomes Main St., Farm to Market Rd.)
17.0	Right onto Bayview Edison Rd.
18.0	Bear left to stay on Bayview Edison Rd. (Becomes Samish Island Rd.)
21.3	Right onto Roney Rd.
21.8	Left onto Halloran Rd.
22.8	Continue straight onto Samish Island Rd.
23.3	Right onto Wharf St.

23.4	Left onto Marshall Rd.
24.0	Left onto Samish Point Rd.
24.1	Left onto Samish Island Rd.
25.1	Right to stay on Samish Island Rd. (Becomes Bayview Edison Rd.)
30.9	Left onto Farm to Market Rd. (Becomes Main St., Bow Hill Rd.)
34.0	Bow Hill. (Steep!)
36.8	Turn left onto Old Hw 99 N. (Burlington-Alger Rd.)
37.6	Left onto Friday Creek Rd.
39.7	Donovan County Park. Restrooms.
41.4	Bear left onto Old Hwy 99 N. (Becomes Nulle Rd.)
44.1	Right onto E. Lake Samish Dr.
46.6	Bear right onto Lake Samish Dr.
47.5	Left onto Old Samish Rd. (Lake Samish Dr.)
52.0	Right onto Chuckanut Dr. (SR 11).
53.3	Bear right as Chuckanut Dr. becomes 12th St. (Becomes 11th St., S. State St., Boulevard St., N. State St.)
55.5	Bear right onto N. Forest St.
55.8	Left onto E. Maple St.
56.0	Right onto Railroad Ave. and return to start.

4 SKAGIT (MOSTLY) FLATS

Difficulty	Easy
Time	2½ to 4 hours
Distance	51.2 miles
Elevation Gain	1240 feet

ROAD CONDITIONS: The busier roads have wide shoulders, those without tend to be lightly traveled with the exception of Farm to Market Rd. Chip-seal surface and some rough patches of pavement on Skagit County roads.

GETTING THERE: From I-5, take exit 231 in Burlington. Head north on SR 11 (Chuckanut Dr.) for 7 miles to Bow Hill Rd. Turn left and follow for about a mile to Edison Elementary School. Park here or look for street parking in the small town of Edison, a couple of hundred yards west.

< Drafting behind another rider can cut down on the workload by up to thirty percent.

Because it's largely sans hills, the Skagit Valley—that amorphous area bordered by the Chuckanut Mountains to the north, northern Puget Sound to the west, Interstate 5 to the east, and Fir Island to the south—is popular with cyclists, especially the hill-phobic variety. This 51-miler does its best to be as flat as possible, gaining only about 1300 feet, much

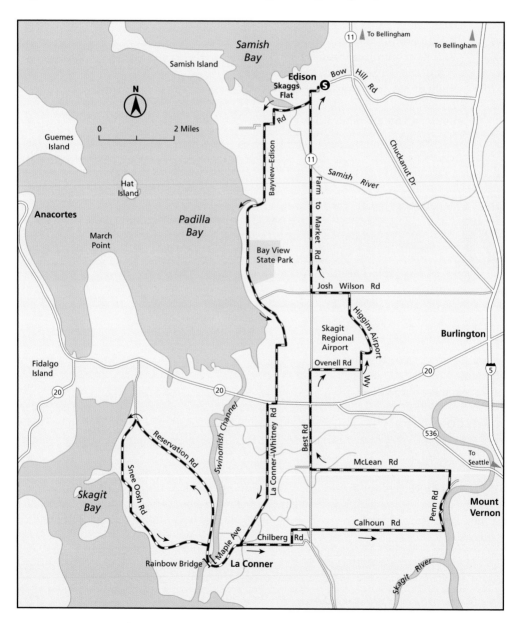

of that on a 10-mile loop around the Swinomish Reservation, across the channel from La Conner. (Skip that part and you have a 40-miler that gains only about 800 feet.)

While this flatland route is certainly scenic—with tulips, swans and snow geese, Cascade views, La Conner's quaintness, and the Padilla Bay ride-by—much of the route is treeless. And given its proximity to the Puget Sound trough between the Cascades and Olympics, it can be windy, especially in the afternoons when a south wind almost always blows through.

From the parking lot follow the sweeping road curve west through charming Edison (doesn't take long) and head south and out of town. Bear right onto Bayview–Edison Road and enter the open, windswept flatlands of the aptly named "Skagit Flats." It's a harrier's paradise out here with raptors of all stripes and feathers scouring the marshy fields and farmlands. It's also a chip-seal paradise, so don't be surprised that even though it's pancake flat, it's not pool-table smooth.

After about 2 miles, Bayview–Edison Road takes a hard left and begins a 4-mile, due-south, mostly straight-arrow push toward Bay View State Park, following the shoreline of Padilla Bay. Along the way, it offers up one of the route's few hills. Across the bay is Fidalgo Island, the refineries of March Point in the foreground. Continue south, crossing State Route 20. At about 15 miles from the start,

reach La Conner, beloved by antique-lovers and cyclists alike. Although stopping for a treat is tempting, perhaps save that for later when you come back this way again.

For now, continue south through town on Maple Avenue and follow it to postcard-worthy Rainbow Bridge, which spans the Swinomish Channel. Once across, continue straight on what becomes Reservation Road and let 'er rip on a 10-mile, mostly forested loop around Swinomish Reservation. (Be sure to turn left onto Snee Oosh Road about 4 miles into the loop, and follow it back to Rainbow Bridge and La Conner.)

Back in La Conner, down a cappuccino or two, then get back at it, heading due east, then due north, then due west, then due north via one flat road after another, eventually crossing to the north side of State Route 20. After a quick foray on smooth roads around Skagit Regional Airport, during which you gain a couple hundred feet of elevation, give it all back on a fast mile down into the flatlands along Farm to Market Road. From here, it's an easy 3.5 miles back to Edison, where the route started.

Variations: Several routes (see Tour 3, Samish Island–Bow Hill Loop; Tour 6, Fidalgo Island–Mout Erie Leg Shredder; and Tour 10, Arlington–La Conner–Stanwood Loop) overlap in the Skagit Valley. Try mixing and matching sections of those routes to create your own Skagit ramble.

MILEAGE LOG

0.0	From Edison Elementary's parking lot, head west on W. Bow Hill Rd. toward Main St.
0.2	Slight left at Main St. (Becomes Farm to Market Rd.)
0.7	Right onto Bayview–Edison Rd.
1.8	Bear left to stay on Bayview–Edison Rd.
2.7	Left to stay on Bayview-Edison Rd. (Becomes La Conner–Whitney Rd.)
10.5	Cross SR 20.
14.6	At traffic circle, right onto Morris St. Enter La Conner.
14.7	Left onto Maple Ave.
15.7	Cross Rainbow Bridge into Swinomish Indian Reservation.
15.9	Bear right onto Pioneer Pkwy. (Becomes Reservation Rd.)

20.3	Left onto Snee Oosh Rd.
25.5	Right onto Pioneer Pkwy. (Cross Rainbow Bridge. Becomes Maple Ave.)
27.0	Right onto Morris St. Continue straight through circle. (Becomes Chilberg Rd.)
29.5	Becomes Higby Rd. and then Calhoun Rd.
33.0	Left onto Penn Rd.
34.1	Left to stay on Penn Rd.
34.6	Left onto McLean Rd.
38.2	Right onto Best Rd. (Becomes Farm to Market Rd.)
40.0	Cross SR 20.
40.8	Right onto Ovenell Rd.
42.2	Left onto Higgins Airport Wy.
44.6	Left onto Josh Wilson Rd.
45.6	Right onto Farm to Market Rd. (Becomes Main St. and then Bow Hill Rd.)
51.2	Right to return to start.

5 BIG LAKE–SR 530–DARRINGTON LOOP

Difficulty	Strenuous
Time	5½ to 8 hours
Distance	104.4 miles
Elevation Gain	3535 feet

ROAD CONDITIONS: A mix of busy highway with narrow shoulder and less-traveled highway with ample shoulder. Long stretch of rural country road with chip-seal surface but low traffic.

GETTING THERE: From I-5, take exit 227 in Mount Vernon. Head east on E. College Wy. (SR 538) for 3.6 miles to the roundabout intersection with SR 9. Turn right and follow SR 9 south for 2.3 miles to W. Big Lake Blvd. Turn right, then take an immediate left onto Lakeview Blvd. and park in the grocery store parking lot or (on weekends) at the elementary school next door.

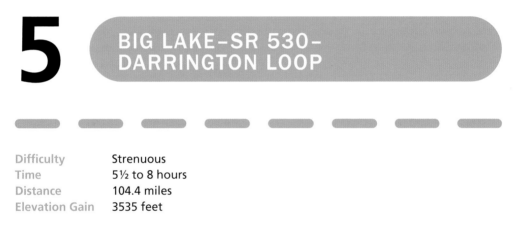

< *Spring daffodils in the Skagit Valley*

Looking for a hundred-miler that's largely off the beaten path, is not too hilly or flat, and is just about right for getting in your early season base-building mileage? (Or fun fall foliage ride?) Then this route is for you.

From the grocery store or elementary school parking lot, head away from State Route 9 up W. Big Lake Boulevard. You'll immediately notice that this isn't the tulip-and-daffodil-fields, straight-arrow-roads side of Skagit County. This is the snaking-roads and forested-foothills side, the side that'll have you standing every so often to get to the top of one little bump and be quickly rewarded with a short descent on the other side. Warm up in this fashion for about 4 miles, following the west side of Big Lake before intersecting with at times busy and in places narrow-shouldered State Route 9.

Go right and follow State Route 9 for about 14 miles to Arlington. The road is smooth, the hills are mostly gentle rollers, but the traffic can be a bit much. Make sure you can be seen whether it's with bright reflective clothing or flashing lights, or both. (In the near future, riders should be able to jump on the Centennial Trail, a paved rail trail, for at least part of this stretch. This section of the trail was under construction at press time.)

In Arlington, which has ample places for eats and drinks, pick up State Route 530 (the Arlington–Darrington Road) and head east. Along with a wider shoulder, the road offers a pleasant riding experience: less traffic and stunning scenery of fields, farmland, and the surrounding Cascade foothills and mountains. Scroll through tiny communities such as Cicero, Oso, Hazel, and Fortson. At 46 miles

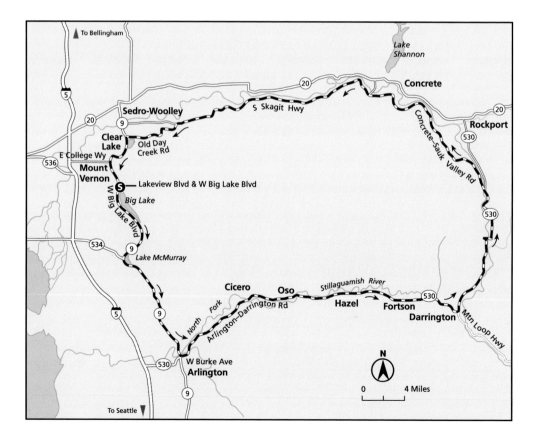

Terrific river riding beside the Sauk River between Darrington and Rockport (Scott Rittscher)

from your start point, you'll find yourself in Darrington, which, as the sign boasts, is the "Bluegrass Capital of the Northwest."

At Darrington (many places here for a midway eat 'n' drink break), State Route 530 (now the Sauk Valley Road) swings north and begins following the scenic Sauk River. Much of this section of 530 is densely wooded, with a more narrow shoulder and some logging truck traffic. About 13 miles north of Darrington, turn left onto Concrete–Sauk Valley Road, cross the Sauk River, and pretty much have the road to yourself.

Concrete–Sauk Valley Road is a bit more chip-sealy than what you've ridden to this point, but it's a beautiful area, especially in the fall when the leaves change color. After 16 miles, turn left onto S. Skagit Highway

and begin heading west, now tracing the serpentine ways of the Skagit River. (If you're in need of a rest/refuel stop, stay on Concrete–Sauk Valley Road, cross the Skagit River, and just ahead enter the town of Concrete, which offers a grocery store and sundry places to eat and drink.)

Follow S. Skagit Highway for about 18 miles and take a left onto Old Day Creek Road. Here, start making your way toward Clear Lake by climbing the steepest hill on the route. Five hundred feet of elevation gain over 3 miles isn't that bad, but coming at the 95-mile mark as it does, it might seem a bit harsh. But hey, you're rewarded with a 3-mile descent back to State Route 9. Turn left onto 9 and follow it for 5 miles to your start point at the grocery store.

Variation: If you're feeling a little beat up from the chip-seal pavement, you can always substitute State Route 20 from Concrete to Sedro-Woolley for the S. Skagit Highway. Be aware, however, that though State Route 20 is smoother and has a mostly wide shoulder, it's one of the state's major east-west routes with a lot of heavy, high-speed traffic.

MILEAGE LOG

0.0	From the grocery store parking lot, head west and then south on W. Big Lake Blvd.
4.3	Keep right onto SR 9 S.
8.1	Left to stay on SR 9 S.
18.3	Right onto W. Burke Ave. (Becomes SR 530.) Arlington.
46.2	Enter Darrington; bear left onto Seeman St.
46.5	Left to stay on SR 530.
58.6	Slight left onto Concrete–Sauk Valley Rd.
65.6	Right to stay on Concrete–Sauk Valley Rd.
74.5	Slight left onto S. Skagit Hwy.
89.0	Left to stay on S. Skagit Hwy.
92.8	Left onto Old Day Creek Rd.
98.6	Left onto SR 9 S. Clear Lake.
102.1	Remain on SR 9 S. through roundabout.
104.4	Right onto W. Big Lake Rd. and back to the start.

6 FIDALGO ISLAND– MOUNT ERIE LEG SHREDDER

Difficulty	Strenuous
Time	3 to 5 hours
Distance	50.6 miles
Elevation Gain	3460 feet

ROAD CONDITIONS: Nice mix of trestle trail, paved pathway, and roads with ample shoulders and/or low traffic. One-mile stretch of busy SR 20.

GETTING THERE: Take I-5 to exit 230 in Burlington and head west on SR 20 for 11 miles. Turn right on March Point Rd. and park in the March Point Park & Ride just ahead.

Fidalgo Island is best known as the home of Anacortes, the place where you catch the ferry to the San Juan Islands. Cyclists know it for another reason—the house of pain that is Mount Erie. An elevation of only 1273 feet sounds harmless enough—after all, other routes in this book climb to over 6000 feet—until you actually start pedaling

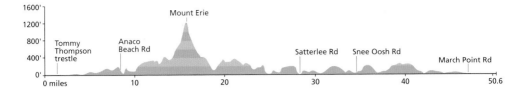

up it. Winding through the thick forest of the Anacortes Community Forest Lands, Erie Mountain Drive climbs 900 feet in just 1.5 miles. Those will be the longest 1.5 miles you'll ever ride.

But there are huge payoffs: the far-reaching views of water, mountains, and islands from the summit; the screaming-fast descent; the knowledge that you came, you saw, you conquered, you kicked its a … ascent. *Because it's there*, and all that . . . .

But Mount Erie is a mere blip on this terrific route. Begin this modified cloverleaf route by heading north on the west side of Jekyll 'n' Hyde March Point. On your left are the peaceful muddy flats and tidewater of Fidalgo Bay, home and feeding ground to harbor seals, kingfishers, eagles, and herons. On your right is a city of industry—oil refineries belching smoke and steam (and a bit of a stench) into the air. No matter; in about a mile, you leave the latter behind and cross the former via the

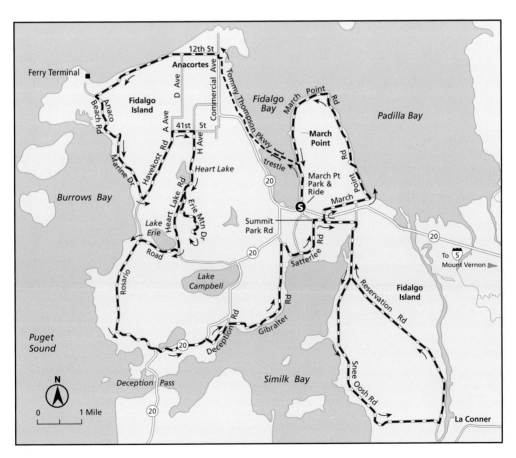

ultra-cool Tommy Thompson Parkway, a trestle trail that continues for several miles as a paved pathway through downtown Anacortes.

At 12th Street, make like a car heading west toward the San Juan Island ferry terminal. If there's a lineup of cars, ha-ha to them: you get to keep on going. Just past the turn-off to the ferry terminal, go left on Anaco Beach Road, which soon turns into Marine Drive. (Is it just me, or does every town in Washington have a Marine Drive?) Washington Park is just ahead. Here, some rolling ups and downs ensue; some of them quite steep and many offering views west across Burrows Bay to nearby Burrows Island and the Olympic Peninsula beyond. Follow the shoreline for a couple miles before heading toward the center of the island—and, gulp … Mount Erie—via Havekost Road. Head north toward the southern outskirts of Anacortes for a couple miles before making a wide U-turn south onto Heart Lake Road and beginning the at-first gradual climb toward Mount Erie. Just after passing peaceful Heart Lake on your right, turn left onto Erie Mountain Drive and let the hill begin.

After you've made it to the top, admired the views, and used the restrooms, head back down to Heart Lake Road. Turn left and continue south. A big downhill awaits and, after a right onto Rosario Road, a return to the west side of Fidalgo Island and its lumpy profile and occasional water views. At the south end of the island you have the only truly unpleasant stretch—1.2 miles of State Route 20—which, given the mega-popularity of Deception Pass State Park just to the south, is often traveled by boat-hauling pickup trucks that seem to make no bones about shoving you off the road. (In fact, many seem to feel it's their God-given duty.) No biggie, just time-trial it like crazy 'til you hit Deception Road, where you turn right. It's lovely residential and country road here, much of it beside the glistening waters of Similk Bay.

Follow the route onto the third cloverleaf—a mostly wooded 10-mile loop around the Swinomish Reservation, just across the channel from La Conner. Finish it off with 7-mile loop of wide-open (save for the refineries in the middle) March Point on the north side of State Route 20. Dead flat (though likely breezy), with expansive views of open water, mudflats, and mountains. You'll probably see more great blue herons than you can count. Complete the loop back at the March Point Park & Ride.

Variation: To skip the Mount Erie climb, just continue straight on Heart Lake Road to Rosario Road and follow the route from there.

MILEAGE LOG

0.0	Leave March Point Park & Ride and turn right onto W. March Point Rd.
1.2	Left onto Tommy Thompson Pkwy. trestle; continue on paved path.
2.3	Arrive in Anacortes.
4.4	Left onto 13th St., followed by immediate right onto Commercial Ave.
4.5	Left onto 12th St. (toward San Juan Island ferry terminal).
7.9	Left onto Anaco Beach Rd. (Becomes Marine Dr.)
10.7	Left onto Havekost Rd.
12.4	Right onto 41st St.
13.0	Right onto H Ave., also called Heart Lake Rd.
14.6	Left onto Erie Mountain Dr.

< The Tommy Thompson Parkway crosses Padilla Bay into Anacortes.

16.1	Turnaround point atop Mount Erie; return to Heart Lake Rd.
17.6	Left onto Heart Lake Rd.
18.9	Right onto Rosario Rd.
19.9	Left at intersection to continue on Rosario Rd.
23.3	Left onto SR 20.
24.3	Right onto Deception Rd.
25.3	Right onto Gibraltar Rd.
27.9	Right onto Satterlee Rd.
29.5	Right onto Summit Park Rd.
29.7	Right onto Thompson Rd., then quick left onto Stevenson Rd.
30.6	Right onto Reservation Rd.
31.8	Right onto Snee Oosh Rd.
37.0	Left onto Reservation Rd.
41.2	Straight on Reservation Rd.
42.4	Left onto Stevenson Rd.
43.2	Right onto Thompson Rd.
43.3	Cross SR 20.
43.6	Right onto S. March Point Rd.
44.5	Left onto E. March Point Rd.
50.5	Left onto W. March Point Rd.
50.6	Left into March Point Park & Ride.

7 ORCAS ISLAND 50-MILER

Difficulty	Strenuous
Time	3½ to 6 hours
Distance	50.7 miles
Elevation Gain	5850 feet

ROAD CONDITIONS: Winding roads with narrow shoulders, short stretch of gravel road, steep 5-plus mile climb up Mount Constitution. Bike turnouts.

GETTING THERE: Take I-5 to exit 230 in Burlington. Head west on SR 20 for 13 miles to Anacortes. Turn right onto Commercial Ave. and, a mile ahead, left on 12th St. following signs for Washington State Ferries. In about 4 miles, turn right on Ferry Terminal Rd. Paid parking in the ferry terminal lots.

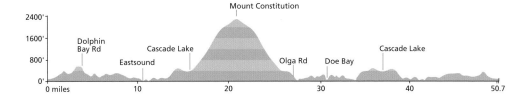

Orcas is my favorite San Juan Island for cycling. Of course, that's because I like challenges, and Orcas doles out challenges in spades: everything from short, steep punches in the nose (rudely repetitive ones at that) to a sustained 5.5-mile uphill slog so steep in parts that you'll keep looking down at your rear cluster, hoping to see one more easier gear to shift into.

But Orcas offers payoffs by the bucketful. Along with the island's hippy-artsy-organic-affluent vibe is world-class scenery that will take your breath away. None more so than from the top of Mount Constitution, where the sweeping views will make you feel as though you're hang-gliding above the glistening straits below. Getting there will take your breath away as well, for Mount Constitution Road climbs some 2100 feet in just 5.5 miles. (Yikes!)

Upon disembarking at the Orcas Island ferry landing, turn right onto Killebrew Lake Road. The winding two-lane country road starts out following the shoreline, offering peek-a-boo views through the red-barked madrone trees across Harney Channel to Shaw Island. Soon enough the route turns inland, bears left onto Dolphin Bay Road, becomes smooth gravel—not overly washboardy or rutted—and throws in a few rolling hills. (Rolling hills is a popular theme on this route.) Pass through forest, farmland, and open fields en route to Eastsound.

After about 4 miles of gravel and dirt road, return to pavement and after a mile or so—at about 7 miles from the ferry landing—turn right, still on Dolphin Bay Road. Not far ahead, continue straight as Dolphin Bay Road merges with Orcas Road, the main thoroughfare from the ferry to Eastsound. Main thoroughfare it may be, but it's narrow and has no real shoulder to speak of. Caution is key.

It's also mostly downhill from here to Eastsound, Orcas Island's biggest town. Along with ample food and drink opportunities (including a grocery store), there's a bike shop. (You'll come back through here later in the ride.) Continue straight through town and after pedaling past the wading herons poking around the mudflats of Ship Bay, crest a short, steep hill, and turn right at the intersection just ahead onto Olga Road. Working your way south down Orcas's east lobe, you'll notice the large forested wall on your left—that is the 2000-foot-high ridgeline of Mount Constitution, which you'll spend the next 9 miles scaling. But first, you've got a share of steep rollers to work through over the 3 miles just to get you into 5000-acre Moran State Park, of which Constitution is the centerpiece.

Once in the park, descend to the shoreline of pleasant Cascade Lake, ringed with campgrounds from which the pleasing aroma of campfires is likely wafting. There are restrooms here and just ahead, a sign that reads "Mount Constitution Summit: 5.5 miles." Not much left to the imagination: as soon as the road pulls away from the lakeside, it begins to climb—about a mile past the lake, bear left following the sign for Mount Constitution Road—and doesn't let up until it reaches the top. It goes like this: steep, followed by really steep, followed by not-so-steep, then steep, followed by really steep. The steepest section is a 2.25-mile stretch in the middle that climbs 1175 feet—that's 10 percent. Thankfully, during a couple tight switchbacks about halfway up the mountain,

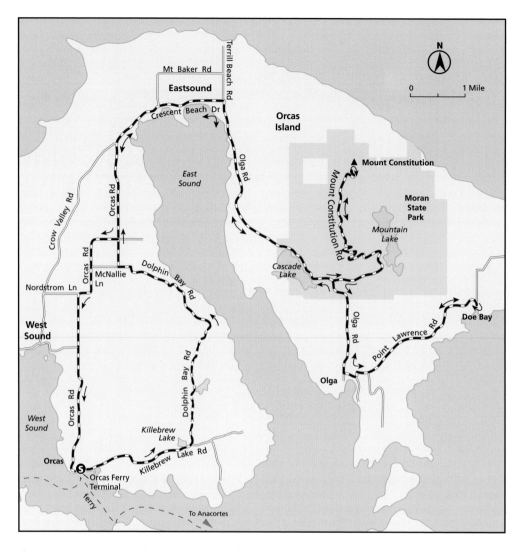

the trees open up on the south side, offering spectacular island, water, and mountain views. There's also a wide pullout area if you need to take a breather

At the top, take time for some well-deserved R&R and for marveling at the views. Depending on the weather and cloud cover, you could see everything from Vancouver, BC, and the British Columbia Coast Mountains; to Bellingham and Mount Baker; to untold numbers of Cascade peaks and Gulf and San Juan islands; to Mount Rainier and everything in between. But you're not done

with this route. When you're ready, hop back on your bike and head down. Carefully. Concentration and caution are key.

Once down the mountain, turn left back onto Olga Road (kind of a tricky 45-degree angle) and continue mostly downhill for another 2 miles to Olga, a tiny waterfront community. Turn left onto Point Lawrence Road (Café Olga is there on the corner in the old strawberry-packing plant building) and head another 3.5 miles to Doe Bay, the turnaround point. There's a resort and retreat here as well as a store.

From Doe Bay, retrace your tire tread back to Eastsound (sans the Mount Constitution climb), negotiating a fair number of slow ups and fast downs along the 11-mile route. Refuel in Eastsound if you like, remembering that you have a ferry to catch. Via Orcas Road, it's 8 rolling-up-and-down miles past fields and llama ranches back to the Orcas ferry landing.

MILEAGE LOG

0.0	From Orcas Island ferry landing, turn right onto Killebrew Lake Rd.
2.5	Bear left onto Dolphin Bay Rd.
7.2	Right, continuing on Dolphin Bay Rd.
7.6	Continue straight onto Orcas Rd.
10.5	In Eastsound, right onto Main St. (Becomes Crescent Beach Dr.)
11.8	Right onto Olga Rd.
16.4	Left onto Mount Constitution Rd.
21.0	Turnaround at top of Mount Constitution.
25.6	Left onto Olga Rd.
27.8	Left onto Point Lawrence Rd.
31.2	Turnaround at Doe Bay.
34.6	Right onto Olga Rd.

A rider pedals ever higher up the 5.5-mile climb to the top of Orcas Island's 2,409-foot Mount Constitution, the highest point in the San Juan Islands. (Jen McQuaide)

36.8	Bear left at intersection with Mount Constitution Rd.
41.4	Left onto Crescent Beach Dr. (Becomes Main St. in Eastsound.)
42.7	Left onto Orcas Rd.
43.8	Left to continue on Orcas Rd.
45.6	Bear right to continue on Orcas Rd.
50.7	Arrive back at ferry landing.

8 SAN JUAN ISLAND CRISSCROSS

Difficulty	Strenuous
Time	3 to 5 hours
Distance	53.9 miles
Elevation Gain	3880 feet

ROAD CONDITIONS: Mostly lightly traveled country roads, but with poorly defined shoulders. Bike turnouts.

GETTING THERE: Take I-5 to exit 230 in Burlington. Head west on SR 20 for 13 miles to Anacortes. Turn right onto Commercial Ave. and, a mile ahead, left on 12th St. following signs for Washington State Ferries. In about 4 miles, turn right on Ferry Terminal Rd. Paid parking in the ferry terminal lots.

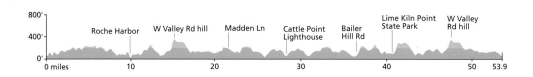

This route bounces back and forth across San Juan Island, touching on most of the island's best attractions: a bit of seaside riding to look for orcas, a pass-through of its two national historical parks (American Camp and English Camp), and lots and lots of pedaling through the bucolic heart of the island, with lavender fields, alpaca ranches, vineyards, and organic farms.

This ride reveals the island's hilly character as well. Though you are never more than 350 feet above sea level, this route climbs over 3500 feet, meaning you're always heading up, heading down, or about to do one or the other.

From the Friday Harbor ferry dock, make your way through town and head northwest across the island on winding rural Roche

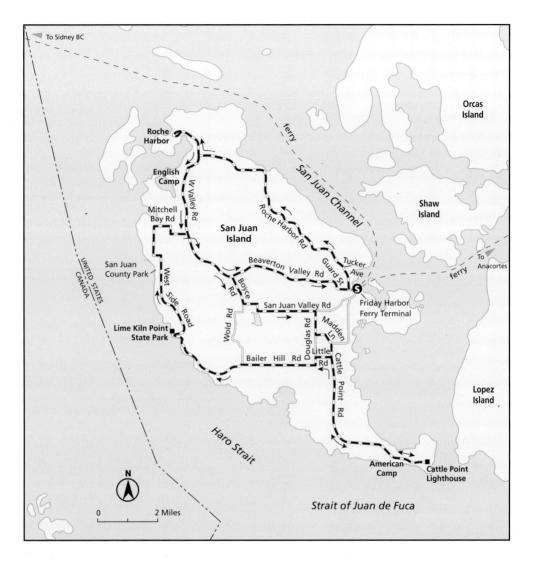

Harbor Road. The shoulder's not super wide and at times (i.e., shortly after a ferry arrival), it can be busy, so concentration is key.

At about 10 miles, reach Roche Harbor, a tony harbor town. As one of the island's top destinations, Roche can be crowded, so don't dally too long—grab something to eat or drink at the small market and then get back at it.

From Roche Harbor, return the way you came via Roche Harbor Road for about 2 miles to W. Valley Road, where you turn right. This forested country road has a lot

of ups and downs as it winds its way south past the English Camp portion of San Juan Island National Historical Park. The park recalls the mid-1800s when both British and American troops occupied the island until an unbiased third party (Kaiser Wilhelm of Germany) determined who owned the San Juan Islands. (In another 12 miles, you'll pass through the American section of the same park.)

A couple miles south of English Camp begins a short (half mile) but very steep stretch, the stiffest climb of the route. (And here's something you should probably know: you will repeat this climb later in the ride.) There is a payoff, however: the next 5 miles, including the right-hand turn onto Boyce Road, is a mostly downhill fun-and-fast fest. You're cutting right across the center of the island here, trending south and east on San Juan Valley and Douglas roads through open farmland. Be prepared for potential winds.

Make your way to the southeast corner of the island at Cattle Point, first passing through American Camp, site of a US Army encampment in those days of yore. The treeless, windswept bluffs are stunningly beautiful and afford views across the Strait of Juan de Fuca south to the Olympics and east to the Cascades. Scan the water for orcas, about 90 of which call these waters their summer home. Descend just about to sea level at the

Riding West Side Road above Haro Strait where summer orca sightings are frequent (Baker McQuaide)

Cattle Point Lighthouse (restrooms here), the easternmost point on San Juan Island. Lopez Island is not much more than a stone's heave away, across Cattle Pass.

Retrace your pedal strokes back through American Camp on Cattle Point Road, this time turning left onto Little Road, which delivers you to Bailer Hill Road. Head west straight across the island through pastoral farmland on a rural country road where more than likely you'll come across cyclists doing the same thing you are. The gradual climb culminates with a stunning descent alongside Haro Strait. This west side of the island is probably the best place for spotting orcas anywhere in the contiguous United States.

Follow the road down a sweeping bend to the right and make your way north up what is now West Side Road. That's Vancouver Island across the strait, and if you're lucky, a pod of orcas might be frolicking in the kelp beds just offshore from the jagged rocks below. Stop in for a look-see at Lime Kiln Point State Park (restrooms here, as well as a lighthouse), then back on your bike to resume the rolling-hill theme you enjoyed earlier, now in forest and away from those killer water (and whale) views.

About 4 miles from Lime Kiln, turn right onto Mitchell Bay Road, which in about 1.5 miles intersects with W. Valley Road. Turn right. Remember that hill I warned you about having to repeat? Well, here it is again. (You're welcome.) But hey, it's short. And once you've crested it, the rest of the ride is mostly downhill for 6 miles through pleasant countryside back into Friday Harbor. Along with a grocery store, the town offers many places to eat, drink, and stay, as well as a bike shop.

Variations: Multitudinous. This route hits all the island's greatest spots, several of which are worthy destinations on their own. Friday Harbor to Roche Harbor and back is about 19 miles with 1100 feet of elevation gain; to Cattle Point and back also about 19 miles with 1200 feet elevation gain; to Lime Kiln Point State Park and back via W. Valley and Mitchell Bay roads about 18 miles and 1100 feet elevation gain.

MILEAGE LOG

0.0	From Friday Harbor ferry dock, right onto Front St. and then left onto Spring St.
0.1	Right onto 2nd St. S. (Becomes Guard St.)
0.5	Right onto Tucker Ave.
0.9	Bear left onto Roche Harbor Rd.
9.5	Left to stay on Roche Harbor Rd.
9.6	Right to stay on Roche Harbor Rd.
9.8	Right onto Reuben Memorial Dr. Arrive Roche Harbor.
10.2	Left onto Roche Harbor Rd., making a small loop.
10.3	Right onto Roche Harbor Rd.
11.5	Right onto W. Valley Rd.
12.3	Pass through English Camp, San Juan Island National Historical Park.
16.8	Right onto Boyce Rd.
17.8	Left onto San Juan Valley Rd.
18.2	Bear right to stay on San Juan Valley Rd.
20.4	Right onto Douglas Rd.
21.2	Left onto Madden Ln.
21.8	Right onto Cattle Point Rd.
25.0	Enter American Camp, San Juan Island National Historical Park.

28.7	Turnaround at Cattle Point Lighthouse.
35.1	Left onto Little Rd.
35.5	Left onto Douglas Rd.
35.7	Bear right onto Bailer Hill Rd. (Becomes West Side Rd.)
41.3	Lime Kiln Point State Park.
45.6	Right onto Mitchell Bay Rd.
46.9	Right onto W. Valley Rd. (Becomes Beaverton Valley Rd., then Guard St.)
53.6	Follow to the right onto 2nd St. S.
53.8	Left onto Spring St.
53.9	Right onto Front St. S.
53.9	Return to ferry dock.

9 CAMANO ISLAND LOOP

Difficulty	Moderate
Time	2 to 3½ hours
Distance	40.8 miles
Elevation Gain	2675 feet

ROAD CONDITIONS: Mostly rolling country roads with ample shoulders; some residential streets.

GETTING THERE: Take I-5 to exit 212 near Silvana. Head west on SR 532 to Camano Island and Terry's Corner Shopping Center at the corner of SR 532 and Sunrise Blvd. Park in the parking lot.

Separated from the mainland by the slimmest of sloughs—Davis Slough—Camano is an island by the slimmest of margins. Roughly 15 miles long, Camano used to be longer before the Great Slide of 1825, when a large chunk of the island's southern tip slid into Puget Sound. The resulting tsunami killed dozens of Native American inhabitants on nearby Hat Island.

Because Camano isn't on the way to somewhere else—no major highways pass through it, no ferries leave from it—it has a definite

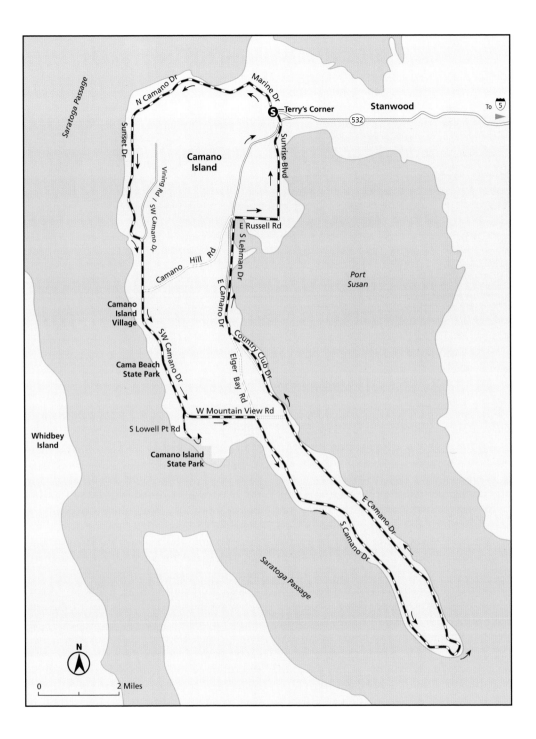

Saratoga Passage

N Camano Dr

Marine Dr

Terry's Corner · S · Stanwood

To 5

532

Sunset Dr

Camano Island

Sunrise Blvd

Vining Rd / SW Camano Dr

Camano Hill Rd

E Russell Rd

S Lehman Dr

Port Susan

Camano Island Village

E Camano Dr

Country Club Dr

Cama Beach State Park

SW Camano Dr

Elger Bay Rd

W Mountain View Rd

Whidbey Island

S Lowell Pt Rd

Camano Island State Park

E Camano Dr

S Camano Dr

Saratoga Passage

N

0   2 Miles

A rider stops to investigate some roadside art—a common sight on Camano Island.

off-the-beaten path feel. Which, along with the stunning water views, smooth roads, and fun rollers, makes it a terrific place to ride a bike. Another plus: Camano's Northwest artist island-laid back vibe, prominently on display during the annual spring art studio tour.

To begin this loop, which traces the island's outline, head north from Terry's Corner via N. Camano Drive. You'll be treated to glimpses of Skagit Bay and La Conner to the north, as well as views of Whidbey Island to the west—Camano Island essentially sits within Whidbey's C-shaped curve. Loosen up those quads with some early rollers that climb a couple hundred feet over a mile or two. As the elevation profile shows, there are really no long, devastating climbs on this ride, just many short and steep ups and downs.

Just past 9 miles, roll into Camano Island's village. You'll be through in a sec, though you might want to take advantage of the village's small country-style grocery store. Continue south, passing Cama Beach State Park (which offers waterfront cabins and bungalows for rent). Three miles south of Camano island Village, on a somewhat rough and forested road, reach Lowell Point Road, where you can make a quick dropdown visit to Camano Island State Park. With more than a mile of shoreline and expansive views of islands and the Olympic Mountains, this 88-site camping park makes for a nice diversion (and rest stop), despite its steep entrance and exit.

Back on the main route, follow W. Mountain View Road, which cuts east to the center of the island, climbing quite steadily for about a mile. After an equally steep descent—probably the fastest of the route—turn right and continue on S. Camano Drive toward the island's less populated southern tip. (Another country grocery shop at the intersection of Mountain View Road and S. Camano Drive offers the opportunity to refill those bottles or pick up something to eat.)

The next 15 miles are fairly straightforward (and rolling and winding), following S. Camano Drive until it reaches the southern tip of the island, then swinging north as E. Camano Drive. There are no open views at that southern tip, but it boasts the route's biggest hill, which climbs some 300 feet over 2 miles.

In order to stay off the busiest section of NE Camano Drive, the route's last 5 miles follow a mix of less-traveled residential streets and pleasant country roads, before closing the loop back at Terry's Corner.

MILEAGE LOG

0.0	Right out of Terry's Corner shopping center parking lot onto Marine Dr. (Becomes N. Camano Dr.)
3.9	Right onto N. Sunset Drive W. (Becomes S. Sunset Dr.)
7.9	Right onto Vining Rd. (also called SW Camano Dr.).
9.4	Camano Island Village.
11.8	Cama Beach State Park.
12.2	Right on S. Lowell Point Rd. (for visit to Camano Island State Park).
13.3	Camano Island State Park.
14.5	Right on W. Mountain View Rd.
16.2	Right onto S. Camano Dr.
24.4	Reach the southern tip of Camano Island; road becomes E. Camano Dr.
32.7	Right onto Country Club Dr. (Becomes S. Beach Dr.)
34.3	Right onto Cavalero Rd.
35.0	Right onto E. Camano Dr.
35.5	Right onto S. Lehman Dr.
37.1	Right onto E. Russell Rd.
38.2	Left onto Nelson Rd. (also called Sunrise Blvd.).
40.5	Sunrise Blvd.–NE Camano Dr. intersection
40.8	Return to Terry's Corner parking lot.

10 ARLINGTON–LA CONNER–STANWOOD LOOP

Difficulty	Moderate
Time	3 to 5½ hours
Distance	62.1 miles
Elevation	1245 feet

ROAD CONDITIONS: Mix of busy state highway with narrow shoulder, paved trail, and rural farm roads with little traffic.

GETTING THERE: From I-5 take exit 206 near Smokey Point. Head east on SR 531 (172nd St. NE) for 2 miles to 67th Ave. NE. Turn left and follow for 2 miles to 204th St. NE (Kent Prairie Rd.) Turn right and park in the large grocery store parking lot on the right, about a half mile south of Arlington.

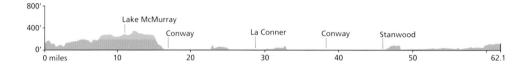

This mostly flat loop courses through the flats of the Skagit and Stillaguamish river deltas with a halfway stop in La Conner, a place beloved by cyclists for its plethora of espresso-'n'-scone (or the like) opportunities. The Skagit Valley means revolving scenery too—whether it's tulip season, swan and snow geese season, raptor season, or any other season you can think of. And of course, every season in La Conner is tourist season, so be aware of that—their cars, I mean—especially on weekends.

Begin by following State Route 9 north, skirting Arlington proper, for just over 10 miles. Admittedly, the shoulder here is narrow but in the near future (maybe even by press time), you'll be able to substitute the paved Centennial Trail for most of these first 10 miles.

Just past Lake McMurray, turn left onto State Route 534 and leave most (but not quite all) of the big, heavy rigs behind. This is a contemplative pastoral stretch past the Foggy Bottom Natural Area and Sixteen Lake. You're trending west here toward Puget Sound and after a fast mile-plus-long descent during which you lose about 250 feet of elevation, you enter the Skagit Flats. But first you cross over the freeway, and just beyond that, cross the Skagit River herself.

After turning right onto Skagit City Road, which hugs a dike that hugs the eponymous flood-prone Skagit River, the route becomes a flat and mellow meander snaking its way through farm- and pastureland. During the

winter and early spring, the fields will be almost white with swans and geese, as the fertile Skagit River delta attracts an estimated thirty thousand snow geese as well as hundreds of trumpeter and tundra swans.

Little communities such as Conway and Rexville offer nice markets and coffee stands. If you want more selection, wait 'til La Conner, which you hit at the 28-mile mark. On weekdays, it's fun to roll through this quaint antique shop- and art-gallery-heavy village; weekends, however, can be crowded.

From La Conner, head back east the way you entered the town, but this time turn right onto Dodge Valley Road and start heading south toward Fir Island. Formed where the Skagit River splits in two just before reaching Puget Sound, Fir Island is a 16-square-mile triangle that's a world-renown hotspot for several species of migrating birds. Thousands of snow geese, swans, eagles, and various other waterfowl species make this their winter home.

Cyclists will note, too, that Fir Island is quite flat. And low, less than 10 feet above sea level. Which, given the braids of river on either side of it, imply that Fir Island is prone to flood. Which it is. (After periods of flooding, watch out for debris on the road.) After 5 miles of Fir Island, cross the Skagit River again, reenter Conway, but this time turn right onto Pioneer Highway and make an 8-mile pancake-flat beeline for Stanwood. Highway is the operative word here because this road can be busy and its shoulder isn't

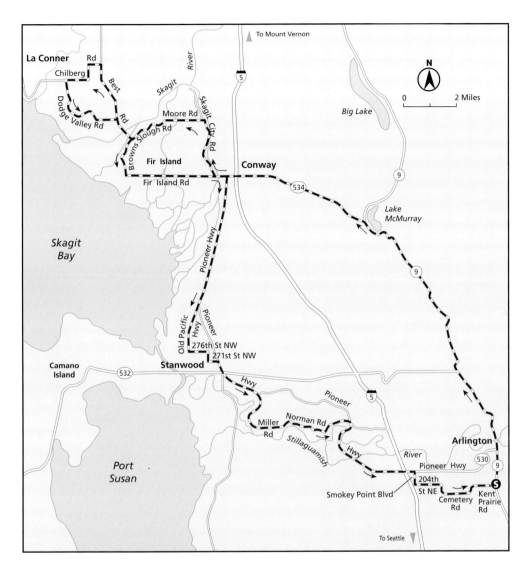

the widest. So take advantage of the second
operative word—flat—and time-trial it like
heck to just north of Stanwood, where this
route exits Pioneer Highway onto more mellow Old Pacific Highway.

After some maneuvering through Stanwood—bike shop and plenty of places here
for food or drink—pick up Pioneer High-

way again. South of town, the highway is not
nearly as crowded as the earlier stretch. You're
on it for only a mile or so before turning right
onto Miller Road, then Norman Road, for a
pleasant 5-mile jaunt along the Stillaguamish
River. From here, it's about 8 miles back to
your starting point in Arlington, most of it
via rural Snohomish County back roads.

0.0	From the grocery store parking lot in Arlington, right onto 204th St. NE (Kent Prairie Rd).
0.2	Left onto SR 9 N.
11.7	Bear right to stay on SR 9 N.
11.8	Left SR 534 W.
17.1	Right onto Fir Island Rd. Roll through Conway.
17.7	Right onto Skagit City Rd.
19.9	Left onto Moore Rd.
22.9	Right onto Best Rd.
24.2	Bear left to stay on Best Rd. (at Rexville Grange Rd. intersection).

With bike-friendly streets and welcoming cafes, La Conner is a favorite among cyclists.

26.0	Left onto Chilberg Rd.
28.4	Continue straight through traffic circle.
28.5	Enter La Conner. Turnaround point.
28.6	At the traffic circle, continue straight to stay on Chilberg Rd.
29.3	Right onto Dodge Valley Rd.
31.8	Left to stay on Dodge Valley Rd. (Also called Sharfenberg Rd.)
32.4	Right onto Best Rd.
33.4	Right onto Browns Slough Rd. (Fir Island Rd.)
34.7	Bear left to stay on Fir Island Rd.
38.5	Right onto Pioneer Hwy.
43.2	Right, then immediate left onto Old Pacific Hwy.
45.2	Turn left at 276th St. NW. (Becomes Lovers Rd., 92nd Ave. NW.) Enter Stanwood.
46.2	Left onto 271st St. NW.
46.6	Right onto Triangle Dr.
46.7	Bear right onto Pioneer Hwy.
48.5	Right onto Miller Rd.
50.0	Bear left onto Norman Rd.
53.1	Left to stay on Norman Rd.
54.3	Right onto Pioneer Hwy.
58.2	Right onto Smokey Point Blvd.
58.7	Left onto 204th St. NE.
59.7	Right onto 43rd Ave. NE.
60.0	Bear left onto Cemetery Rd. (Becomes Kent Prairie Rd.)
62.1	Return to grocery store parking lot.

11 GRANITE FALLS–BARLOW PASS (MOUNTAIN LOOP HIGHWAY)

Difficulty	Moderate
Time	3 to 5½ hours
Distance	61.6 miles
Elevation Gain	3270 feet

ROAD CONDITIONS: Fairly smooth rural highway with varying shoulder widths; some heavy truck traffic near Granite Falls. *Note:* Because of seasonal snow, the Mountain Loop Hwy. is gated most years from sometime in November until spring at Deer Creek Rd., about 7 miles west of Barlow Pass and 23 miles east of Granite Falls.

GETTING THERE: From I-5, take exit 199 in Marysville. Go east through town on SR 528 about 3.4 miles to the T intersection with SR 9. Turn right and go south on SR 9 for 1.8 miles and then turn left on Granite Falls Hwy. (SR 92). Continue for 8.2 miles into Granite Falls and turn left onto N. Granite Ave. Park in the grocery store parking lot just ahead on the right.

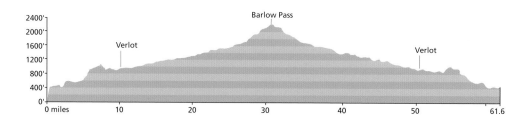

This 60-mile out-and-back might just trick you into thinking you're the strongest cyclist in the world. As the elevation profile suggests, it's pretty much one long uphill on the way out and one long descent on the way back. It's not a particularly steep hill—the climb's average gain is less than 100 feet per mile—so it won't whoop you on the way out, but it will make you feel like you're flying on the descent.

In Granite Falls, begin by making a left onto Granite Avenue, then a quick left onto E. Stanley Street, then just ahead a left onto N. Alder Avenue, which becomes the Mountain Loop Highway. From there, stay straight for 30 miles or so to your turnaround point at Barlow Pass, elevation 2361 feet.

Take care over the first few miles close to town where the road's narrow shoulders and the large equipment trucks can cause some anxious moments. But soon enough, the big trucks scatter, the shoulder widens, and the anxiety fades. At 4 miles, hit the route's one stiff climb, a 3-mile bump that features one stretch of 8 to 10 percent grade, but it's nothing you can't handle.

Sections of the highway follow the Still-aguamish River as well as the old Everett and Monte Cristo Railway route, which was built

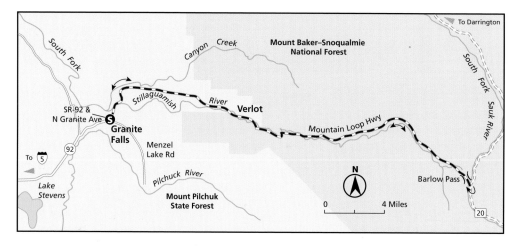

The aptly named Mountain Loop Highway affords stunning views of the North Cascades. >

in the 1890s during the rush for gold and silver. The area is steeped in mining history; Barlow Pass is also the trailhead for the site of the old mining town (now a ghost town) of Monte Cristo. The area has plenty of scenic beauty too. Dozens of big-name Cascade peaks surround you on all sides and the highway offers access to some of the region's most beloved hiking trails and picnic spots—Mount Pilchuck, Lake Twenty-Two, the Big Four Picnic Area, and Ice Caves trail, among others. (For information on these and other trails, duck your head into the Verlot Ranger Station located on the highway, about 10 miles east of Granite Falls. Restrooms available.)

The road steepens a bit for the last couple miles before Barlow Pass, but again, nothing too terrible. At Barlow Pass (where there are Forest Service pit toilets), turn around and head back down on what's a truly fun return ride to Granite Falls.

Variation: Pavement ends at Barlow Pass and the next 14 miles of the Mountain Loop Highway—also called Forest Road 20—are gravel, much of it one lane. But if you have beefy tires, or don't mind chancing punctures, you can ride the entire Mountain Loop Highway for a 90-plus miler. At Barlow Pass, follow the road for 25 miles to Darrington; the last 11 miles to the town are paved. From Darrington, go left on State Route 530 and head west for about 30 miles to Arlington. (Tour 10, Arlington–La Conner–Stanwood Loop, describes this stretch heading east.) From Arlington, it's about 13 miles to Granite Falls, following Burn Road most of the way.

MILEAGE LOG

0.0	From grocery store parking lot in Granite Falls, left onto N. Granite Ave.
0.1	Left onto E. Stanley St.
0.3	Left onto N. Alder Ave. (Becomes Mountain Loop Hwy.)
30.8	Turnaround at Barlow Pass.
61.1	Back in Granite Falls, right onto E. Stanley St.
61.3	Right onto N. Granite Ave.
61.6	Arrive at start.

12 TOUR DE NORTH WHIDBEY

Difficulty	Strenuous
Time	3½ to 6 hours
Distance	59.7 miles
Elevation Gain	4015 feet

ROAD CONDITIONS: Mostly rural roads with low traffic; a couple short stretches of busy state highway.

GETTING THERE: From I-5 just south of Everett take exit 189 and head west on SR 526 for 5 miles. Turn right onto SR 525 (Mukilteo Speedway), follow it for 2 miles to the Mukilteo ferry terminal, and drive aboard. From Clinton, take SR 525 and go north for 17 miles. Turn right on Wonn Rd. Park at Greenbank Farm, just ahead on the left.

With the advent of cell phones, there will come a day when to describe Whidbey Island as shaped like a telephone receiver will be met with a blank stare. Maybe we're already there. No matter, Whidbey Island is shaped like a telephone. This route features the island's northern reaches—Oak Harbor and surrounding area, including the Naval Air Station Whidbey Island—as well as its central region: a mix of rural roads, lovely farms, scenic fields, and artist studios. The sort of fare typical of Washington island communities. This route roughly follows the northern 60-mile route of the Tour de Whidbey, a fundraising ride for Whidbey General Hospital Foundation held annually in September.

Begin at Greenbank Farm, one of Whidbey's historic farms. Its produce and crafts market makes it a great place for pre- or post-ride R&R. Turn left onto N. Bluff Road and warm up with a pleasant seaside ride along glistening Saratoga Passage, which separates Whidbey and Camano islands. If the skies cooperate, you should have views of Mount Baker and the North Cascades. Later, you'll have equally stunning views of the Olympics across the Strait of Juan de Fuca, and even Mount Rainier to the southeast. More than likely, however, what you'll notice most over the early miles of this ride is that Whidbey is one hilly island. Traffic is sparse on these mostly rural roads, but make no mistake: they're a roller coaster. This route's high point is less than 400 feet above sea level, but over

its 60 miles, the route climbs more than 4000 feet. Look at that elevation profile—it resembles the teeth on your big chainring.

After 4.5 miles of these rural, largely forested rollers, turn right onto State Route 525, which, though often busy (especially on summer weekends), offers a wide shoulder. In less than 2 miles, you return to the rural rollers via Race Road. The upside (literally, downside) of the rollers is they offer a plethora of fast descents on smooth road. Begin making your way toward Coupeville, an artsy historic waterfront town that dates back to the 1850s. Plenty of food and drink places available. (This, by the way, is the driest part of Whidbey Island, with an annual rainfall of 18 to 20 inches, about two-thirds that of Seattle.)

Through Coupeville, follow Madrona Way and, for a short stretch, State Route 20, tracing the shoreline of Penn Cove. The island is not much more than a mile wide here and after turning right onto Penn Cove Road and beginning your jaunt north toward Oak Harbor via Scenic Heights Road, another of the ride's themes will likely become apparent—the fact that Whidbey Island can be a breezy, windy, gusty place. No wonder, since it is located pretty much at the intersection of Puget Sound Drive and Strait of Juan de Fuca Way. Winds from the Pacific Ocean and the Olympic Mountains clash here with winds from the Cascades. (Best to ride behind large-framed friends who can block the wind.)

About 25 miles into the ride, reach Oak Harbor and for the next couple miles, it's

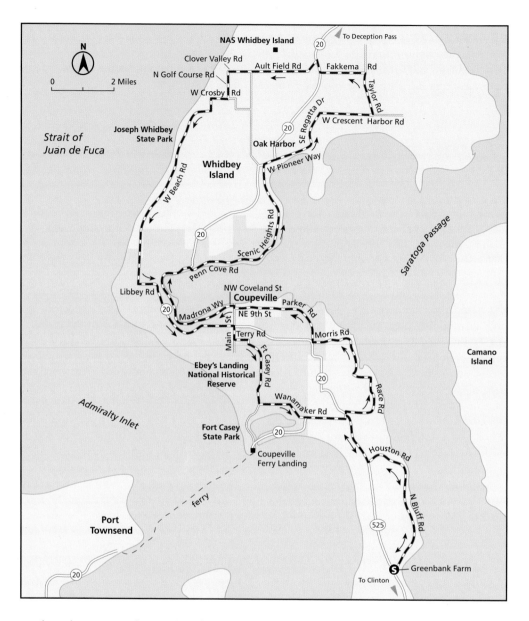

residential in-town riding with a few blocks of State Route 20 fast-food-and-mini-mart sprawl. The upside is that there are plenty of places to eat. Oak Harbor also has a bike shop.

Head north out of town and after another short State Route 20 stretch, turn left onto Ault Field Road by the twin jet fighters just outside the Naval Air Station Whidbey Island. With the air station to your right, head due west via a smooth, wide-shouldered, if a tad busy roadway, eventually reaching Joseph Whidbey State Park and W. Beach Road, on the dramatic shoreline of the Strait of Juan de Fuca. Whidbey, who served on George Vancouver's 1791–95 expedition, is of course the source of the park's and the island's names (and of many places on the island). Views here are huge—not only of the great expanse of the strait but also of Vancouver Island and the icy, 7000-foot Olympic peaks, which appear to rise right out of the water.

Continuing straight, the road leaves sea level in a hurry, with a steep climb of almost a mile. It then heads back to State Route 20 for a 3.5-mile stretch that includes a ride-by of Ebey's Landing National Historical Reserve, popular with the mountain bike crowd for its Kettles area. At Coupeville, turn right and head south toward the windswept fields just north of Fort Casey State Park and the Coupeville (formerly Keystone) Ferry Terminal. Go left on Wanamaker Road and up yet another couple-hundred-foot hillock out to State Route 525. Turn right and retrace your pedal strokes for the final 4.5 up-and-down miles back to Greenbank Farm.

MILEAGE LOG

0.0	Left out of Greenbank Farm onto Wonn Rd.
0.1	Left onto N. Bluff Rd. (Becomes Houston Rd.)
4.7	Right onto SR 525.
6.2	Right onto Race Rd. (Becomes Harrington Rd., then Morris Rd.)
11.1	Right onto SR 20. Just ahead, continue straight onto Parker Rd., which becomes NE 9th St. in Coupeville.
14.3	Right onto Main St.; quick left onto NW Coveland St.
14.5	Left onto Madrona Wy.
17.7	Right onto SR 20.
18.6	Right onto Holbrook Rd.
18.7	Left onto Penn Cove Rd. (Becomes Scenic Heights Rd.)
24.0	Enter Oak Harbor.
24.5	Right onto W. Pioneer Wy. (SR 20). (Becomes SE Pioneer Wy.)
26.1	Left onto SE Regatta Dr.
27.5	Right onto W. Crescent Harbor Rd.
29.3	Left onto Taylor Rd.
30.5	Left onto E. Fakkema Rd.
32.0	Right onto SR 20.
32.3	Left onto Ault Field Rd. (Becomes Clover Valley Rd.)
35.2	Bear left onto N. Golf Course Rd.
36.2	Right onto W. Crosby Rd. (Becomes W. Beach Rd.)
43.3	Left onto Libbey Rd.
43.9	Right onto SR 20.
47.4	Right onto Main St., Coupeville.
47.7	Left onto W. Terry Rd.
48.3	Right onto Fort Casey Rd.
50.4	Left onto W. Wanamaker Rd.
52.1	Left to continue on Wanamaker Rd.
53.4	Right onto SR 525.
54.9	Left onto Houston Rd. (Becomes N. Bluff Rd.)
59.6	Right onto Wonn Rd.
59.7	Return to Greenbank Farm.

13 SOUTH WHIDBEY ISLAND

Difficulty	Strenuous
Time	3 to 5 hours
Distance	54.9 miles
Elevation Gain	4100 feet

ROAD CONDITIONS: Rolling low-traffic rural roads with narrow shoulders and some chip-seal surfaces; state highway with wide shoulder. Some residential and small-town riding.

GETTING THERE: From I-5 north of Lynwood, take exit 189 and head west on SR 526 for 5 miles. Turn right onto SR 525 (Mukilteo Speedway) and follow it for 2 miles to the Mukilteo ferry terminal. Paid parking at ferry terminal.

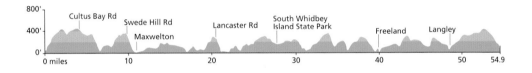

Many folks escape to the islands of Puget Sound for, in the words of Elmer Fudd, some "west" and "wewaxation": lazy strolls along driftwood beaches, mellow museum tours and gallery gazing, topped off with lingering lunches in seaside eateries.

Well, screw that!

Why "west" and "wewax" when you can hitch a ride on a ferry and experience what the islands serve up on a silver platter: low-traffic roads by the dozen, challenging quad- and character-building climbs (all of which are thankfully short), and of course, those stunning island-mountain-seaside vistas that you can't get anywhere else. But you *can* do both: do the ride, then do the "wewaxing." Whidbey Island is perfect for both.

From the Clinton ferry dock, head toward Whidbey Island's interior by climbing up State Route 525 on smooth bike lane. It's a 2-mile sustained climb that serves a couple purposes. One, to get your heart pumping and the blood flowing through your legs, and two, to enlighten you to one of the basic truths of island riding. That being: anytime you find yourself near the water (in this case, disembarking from a ferry), you will soon be climbing to get away from it. Look at the elevation profile and you'll see that most of the climbs are short and steep. However, at 2 miles or so, this one's longer than most.

State Route 525 can be busy, especially after a ferry arrives, but the shoulder is wide and you're on it for less than 3 miles before

< Along with excellent cycling, Whidbey Island boasts beautiful beaches along the Strait of Juan de Fuca.

you turn left onto Cultus Bay Road. Here's where the low-traffic rural roads kick in, as you pedal south rolling up and down a series of winding rural roads through dense woods, horse farms, and bucolic valley meadows. Steep climbs are followed by rollicking descents (some up to a 10 percent grade, both up *and* down) with almost nothing in between—you're a yo-yo on a bike.

At about 11 miles, reach Maxwelton, a tiny beachside community on Useless Bay, so named because early explorers found the inviting bay's waters too shallow for their tall ships. As a quick stop at Mackie County Park

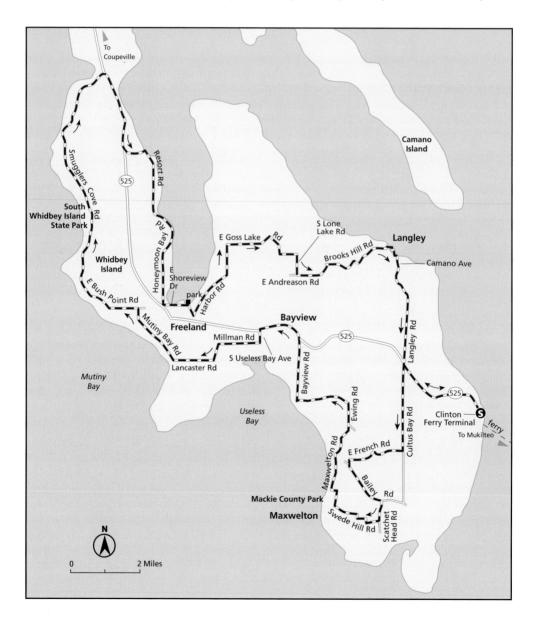

Set on a bluff overlooking Saratoga Passage and Camano Island, charming Langley makes a great lunch stop on a riding tour of South Whidbey Island.

illustrates (just a couple hundred yards to the left on Maxwelton Road), the bay might've proved useless but the views west toward Marrowstone Island and the Olympic Mountains are priceless.

Continuing inland (interestingly, not that steeply) and north, find yourself back on State Route 525 at Bayview, a small sort-of town with refreshment options. You're on potentially busy, but wide-shouldered State Route 525 for a little more than a mile before turning left onto rural roads that roll up and down through fields, forest, farms, and valleys before descending to waterside riding along Mutiny Bay.

And on and gloriously on much of this route goes: past forested South Whidbey Island State Park, which offers restrooms and seaside views; long stretches of smooth, wide-shouldered road with "Bike Route" signs; and cute seaside towns such as Freeland, a small village founded in the early 1900s as a socialist community. (There's a tiny park here.) Charming Langley is adorned with outdoor sculptures, colorful public art installations, and is fairly bursting at the seams with artsy-island vibe.

There are two more stretches of potentially busy State Route 525—one at about the 32-mile mark, the other the final 2.5-mile return to the Clinton ferry terminal.

MILEAGE LOG

0.0	From the Clinton ferry dock, head west on SR 525 N.
2.6	Left onto Cultus Bay Rd.
5.0	Right onto E. French Rd.
6.6	Left onto Bailey Rd.
8.3	Right onto Scatchet Head Rd.
8.7	Bear right onto Swede Hill Rd.
9.1	Right to stay on Swede Hill Rd.
10.8	Right onto Maxwelton Rd. Mackie County Park to left.
12.8	Left onto Ewing Rd. (Becomes Bayview Rd.)
16.8	Left onto SR 525 N.
18.0	Left onto S. Useless Bay Ave. (Becomes Millman Rd., Lancaster Rd.)
21.2	Becomes Mutiny Bay Rd.
23.1	Left onto E. Bush Point Rd. (Becomes Smugglers Cove Rd.)
27.2	South Whidbey Island State Park.
31.6	Right onto SR 525 S.
34.0	Left onto Resort Rd. (Becomes Honeymoon Bay Rd.)
39.3	Left onto E. Shoreview Dr. (Becomes E. Stewart Rd.) Freeland Park.
40.3	Left onto Harbor Rd. (Might be unsigned.)
42.7	Right onto E. Goss Lake Rd.
44.9	Right onto S. Lone Lake Rd.
45.6	Left onto E. Andreason Rd.
46.1	Left onto Bayview Rd. (Becomes Brooks Hill Rd., 3rd St. in Langley.)
48.3	Enter Langley.
48.5	Left onto Anthes Ave.
48.5	Right onto 2nd St.
48.7	Right onto Cascade Ave.
49.0	Left onto Camano Ave. (Becomes Langley Rd.)
52.3	Left onto SR 525 S.
54.9	Return to ferry dock.

SEATTLE METRO

With a network of paved pathways and dedicated bike lanes, Seattle is perennially ranked as one of America's most bike-friendly metropolitan areas. Its outlying area is a bit of cycling nirvana as well. Many of this section's routes begin on Seattle's urban roadways but soon enough—often after transitioning to paved trail—lead to quiet country roads through farmland and outlying towns and communities.

14 SNOHOMISH–GRANITE FALLS–MONROE LOOP

Difficulty	Moderate
Time	2½ to 4 hours
Distance	47.6 miles
Elevation Gain	1630 feet

ROAD CONDITIONS: Paved rail trail and winding country roads, some with narrow shoulders.

GETTING THERE: Drive US Hwy 2 to Snohomish and take the 88th St. SE exit. Head west toward Snohomish on 88th St. SE, which becomes 92nd St. SE, and then becomes 2nd St. At 0.7 mile, turn right onto Maple Ave. Continue for 0.7 mile to the Centennial Trail on your right. On-street parking is available.

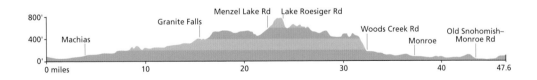

A mix of flat rail trail and roller-coaster hills awaits riders on this terrific rural Snohomish County route. Start by heading north from Snohomish on the epic Centennial Trail, the 23-mile paved rail trail that reaches from Snohomish to just north of Arlington in Bryant. (Begun in 1989 as part of a celebration for Washington State's 100th anniversary, the Centennial Trail will one day reach far into Skagit County.) The paved trail passes through bucolic pastureland along the scenic Pilchuck River. Enjoy the peace of no cars, SUVs, or pickup trucks with insanely wide side-view mirrors.

In just under 5 miles, leave the Centennial (perhaps after a visit to the plush Machias

The flat, fast run-in to Snohomish via Old Snohomish-Monroe Road

restrooms) and after a short stretch on Machias Road, turn right and cross the Pilchuck River. Just ahead, go left and begin a pleasant stretch on winding, low-trafficked country roads with here and there a roller of sorts.

The pleasantness is interrupted by a couple-mile stint on State Route 92 (Granite Falls Highway)—you'll know it by the fast-moving traffic and the aforementioned big-eared pickups—but thankfully, the shoulder is wide. After some more country riding, and a very short stretch again on State Route 92, enter Granite Falls, where all sorts of food and drink establishments await.

Work your way east through town on E. Pioneer Street. Pioneer becomes Menzel Lake Road, marking the beginning of a 20-plus mile stretch of mostly (though not always) gentle ups and downs. Though the rolling, winding road doesn't feature a lot of traffic, its shoulder is narrow and the vehicles that do travel it tend to be on the heavy-duty, wide side-mirrored side. Be careful.

About 6 miles past scenic Lake Roesiger and its accompanying day-use and camping park (water here, if needed), begin a fast mile-plus-long descent into Woods Creek. Enjoy this last little bit of Snohomish County nirvana-esque riding because in about 5 miles you'll pass through the aesthetically challenged sprawlville of Monroe. The upside is that all kinds of grocery stores, mini-marts, and espresso joints line the highway along this strip.

Carefully cross US Highway 2 and after pedaling east down W. Main Street, continue west out of town toward flat and potentially rocket-fast Old Snohomish–Monroe Road. At the intersection with State Route 522, there is a semi-tricky rotary to negotiate and just past that, a bit of a narrow shoulder, but soon enough traffic thins out, you're out in flat farmland, and, with the likely south wind at your back, it's a fun final 5 miles back into Snohomish.

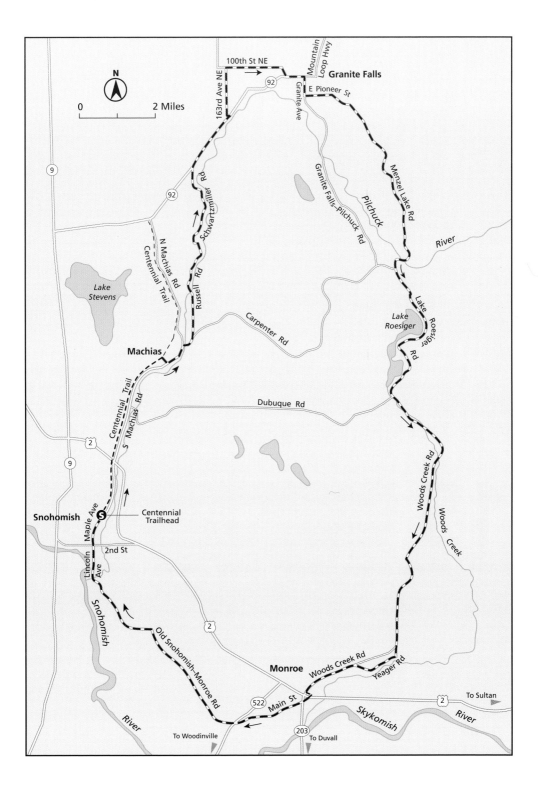

N

0   2 Miles

100th St NE

Mountain Loop Hwy

Granite Falls

163rd Ave NE

92

E Pioneer St

Granite Ave

9

92

Schwartzmiller Rd

N Machias Rd
Centennial Trail

Russell Rd

Menzel Lake Rd

Granite Falls–Pilchuck Rd

Pilchuck

River

Lake Stevens

Carpenter Rd

Lake Roesiger

Lake Roesiger Rd

Machias

Centennial Trail

S Machias Rd

Dubuque Rd

2

9

Woods Creek Rd

S

Centennial Trailhead

Snohomish

Maple Ave

Woods Creek

2nd St

Lincoln Ave

Snohomish River

Old Snohomish-Monroe Rd

2

Monroe

Woods Creek Rd

Yeager Rd

522

Main St

To Sultan

2

Skykomish River

To Woodinville

203

To Duvall

0.0   In Snohomish, head north on Centennial Trail.
4.8   Right onto Division St. at Machias Trailhead.
5.0   Left onto S. Machias Rd.
5.5   Right onto OK Mill Rd.
6.0   Left onto 147th Ave. NE. (Becomes Russell Rd.)
8.7   Right onto Schwartzmiller Rd.
10.7   Right onto SR 92 (Granite Falls Hwy.).
12.5   Left onto 84th St. NE.
12.6   Right onto 163rd Ave. NE.
13.6   Right onto 100th St. NE.
15.0   Right onto 187th Ave. NE (Jordan Rd.).
15.4   Left onto SR 92 (Granite Falls Hwy.). Enter Granite Falls.
15.7   Right onto Granite Ave.
15.9   Left onto E. Pioneer St. (Becomes Menzel Lake Rd. and eventually Lake Roesiger Rd.)
27.1   Left onto Woods Creek Rd.
34.4   Left onto Yeager Rd.
36.3   Left onto Woods Creek Rd.
37.6   Left onto Oaks St.
38.0   Right onto Old Owen Rd., which becomes Main St. in Monroe. Follow through Monroe; road becomes Old Snohomish–Monroe Rd.
46.9   Left onto 2nd St. (in Snohomish).
47.0   Right onto Maple Ave.
47.6   Back to starting point.

15 KENMORE–SULTAN LOOP

Difficulty	Strenuous
Time	3½ to 6 hours
Distance	69.7 miles
Elevation Gain	2950 feet

ROAD CONDITIONS: Paved trail, short stretches of urban roadways, winding country roads with narrow shoulders but low(ish) speed limits. Many city streets have bike lanes.

GETTING THERE: From I-5 in north Seattle, take exit 171 and head northeast on Lake City Wy. (SR 522) for 6.3 miles. (The road becomes NE Bothell Wy. after 4 miles.) Turn right onto 61st Ave. NE and at the bottom of the hill, turn right into Log Boom Park.

Burke-Gilman/
Sammamish
River Trails
Broadway Ave
Old Owen Rd
Fales Rd
Woodinville
Woodinville
Duvall Rd
Snohomish
Sultan
Tualco Rd

800'
400'
0'

0 miles   10   20   30   40   50   60   69.7

Head north from Kenmore on this serpentine Snohomish County tour that takes in Snohomish and Monroe before making the turnaround at Sultan, a tiny burg whose name is an anglicized version of Tsul-tad, a local Native American chief in the 1870s. (In the late 1960s, this town hosted the Sky River Rock Festival and Lighter Than Air Fair, which featured, among others, Santana, the Grateful Dead, Pink Floyd, and comedian Richard Pryor.) Though much of this route's road shoulders are narrow, the thoroughfares are lightly traveled and speed limits are generally low—35 miles per hour and below.

From Log Boom Park, head east on the paved Burke-Gilman Trail, the granddaddy of Puget Sound's paved pathways and, as signs along the way point out, member of the Rail Trail Hall of Fame. Obey the stop signs and be aware of families on bikes (which often include wobbly kids learning how to ride), runners, walkers, pet owners whose pets aren't as well mannered as their owners imagine, and the like. Also watch for cracked bits in the pavement and spots where growing roots are emerging from below. Try not to feel snootily superior to those poor schlubs in cars and trucks stuck in traffic mere yards to your left whilst you zoom past, enjoying the freedom of human pedal power.

At 2.5 miles, turn left onto the Sammamish River Trail. The route follows said river for 3 miles to Woodinville Fields. Here, you're momentarily thrust into a world of

A winter ride through Snohomish County

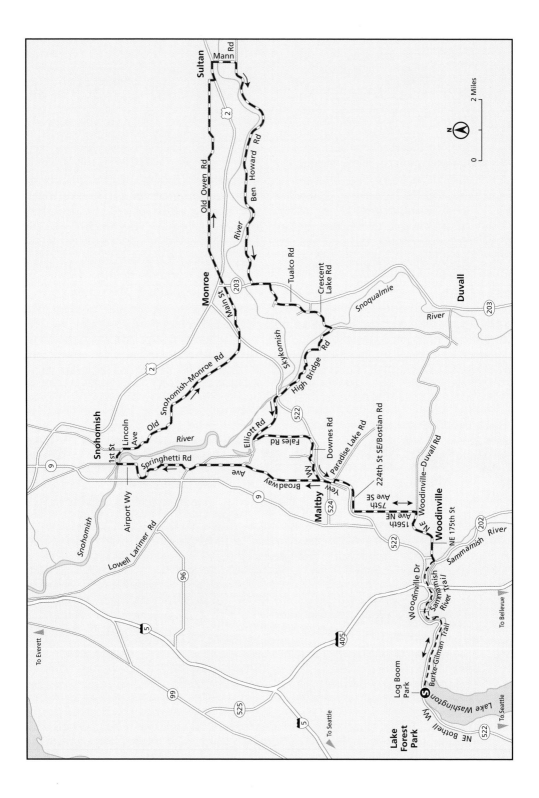

mega-traffic, fast food joints, and gas stations. Maneuver your way onto NE 175th Street and head east through Woodinville and then up. The road climbs almost 400 feet in 1.5 miles, with a stretch or two tickling 9 percent. But fret not; it's the steepest pitch on this ride and, coming so early, is a good warm-up. At the top of the climb, turn left and soon you're in Snohomish County.

The roads are a tad rougher, the scenery more rural, the hills more rolling, and where the road shoulder is narrower, the speed limits are generally lower. (Except when they're not.) After maneuvering across State Route 522 at Maltby, continue north toward Snohomish through an ever more agricultural landscape, dropping speedily when you swoop down into the Snohomish River floodplain. Just after crossing the river, roll into the town of Snohomish at the 20-mile point—a lot of of nice places for food, drink, 'n' restrooms here, as well as a bike shop. Turn right onto 1st Street and follow it for a little more than a half mile through town to Lincoln Avenue.

Go right—Lincoln soon becoming Old Snohomish–Monroe Road—and pick up some speed on the flat 6-mile run across the Snohomish floodplain into Monroe. Continue straight through town on what's now become its main street, following it to the intersection with US Highway 2, which, thankfully, you'll be crossing, not riding on. That comes later.

Like a lot of Washington towns (towns everywhere?), Monroe boasts a nice downtown but its outskirts are ravaged by an absolute hell of a sprawl, which, if you're like me, you'll want to sprint through as quickly as possible. But if you need eats or drinks—or a bike shop, which is located right on Main Street—stop and then go, go, go.

Across US Highway 2, continue straight onto what is now Old Owen Road, a lovely road that, though a bit chip-sealy in spots, winds through rural countryside offering big-

time views of the Cascades. Climbing gradually, Old Owen continues this way for about 6 miles before dropping sharply in a winding descent that delivers you back to US Highway 2, just west of Sultan. Here's where you *do* ride along the highway, turning left and heading east, but for less than a mile. In Sultan, turn right onto Mann Road, cross the Skykomish River, and just ahead, go right on Ben Howard Road and begin making your way west back toward the Monroe end of the world.

Similar to Old Owen, Ben Howard offers a pleasant rural riding experience, albeit with a different flavor. Largely forested and potentially damp, the road rolls up and down for almost 10 rollicking miles, tracing the meanderings of the Skykomish River and offering several spots to stop and gaze riverward. The speed limit's low (35 mph), so the few vehicles that do pass you shouldn't be doing it at scary-fast speeds. At the T intersection with busy State Route 203, just south of Monroe, go left and follow 203 for about three-quarters of a mile to Tualco Road, where you turn right.

After a terrifically fun flatland traverse of the Snoqualmie-Skykomish floodplains, turn right onto High Bridge Road and enjoy a challenging series of winding rollers along and above the confluence of the rivers. After a short steep descent on Elliott, keep your eyes peeled for Fales Road, where you have to make a nearly 180-degree left turn and then head straight up. This segment might seem a bit cruel, but hey, if you were looking for easy, you'd be playing golf.

This last big climb of the day (Fales Road and then Downes Road, which you turn right onto) climbs about 400 feet over 3 miles. This may not sound bad, but it does so via a series of steep steps. At the top of the hill, turn left onto Yew Way and follow for a mile to tiny Maltby, where you rejoin the route at the State Route 522 intersection that you negotiated on the way out. Return the same way for the last 12 miles back to Kenmore.

0.0	From Log Boom Park, head east on Burke-Gilman Trail.
2.6	Left onto Sammamish River Trail.
5.5	Exit trail at 131st Ave. NE near Woodinville Fields.
5.6	Left onto 131st Ave. NE.
5.7	Right onto NE 175th St. (Becomes NE Woodinville–Duvall Rd.)
7.1	Right to stay on NE Woodinville–Duvall Rd.
7.7	Left onto 156th Ave. NE.
11.3	Left onto Paradise Lake Rd.
11.4	Right onto Yew Wy.
11.9	Left onto Broadway Ave.
16.6	Right onto Springhetti Rd. (Becomes Airport Wy.)
19.7	Right onto 1st St. (in Snohomish)
20.3	Right onto Lincoln Ave. (Becomes Old Snohomish–Monroe Rd.)
26.1	Becomes 164th, then 162nd St. SE, then Main St. in Monroe.
28.5	Cross US Hwy 2; road becomes Old Owen Rd.
35.2	Left onto US Hwy 2.
36.0	Right onto Mann Rd.
36.8	Right onto Ben Howard Rd.
45.2	Left onto SR 203 S. (Monroe–Duvall Rd.).
45.8	Right onto Tualco Rd.
46.5	Left to stay on Tualco Rd.
47.5	Left onto Crescent Lake Rd.
48.8	Right onto High Bridge Rd. (Becomes Elliott Rd.)
52.2	Slight right onto Elliott Rd.
54.1	Left onto Fales Rd.
56.0	Right onto Downes Rd.
56.8	Left onto Yew Wy.
57.8	Bear left to stay on Yew Wy.
58.3	Left onto Paradise Lake Rd.
58.4	Right onto Bostian Rd. (91st Ave. SE). (Becomes 156th Ave NE.)
62.0	Right onto NE Woodinville–Duvall Rd.
62.5	Left to stay on NE Woodinville–Duvall Rd. (Becomes NE 175th St.)
64.0	Left onto 131st Ave NE.
64.1	Right onto Sammamish River Trail by Woodinville Fields.
67.1	Right onto Burke-Gilman Trail.
69.7	Return to Log Boom Park.

16 SUPER TORTURE METRIC CENTURY

Difficulty	Very Strenuous
Time	4 to 7 hours
Distance	58.2 miles
Elevation Gain	6250 feet

ROAD CONDITIONS: Urban and residential streets, many with bike lanes and wide shoulders. Some not so wide. A couple stretches of paved bike paths.

GETTING THERE: From SR 520 near Redmond, take the W. Lake Sammamish Pkwy. NE exit. Head south on W. Lake Sammamish Pkwy. NE for 0.6 mile and turn left into Marymoor Park. Park in the east Marymoor parking lot.

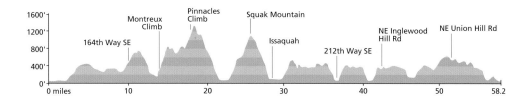

This route follows the first half of the loosely organized Torture Century, which is hosted (sort of) by Native Planet and the Cascade Bicycle Club. The route has basically one goal: to get you climbing as many hills as possible in as short a distance as possible. It features several well-known Seattle-area climbs, including Montreaux, Cougar Mountain, Squak Mountain, and Zoo Hill (though on this route, Zoo Hill is a descent). You average more than 1000 feet of climbing for every 10 miles, but these are not long, steady climbs. Rather, they're short, steep pitches with their own painful charms.

From Marymoor Park, head south through mostly residential area via 164th Avenue NE and SE. A few rollers here and there will warm you up for what's in store. Approach-

ing Interstate 90, jump on the I-90 Trail Walk and follow it for about a mile. It is paved, but watch for spots where tree roots are cracking the pavement. On the south side of the freeway, begin your first real climb of the day, ascending 450 feet over 2 miles, first on Newport Way and then on 164th Way SE.

Like most of the route on the south side of the freeway, this section follows residential streets and thoroughfares. The streets are wide but pose their own potential dangers: folks backing out of driveways, errant Frisbees and/or soccer balls, and so forth.

Once at the top, turn left on Lakemont Boulevard and enjoy the ride's other major theme: fast descents. Control your speed. Repeat: Control your speed. See previous paragraph about this being a residential area with the potential for errant soccer balls, sometimes with small soccer players in pursuit.

After quickly losing all that elevation you worked so hard to gain (along with a few millimeters of brake pads), turn right onto NW Village Park Drive and begin the longest climb of the day. The first part is known as the Montreux Climb—starting as it does in the tony neighborhood of that name—and climbs 650 feet in less than a mile and a half.

After that, spend about a mile on mostly flat, even slightly downhill Lakemont Boulevard SE (consider a break at Lewis Creek Park, which has restroom facilities). Next, turn left onto SE Cougar Mountain Way, where the road once again tilts skyward, climbing 530 feet in little more than a mile. This is known as the Pinnacles Climb. At the top, turn around and head back down, taking a moment to enjoy the spectacular view of Seattle's downtown buildings, set against a backdrop of Puget Sound and the Olympic Mountains.

Continue your descent, keeping in mind all safety considerations. The rip-roaring 3.5-mile drop includes Zoo Hill, so named because of the nearby Cougar Mountain Zoological Park. (Zoo Hill is the site of an annual hill climb time trial—ridden in the opposite direction, of course—that also acts as a cancer fundraiser.)

After another stiff residential climb—the epic Squak Mountain Loop Climb, which gains roughly 1000 feet in not quite 3 miles—the route comes back down to earth. Zip through Issaquah (unless you want a break to resupply), cross Interstate 90, and follow a paved pathway up a hill toward the Issaquah Highlands on the east side of Lake Sammamish.

From here, the theme largely continues—up, then down, then up, then down—though this time on country roads and highways with longer, straighter sections. At times, the traffic is sparse, but when it's not, be on your toes for fast-moving vehicles. The route approaches Lake Sammamish, then turns east into the nearby hills, approaches the lake again, then heads for Ames Lake before turning west toward Redmond via the rollers of Union Hill Road.

The return to Redmond and Marymoor Park includes 1.5 miles of busy and fast-moving traffic on Redmond–Fall City Road and Redmond Way, where concentration and good bike sense are key.

MILEAGE LOG

0.0	From the Marymoor Park east entrance parking lot, head toward the main entrance at the park's west side. (Your return is to the park's east entrance.)
1.3	Left onto W. Lake Sammamish Pkwy. NE.
2.1	Bear left to stay on W. Lake Sammamish Pkwy. NE.
2.4	Right onto 172nd Ave. NE.
3.3	Right onto NE 30th St.
3.8	Left onto 164th Ave. NE.
6.5	Left onto SE 14th St. (Becomes 168th Ave. SE.)
7.4	Bear right on SE 24th St.
7.6	Left onto 161st Ave. SE.
8.4	Left onto SE Eastgate Wy. (Enter bike path just ahead from small parking lot on the right.)
9.5	Cross over I-90 via pedestrian bridge.
9.6	Right onto SE Newport Wy.
10.0	Left on 164th Wy. SE. (Name changes a couple times, returns to 164th Wy. SE.)

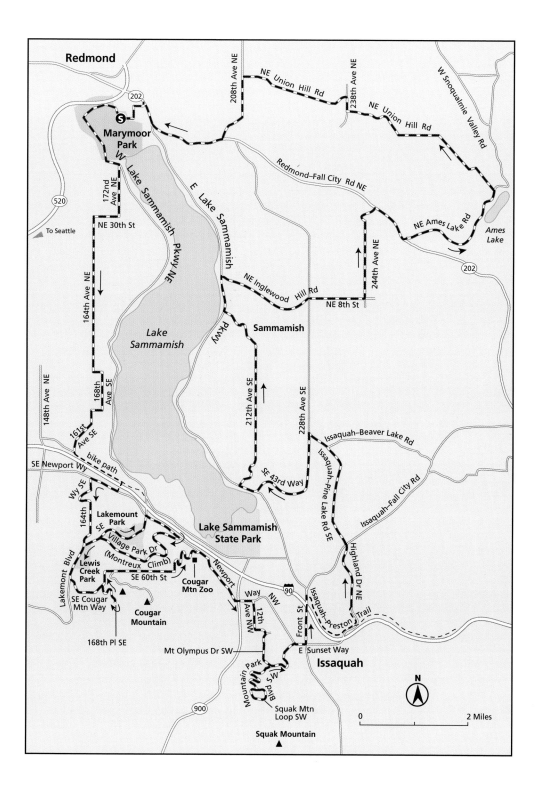

Redmond

208th Ave NE

NE Union Hill Rd

238th Ave NE

NE Union Hill Rd

W Snoqualmie Valley Rd

202

S

Marymoor
Park

Redmond–Fall City Rd NE

NE Ames Lake Rd

Ames
Lake

520

172nd Ave NE

NE 30th St

E Lake Sammamish Pkwy NE

W Lake Sammamish Pkwy NE

244th Ave NE

202

To Seattle

164th Ave NE

NE Inglewood Hill Rd

NE 8th St

168th Ave SE

E Lake Sammamish Pkwy

Lake
Sammamish

Sammamish

148th Ave NE

161st Ave SE

212th Ave SE

228th Ave SE

Issaquah–Beaver Lake Rd

SE Newport Wy

bike path

SE 43rd Way

Issaquah–Pine Lake Rd SE

Issaquah–Fall City Rd

Wy SE

164th SE

Lakemount
Park

Village Park Dr

(Montreux Climb)

Lake Sammamish
State Park

Highland Dr NE

Lakemont Blvd

Lewis
Creek
Park

SE 60th St

Cougar
Mtn Zoo

Newport

Way

90

Issaquah–Preston Trail

SE Cougar
Mtn Way

168th Pl SE

Cougar
Mountain

NW

12th Ave NW

Front St

Mt Olympus Dr SW

E Sunset Way

Issaquah

Mountain Park Dr SW

N

Squak Mtn
Loop SW

0   2 Miles

Squak Mountain

900

11.6	Left onto Lakemont Blvd. SE.
13.3	Right onto SE Newport Wy.
14.1	Right onto NW Village Park Dr.
16.5	Left onto Lakemont Blvd. SE.
17.1	Lewis Creek Park (restrooms).
17.5	Left onto SE Cougar Mountain Wy.
18.4	Right onto 168 Pl. SE. (Becomes 169th and 170th Pl. SE.)
19.1	Turnaround.
19.6	Bear right to stay on 168 Pl. SE.
19.9	Bear right onto SE 60th St.
21.1	Left onto 189 Ave. SE.
22.5	Right onto Newport Wy. NW.
23.7	Right onto 12th Ave. NW.
24.2	Bear left onto Mount Olympus Dr. NW.
24.4	Right onto Mount Olympus Dr. SW.
24.9	Bear left onto Mountain Park Blvd. SW.
25.0	Right onto Mountainside Dr. SW.
26.0	Right onto Squak Mountain Loop SW.
26.8	Right onto Mountainside Dr. SW.
27.7	Right onto Mountain Park Blvd. SW.
28.6	Left onto Front St. N. in Issaquah.
30.0	Cross I-90 via sidewalk and bike trail, then turn right onto Issaquah–Preston Trail.
31.4	Right onto Highland Dr. NE.
32.3	Straight on Issaquah–Pine Lake Rd. SE.
34.6	Left onto 228th Ave. SE. (Becomes SE 43rd Wy.)
36.7	Right onto E. Lake Sammamish Pkwy. SE.
37.2	Right onto 212th Wy. SE. (Becomes 212th Ave. SE then Louis Thompson Rd. SE.)
40.8	Right onto E. Lake Sammamish Pkwy. NE.
41.4	Right onto NE Inglewood Hill Rd. (Eventually becomes NE 8th St.)
44.2	Left onto 244th Ave. NE.
45.9	Right onto SR 202 (Redmond–Fall City Rd. NE)
46.7	Left onto NE Ames Lake Rd.
49.0	Left onto NE Union Hill Rd.
52.2	Right onto 238th Ave. NE.
52.5	Left onto NE Union Hill Rd.
54.5	Left onto 208th Ave. NE.
55.8	Right onto SR 202 (Redmond–Fall City Rd. NE)
57.4	Left onto E. Lake Sammamish Pkwy. NE.
57.5	Right onto NE 65th St.
57.8	Bear left on NE Marymoor Wy.
58.2	Reenter Marymoor Park near the east entrance parking lot.

< *A rider tilts at Squak Mountain's 17-percent grade.*

17 MARYMOOR–MONROE–SNOHOMISH LOOP

Difficulty	Moderate
Time	2½ to 4 hours
Distance	51.4 miles
Elevation Gain	1935 feet

ROAD CONDITIONS: Everything from busy urban streets and suburban roadways to lightly traveled, rural roads. Road surface and shoulder widths run the gamut too.

GETTING THERE: From SR 520 near Redmond, take the W. Lake Sammamish Pkwy. NE exit. Head south on W. Lake Sammamish Pkwy. NE for 0.6 mile and turn left into Marymoor Park. Park in the east Marymoor parking lot.

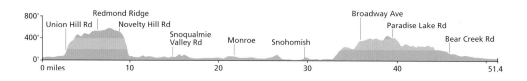

Here's a 50-miler that transports you from the hustle and bustle of the city to the scenic beauty and winding rural roads of the Snoqualmie River Valley, all in a matter of about 10 miles. This tour throws in a visit to a couple Snohomish County towns too—Monroe and Snohomish, each with bike shops and places to eat and drink. As for hills, the elevation profile resembles a dumbbell—expect a good bit of climbing in the first 8 miles, a flat 25 miles in the middle, and a final bit of climbing on the way out of Snohomish. Nice reward toward the end: the last 10 miles are downhill or flat.

From Marymoor Park in Redmond, carefully pick your way across E. Lake Sammamish Parkway and Redmond Way, get on 180th Avenue NE, and begin inching your way out of suburbia. Redmond's bike lanes will provide a bit of breathing room. Go right onto Union Hill Road and begin warming up those quads, calves, and lungs as you make your way up the hill. Overall, the route climbs for the next 5 miles—with some dips and doodles along the way—the first 1.7 miles being the steepest. Unfortunately, some bits have a narrow road shoulder too, but that widens out a bit when you turn left onto 238th Avenue NE (which becomes Redmond Ridge Drive NE).

At 8.1 miles, turn right onto Novelty Hill Road, the novelty here being that, for the most part, you're done with climbing for the next 25 miles. But not with descending. Just ahead is a potentially hair-raising descent into the Snoqualmie River Valley, clinging to a road shoulder that is balance-beam skinny. Be careful, minding those flashing "SLOW DOWN" signs while you drop at what feels like free-fall speed. (You're losing 450 feet of elevation in little over a mile.)

Not far from the bustle of suburban Seattle, riders can enjoy the slower pace and rural farmland of the Snoqualmie River Valley.

Once at the bottom, turn left onto Snoqualmie Valley Road, and follow the wide swath cut over the millennia by the Snoqualmie River. The road is a bit narrow and winding, so be careful and keep your eyes on the road and not on the emerging mountain views (including Mount Baker) to the east. After about 7 miles of this, drop down into the floodplain via Crescent Lake Road, then cross it via Tualco Road, and enjoy a 3-mile zigzag across the valley floor.

Emerge just south of Monroe and turn left onto State Route 203. Exercise caution on this major thoroughfare; in a half mile, it enters Monroe and the speed limit drops to 25. Turn left onto Main Street (where there's a bike shop), and begin heading west out of town toward the town of Snohomish. Main Street becomes 162nd Street SE, then 164th Street SE, and, once past the rotary at the State Route 522 intersection, Old Snohomish–Monroe Road. If you have a southern tailwind on this enjoyable, mostly flat 6-mile jaunt across the Skykomish River Valley, you'll think you're Fabian Cancellara winning yet another time-trial world championship.

Upon entering Snohomish, take the first left—aptly named 1st Street. Go west and then turn left on Avenue D to head south out of town. Should you need a break, Snohomish has plenty of places to eat and drink as well as a bike shop. Back on the route, cross the Snohomish River, Avenue D now becoming Airport Way (then Springhetti Road). Enjoy your last 3 miles of hill-less riding before turning left onto Broadway and undertaking your first real hill in 25 miles. It's not killer, climbing only about 250 feet in a mile, and sets you up nicely for the series of roller coaster ups and downs over the ensuing 8 miles.

Both the road and the shoulder of Broadway are fairly narrow so concentration is key. Also requiring a heads-up is a stretch near Maltby. Veer right onto Yew, continue south

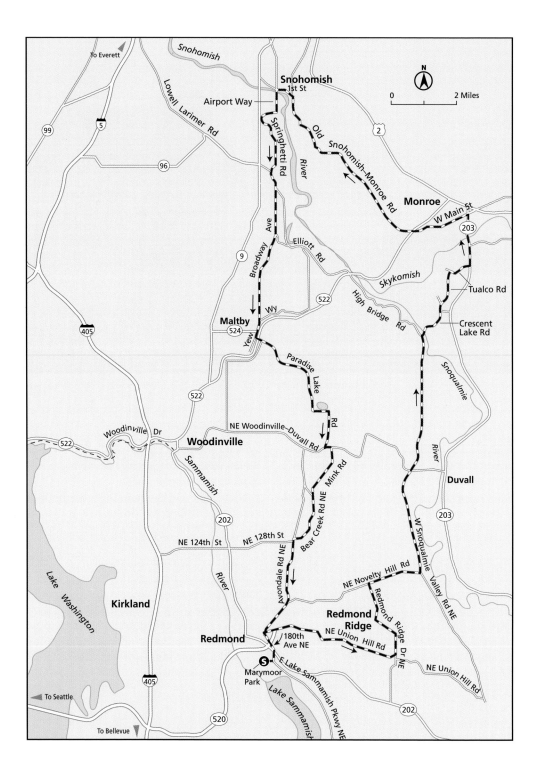

To Everett

Snohomish

Lowell Larimer Rd

99

5

96

9

Snohomish
1st St
Airport Way

Springhetti Rd

River

Old Snohomish-Monroe Rd

2

N

0   2 Miles

Monroe
W Main St
203

Tualco Rd

Broadway Ave

Elliott Rd

Skykomish

High Bridge Rd

Crescent
Lake Rd

405

Maltby
524
Wy
Yew

Paradise Lake Rd

522

Snoqualmie

NE Woodinville-Duvall Rd

River

Woodinville Dr

522

Woodinville

Sammamish

Duvall

203

202

NE 124th St   NE 128th St

Bear Creek Rd NE   Mink Rd NE

Avondale Rd NE

NE Novelty Hill Rd

Redmond Ridge Dr NE

W Snoqualmie Valley Rd NE

Lake Washington

Kirkland

River

Redmond
Ridge
NE Union Hill Rd

NE Union Hill Rd

Redmond
180th Ave NE

S Marymoor Park

E Lake Sammamish Pkwy NE

Lake Sammamish

405

520

202

To Seattle

To Bellevue

toward the intersection with State Route 522, and after turning left and crossing to the east side, continue straight on what is now Paradise Lake Road. Perhaps not quite paradise, the wide smooth road offers ample shoulder as well as some gentle ups and downs. Soon, cross the King County line, pass into more residential areas via Mink and Bear Creek roads, and then into Redmond itself, where you started. The return into Marymoor Park's east entrance requires concentration and the ability to see in about twelve directions at once.

MILEAGE LOG

0.0	Head northeast out of Marymoor Park on NE Marymoor Wy.
0.2	Bear right onto NE 65th St.
0.5	Left onto E. Lake Sammamish Pkwy. NE.
0.7	Continue straight onto 180th Ave. NE.
1.3	Right onto NE 80th St. (NE Union Hill Rd.)
5.4	Left onto 238th Ave. NE. (Becomes Redmond Ridge Dr. NE.)
8.1	Right onto NE Novelty Hill Rd.
9.9	Left onto W. Snoqualmie Valley Rd. NE. (Becomes High Bridge Rd.)
17.1	Right onto Crescent Lake Rd.
18.5	Right onto Tualco Rd.
19.4	Right to stay on Tualco Rd.
20.2	Left onto SR 203. (Monroe–Duvall Rd.; becomes S. Lewis St.)
21.0	Enter Monroe.
21.7	Left onto W. Main St. (Becomes 162nd, then 164th St. SE.)
23.9	164th St. SE becomes Old Snohomish–Monroe Rd.
29.6	In Snohomish, left onto 1st St.
30.2	Left onto Avenue D. Cross bridge. (Becomes Airport Wy., Springhetti Rd.)
33.3	Left onto Broadway Ave.
38.1	Bear right onto Yew Wy.
38.5	Left onto Paradise Lake Rd.
43.3	Left onto NE Woodinville–Duvall Rd.
43.6	Right onto Mink Rd. NE. (206th Ave. NE).
45.2	Bear left onto Bear Creek Rd. NE. (Becomes NE 132nd St.)
46.7	Left onto Avondale Rd. NE.
49.8	Slight left onto Avondale Rd.
50.0	Left onto NE 80th St. (NE Union Hill Rd.).
50.1	Right onto 178th Pl NE. (Becomes 180th Ave. NE).
50.9	Right onto NE 65th St.
51.4	Return to Marymoor Park.

18 FLYING WHEELS 42-MILER

Difficulty	Moderate
Time	2 to 3½ hours
Distance	42 miles
Elevation Gain	2120 feet

ROAD CONDITIONS: Urban roadways with bike lane and rural roads with shoulders of varying width.

GETTING THERE: From SR 520 near Redmond, take the W. Lake Sammamish Pkwy. NE exit. Head south on W. Lake Sammamish Pkwy. NE for 0.6 mile and turn left into Marymoor Park. Park in the east Marymoor parking lot.

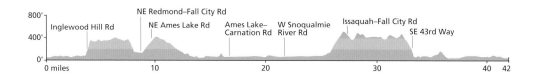

This route begins with an urban riding experience that surprises and delights with how quickly it takes a turn for the rural. From meandering along scenic Lake Sammamish, it heads inland and up, eventually dropping back down into the agriculturally rich Snoqualmie River Valley. (This is roughly the route of the 45-mile loop of Cascade Bicycle Club's Flying Wheels Summer Century.)

From Marymoor Park, head south along Lake Sammamish via E. Lake Sammamish Parkway for about 3.5 miles. You can take advantage of the bike lane, or, if you like to pretend you're riding the cobbled roads of Europe, jostle along the gravel surface of the Lake Sammamish Trail, which parallels the road. (Eventually the trail will be paved; as of press time, it was not.) At Inglewood, after negotiating a roundabout, head up, up, and away toward the more rural reaches of

King County. NE Inglewood Hill Road is a stiff climb—it gains about 280 feet in a half mile with pitches up to 12 percent—but it's not long and the shoulder offers some space should you get a case of the weavie-wobblies. Once at the top, you've got a series of rollers on smooth, tree-lined residential roads— some with bike lanes, some without—before dropping down via a fast, sweeping descent to NE Redmond–Fall City Road.

Busy roadway this is, with not much shoulder, but your passage on it is short (less than a mile). At NE Ames Lake Road, turn left and begin a steep ascent up a winding, just-over-a-mile-long climb that has a pitch or two at 16 percent. (Try not to think about that last bit.)

But you're soon rewarded, for the sweeping descent delivers you into the Snoqualmie River Valley, where the route veers right and heads south following the serpentine river for

Just outside Carnation, a rider crosses the Snoqualmie River via the Tolt Hill Bridge.

about 12 miles. Along the way, the route dips and doodles past farms, fields, and ranches with stunning views of hills and mountains beyond. At the 19-mile mark, pass through Carnation, which offers grocery stores and mini-marts. A true highlight of this stretch is W. Snoqualmie River Road, a mellow riverside ramble that passes the Carnation Marsh Natural Area.

At the 25-mile mark, shortly after crossing SE Redmond–Fall City Road, strap your climbing legs back on for the next hilly ride: almost 400 feet of up in the next 1.3 miles, followed by 5 miles of rolling ups and downs on ever-more residential roadway (mostly with wide shoulders or bike lanes). A final smooth descent delivers you back to the shores of Lake Sammamish. From here, it's a little more than 8 miles back to Marymoor Park via E. Lake Sammamish Parkway, bike lane and bike signs aiding and abetting your ride.

MILEAGE LOG

0.0	From Marymoor Park, go east on E. Lake Sammamish Trail toward E. Lake Sammamish Pkwy.
0.5	Left, followed by two quick rights to exit trail and enter E. Lake Sammamish Pkwy.
3.7	Left onto Inglewood Hill Rd.
6.5	Left onto 244th Ave. NE.
8.2	Right onto NE Redmond–Fall City Rd.
9.0	Left onto NE Ames Lake Rd.
12.8	Left onto W. Snoqualmie Valley Rd.

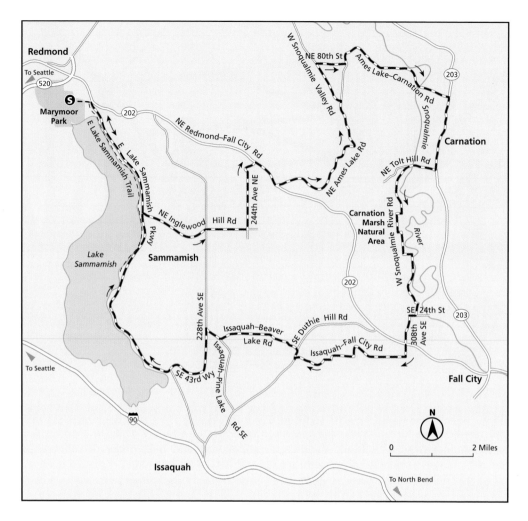

13.9	Right onto NE 80th St.
14.6	Left onto Ames Lake–Carnation Rd.
17.9	Right onto SR 203.
18.7	Enter Carnation.
19.7	Right onto NE Tolt Hill Rd.
20.4	Left onto W. Snoqualmie River Rd.
24.5	Right onto SE 24th St.
24.6	Left onto 309th Ave SE.
25.0	Bear left onto 308th Ave. SE. (Cross Redmond–Fall City Rd. just ahead.)
25.6	Right onto SE 40th St. (Becomes Issaquah–Fall City Rd.)
27.2	Bear right to stay on Issaquah–Fall City Rd.
28.8	Right onto SE Duthie Hill Rd.
29.0	Left onto Issaquah–Beaver Lake Rd.
31.0	Bear right at roundabout onto Issaquah–Pine Lake Rd SE.
31.5	Left onto 228th Ave SE. (Becomes SE 43rd Wy.)

33.5	Right onto E. Lake Sammamish Pkwy.
41.4	Left onto E. Lake Sammamish Trail.
42.0	Reenter Marymoor Park.

19 RENTON–BLACK DIAMOND

Difficulty	Moderate
Time	2 to 3½ hours
Distance	43.2 miles
Elevation Gain	1895 feet

ROAD CONDITIONS: Paved trail, winding and rolling country roads with narrow shoulders but low speed limits. Residential roads, some with bike lanes.

GETTING THERE: From I-405 in Renton, take exit 4 and head east on Maple Valley Hwy. (SR 169) for a half mile to Cedar River Park Dr. Turn right and park at the aquatic center or Renton Community Center.

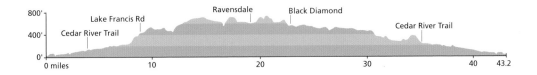

This urban-to-rural route takes you out to the roller-coaster rollers of the Ravensdale–Black Diamond part of the world. (And yes, to Black Diamond, which to Puget Sound cyclists means one thing: a stop at the venerable Black Diamond Bakery.) The route begins and finishes with 8 miles of the Cedar River Trail, one of the many paved bike trails in the Puget Sound area.

From the Renton Community Center, cross to the south side of the Cedar River and go left on the obvious paved trail. (**Note:** The speed limit on the first mile or so of this first stretch is 10 mph.) The trail parallels busy State Route 169, and you'll be thankful that you're not sharing the road with the scrum of high-speed cars, trucks, buses. Follow the trail as it goes under the highway and passes first Maplewood Golf and Country Club and then Cedar River Park. At Cedar Grove Road, say goodbye to the trail and start climbing away from the Cedar River. Turn right onto SE Lake Francis Road and, continuing to climb, follow as your surroundings become more and more rural. Eventually, the road flattens out, but only briefly, for you're soon treated to a series of rolling ups and downs.

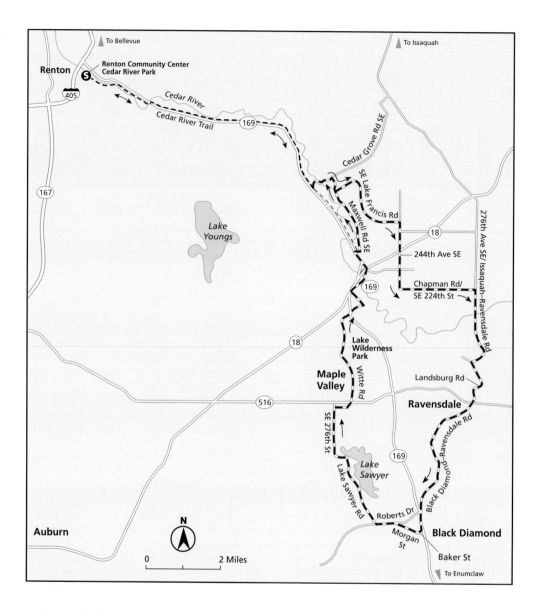

To Bellevue

To Issaquah

Renton

Renton Community Center
Cedar River Park

Cedar River

Cedar River Trail

169

405

167

Lake
Youngs

Cedar Grove Rd SE

SE Lake Francis Rd

Maxwell Rd SE

18

244th Ave SE

169

Chapman Rd/
SE 224th St

276th Ave SE/ Issaquah-Ravensdale Rd

18

Lake
Wilderness
Park

Landsburg Rd

**Maple
Valley**

Witte Rd

Ravensdale

516

SE 276th St

Lake Sawyer Rd

169

Lake
Sawyer

Black Diamond-Ravensdale Rd

Auburn

N

Roberts Dr

Morgan
St

Black Diamond

Baker St

0   2 Miles

To Enumclaw

On 276th Avenue (which becomes Lands-burg Road), return to the Cedar River via a steep descent, only to encounter an even steeper climb (up to 9 percent) on the other side. About halfway up, bear to the left on Landsburg Road SE and continue south toward Ravensdale. Various pulp mills and logging concerns funnel a fair number of big trucks onto the roadways, so be alert as you enjoy this section of rollers between Ravens-dale and Black Diamond.

In Black Diamond, make for the Black Diamond Bakery—it's sort of a cycling rite of passage. After you've had your fill, head north out of town, first via Roberts Drive and then Lake Sawyer Road (which changes names a couple times—just stay on the arterial). You'll follow these streets for 3-plus miles as you skirt the west shore of Lake Sawyer through mostly residential neighborhood.

Riders refuel during a break.

Turn right on SE 276th Street (which becomes Witte Road), maneuver through Maple Valley's newish development (sometimes via bike lane; sometimes not), and after a couple close encounters with State Route 169—one in which you cross it; a second in which you ride north on it for a hundred yards or so—turn right onto SE 216th Way. Just ahead, go left on Maxwell Road SE. (Yes, I know it looks a bit under-the-freeway-bridge scary, but coming up is a truly nice stretch of riding.) That's the Cedar River Trail there on your left, which you can jump back on now if you'd like, but I recommend following Maxwell, turning right just ahead onto SE 208th Street (which becomes Maxwell again) for a 2-mile meander through fields, farms, and forest. A short steep pitch returns you to Lake Francis Road, where you turn left and retrace your pedal strokes back to the start of this route.

MILEAGE LOG

0.0   In Renton, cross the Cedar River behind community center.
0.1   Left onto Cedar River Trail.
8.0   Left onto Cedar Grove Rd. SE.
8.6   Right onto SE Lake Francis Rd.
11.3   Right at 244th Ave. SE.
13.0   Left onto Chapman Rd. (SE 224th St.).
15.0   Right at 276th Ave. SE (Issaquah–Ravensdale Rd.) at Levdansky Park.
17.1   Left onto Landsburg Rd. SE (276th Ave SE).
18.4   Cross through intersection, bearing to the right. Becomes SE Ravensdale Wy.
18.8   Enter Ravensdale.

19.3	Becomes Black Diamond–Ravensdale Rd.
21.9	Left onto SR 169 (3rd Ave.). Enter Black Diamond.
22.5	Right onto Baker St.
22.7	Right onto Morgan St. (Railroad Ave.).
23.3	Left onto Roberts Dr.
23.8	Right onto Lake Sawyer Rd. SE. (Becomes 228th Ave. SE, 224th Ave SE, SE 296th St., 216th Ave. SE.)
27.3	Right onto SE 276th St. (Becomes Witte Rd.)
31.6	Right onto SR 169 N.
31.7	Right onto SE 218th St.
31.9	Left onto Maxwell Rd. SE.
32.5	Right onto SE 208th St.
32.6	Becomes 225th Ave. SE/Maxwell Rd SE.
34.4	Left onto SE Lake Francis Rd.
34.6	Left onto Cedar Grove Rd. SE.
35.2	Right onto Cedar River Trail.
43.2	Return to Renton Community Center.

20 ENUMCLAW–RAVENSDALE

Difficulty	Moderate
Time	2 to 3½ hours
Distance	41.1 miles
Elevation Gain	1575 feet

ROAD CONDITIONS: Quiet, low-traffic farm roads with varying shoulder widths; some rural chip-seal pavement; state highway with ample shoulder.

GETTING THERE: From I-5 near Federal Way, take exit 142. Head east on SR 18 for 4.4 miles to SR 164 E. Go right and follow for 13 miles to 244th Ave. SE in Enumclaw. Turn right and follow for 1 mile to Warner Ave. Turn left. Park on the street or in the high school parking lot just ahead.

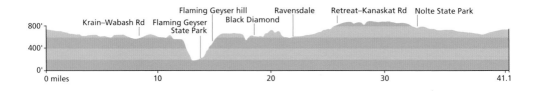

This south King County route features so many farms and pastures, you'll probably find yourself mooing—that is, when you're not ohhing and ahhing at the huge vistas of Mount Rainier. Also on this route are the much lusted-after Black Diamond Bakery and the not-so-lusted-after Flaming Geyser Climb, a mile-long ascent with pitches of 13 percent.

From Warner Avenue adjacent to Enumclaw High School, familiar to RAMROD (Ride Around Mount Rainier in One Day) veterans as the start/finish line, head west, pedaling through the flat dairy land that surrounds the town. Enjoy mega-views of Mount Rainier, just 25 miles away. Its sheer size never ceases to amaze.

Working your way north via rural roads—some smooth and ample shouldered, some with chip-seal surface and sans shoulder, but most not heavily traveled—find yourself at the precipice of a steep, mile-long curving descent into the Green River Valley. Shout "Wheee!!!"

really loud. (Which is exactly what you won't be shouting a mile or so later when you have to climb out of the same valley.) At the bottom of the hill, roughly the 14-mile mark, turn right onto SE Green Valley Road. On the right is Flaming Geyser State Park, should you need restrooms or a psyche-yourself-up-for-a-giant-hill meditation break. The park gets its name from the "flaming geyser" (only about six inches high, but once much higher) that is fueled by underground coal seams.

Now, that hill. In its entirety, the winding Flaming Geyser hill climbs more than 500 feet in about 1.5 miles, mostly at 6 to 8 percent grade with a pitch or two at 13 percent. It's one of the region's classic climbs. Need motivation? Consider this: once you reach the top, you're less than 3 miles from Black Diamond and its famed bakery. Climb done, head to Black Diamond by turning left onto State Route 169 (a bend in the road makes visibility challenging, so be careful making this

Before the annual Ravensdale road race, members of the Fanatik Bike Company team discuss strategy.

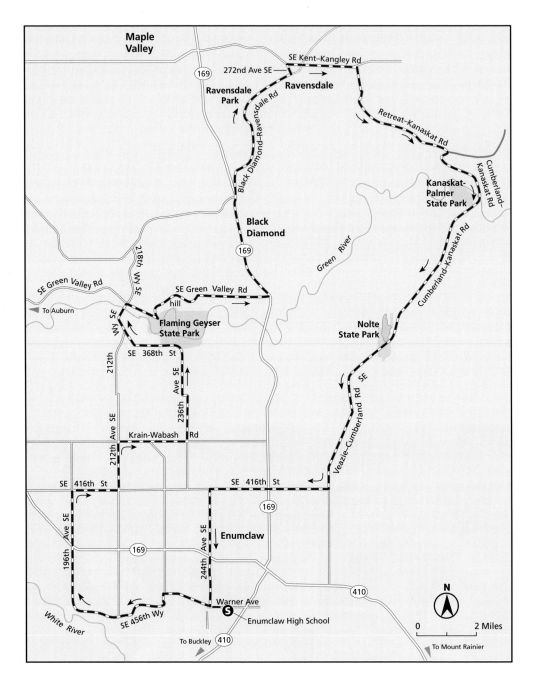

Maple
Valley

SE Kent–Kangley Rd

(169)

272nd Ave SE

Ravensdale
Park

Ravensdale

Retreat–Kanaskat Rd

Black Diamond–Ravensdale Rd

218th Wy SE

Cumberland–
Kanaskat Rd

Kanaskat–
Palmer
State Park

Black
Diamond

(169)

Green River

Cumberland–Kanaskat Rd

SE Green Valley Rd

To Auburn

SE Green Valley Rd

hill

Wy SE

212th

Flaming Geyser
State Park

Nolte
State Park

SE 368th St

Ave SE

236th

Veazie–Cumberland Rd SE

212th Ave SE

Krain–Wabash Rd

SE 416th St

SE 416th St

(169)

196th Ave SE

(169)

244th Ave SE

Enumclaw

(410)

White River

SE 456th Wy

Warner Ave

S

Enumclaw High School

N

To Buckley (410)

0   2 Miles

To Mount Rainier

turn). Though potentially busy, State Route
169 boasts a wide shoulder. (To get to Black
Diamond Bakery, turn left onto Railroad
Avenue/Jones Lake Road; the bakery is about
a half mile ahead on the left.)

Continuing through Black Diamond, turn
right onto Black Diamond–Ravensdale Road,
a winding roller-riffic romp with one biggish
climb followed by a biggish descent that drops
you into Ravensdale, an old coal-mining burg.

There's a market and park (restrooms) here should you need them; otherwise continue east and south through the rolling forestlands of Kanaskat and Cumberland. (Parts of this section show up on the Ravensdale Road Race, held each May.) The next 10 miles meander up and down through working forest and off-the-beaten-path farmland. The road is a bit rough, but that's sometimes the price you pay for quieter, low-traffic routes.

A couple state parks—Kanaskat-Palmer and Nolte—offer restrooms and respite.

Eventually, you pop back out onto Enumclaw's outlying farmland, with Mount Rainier looming in front of you, and hopefully, headwinds not pushing you backward. After a series of perpendicular farm roads, on which you make one 90-degree turn after another, return to Warner Avenue and Enumclaw High School.

MILEAGE LOG

0.0	From Enumclaw High School, head west on Warner Ave.
0.3	Left onto 244th Ave. SE.
0.3	Right onto SE 456th Wy.
1.3	Turn left at 228th Ave. SE. (Becomes 196th Ave. SE.)
6.0	Right onto SE 416th St.
7.0	Turn left at 212th Ave. SE.
8.0	Right onto Krain-Wabash Rd. (SE 400th St.).
9.5	Left onto 236th Ave. SE.
10.5	Left onto SE 384th St.; immediate right back onto 236th Ave. SE. (Becomes SE 368th St.)
12.8	Bear right onto 212th Wy. SE.
13.5	Right onto SE Green Valley Rd.
14.1	Flaming Geyser State Park.
14.3	Big hill.
16.9	Left onto SR 169 N. (Enumclaw Black–Diamond Rd. SE).
18.9	Black Diamond.
19.1	Right onto Black Diamond–Ravensdale Rd.
22.5	Left onto 272nd Ave. SE.
22.7	Right onto SE Kent–Kangley Rd. (SE 272nd St.).
24.0	Right at Retreat–Kanaskat Rd.
27.1	Right at Cumberland–Kanaskat Rd. (Becomes Veazie–Cumberland Rd.)
29.0	Kanaskat-Palmer State Park.
32.5	Nolte State Park.
35.8	Right onto SE 416th St.
38.3	Left onto 244th Ave. SE.
40.8	Left onto Warner Ave.
41.1	Return to start.

21   SUMNER–CARBONADO–ORTING

Difficulty	Strenuous
Time	3½ to 6 hours
Distance	69.7 miles
Elevation Gain	3430 feet

ROAD CONDITIONS: Rural roads and busy highways with varying shoulder widths. Mountain road with potentially rough surface.

GETTING THERE: From I-5 near Des Moines, take exit 149 and head east on SR 516 for 3 miles to SR 167. Turn right and head south for 12.6 miles toward Sumner. Take the SR 410 exit going east and then take the first exit off SR 410 (E. Main Traffic Ave.). Turn left onto Linden Dr. E., which becomes Traffic Ave., then Traffic St. and once it crosses Main St. in Sumner, Fryar Ave. Park at Pierce County Library just ahead on the left.

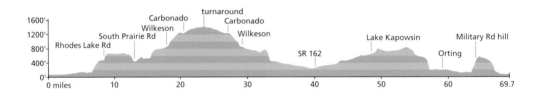

This 70-mile ramble takes in a bevy of Pierce County towns—Sumner, South Prairie, Wilkeson, Carbonado, Orting—and is dominated in one way or another by Mount Rainier, either by stunning views of the towering 14,441-foot volcano or by the scenic river valley you ride through, which was gouged eons ago by the mountain's glaciers.

Begin by maneuvering your way out of Sumner and south via State Route 162, basking in the pancake-flat landscape created over the millennia by the Puyallup River. Though this road can be busy, its shoulder is wide. A little more than 5 miles in, turn left onto 128th Street E. (which becomes McCutcheon Road E., then Rhodes Lake Road) and climb consistently for about 2.5 miles with

one steep stretch at 12 percent. The road is narrow and winding, but the speed limit is only 35.

At the top, after turning left onto 120th Street E., the route mellows out for a little, throws in a roller here and there, and after turning right onto South Prairie Road, drops precipitously with a screaming fun, snaking descent just a few hundred yards east of the small town of South Prairie. Later in the ride, you'll pass through the city center, as it were. The small town offers a few places to resupply, including a roadside convenience store at the South Prairie Creek RV Park. Otherwise, turn left onto Pioneer Way E. (State Route 162) for less than a mile to Lower Burnett Road E. Turn right, leave just about all traffic

Along with offering some terrific rural riding, historic Wilkeson is home to an annual handcar and lawnmower festival.

behind, and drop down onto a pleasing country lane along South Prairie Creek for a short but lovely stretch through a forested canyon.

After bearing right at a T intersection with Fetig Road, climb out of the gorge and go right onto Carbonado–South Prairie Road (State Route 165) and head for Wilkeson, about 2 miles ahead. (Take note when you pass Johns Road that on your return trip, you'll be turning left here.) Wilkeson has a rich history in coal mining and sandstone quarrying, and though small, offers a place or two to refuel as well as public restrooms right on Church Street. Something else you'll note is that Wilkeson boasts a steep climb just south of town. Parts are at 7 to 9 percent, with a sustained stretch that climbs about 400 feet in 1.4 miles.

But hey, it gets you to Carbonado, home of the Carbonado Saloon (popular with bikers of the motorized variety). Past Carbonado, the route continues south and up for almost 4 miles, becoming a remote mountain road climbing its way up a steep rocky gorge (with narrow to nil shoulder) as it approaches Mount Rainier National Park. Watch for falling rocks. The turnaround point is at the intersection with Carbon River Road, but a better spot is the historic Fairfax Bridge about 0.8 mile before, where you can look deep into the Carbon River gorge.

On your return trip, you'll reap the benefits of your recent uphill pedaling, which now translates into a mostly downhill or flat grade for 10 plus miles back through Carbonado and Wilkeson, and, after turning left

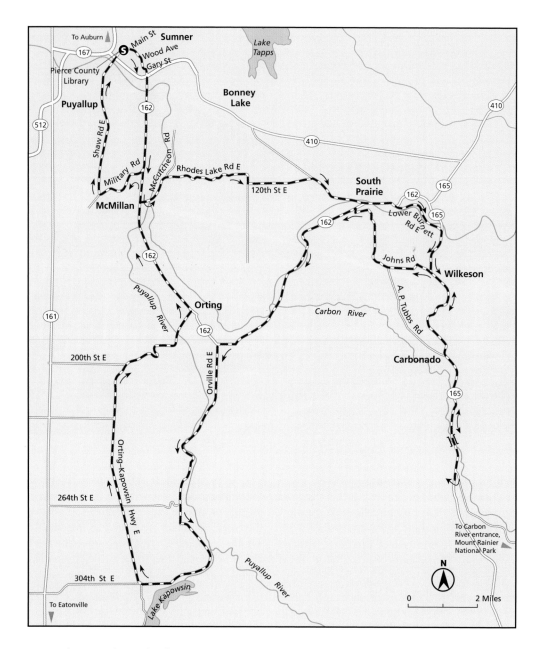

onto Johns Road, nearly all the way to South Prairie, which you approach this time from the south.

In South Prairie, turn right onto Emery Avenue and after crossing the Foothills Trail, go left onto State Route 162, also called Pioneer Way. Head west on the smooth, wide-shouldered (if well-traveled) road for about 6 miles before you begin linking together one rural roadway after another for an open-road tour of central Pierce County, largely through farmland, pastures, and riparian stretches alongside the Puyallup River and Lake Kapowsin. Eventually, make your way north back toward more populous Orting where, now back on State Route 162, you pass through tiny McMillan on your way toward the outskirts of Puyallup.

Just past the turnoff to 128th Street E, which you took on your journey out, look for the left turn to Military Road—and be prepared. It's steep, with an 11 to 13 percent grade in stretches, and climbs almost 400 feet in a mile. At the top, turn right onto Shaw Road and drop like a stone over the next 2-plus miles into Puyallup. At the end of Shaw, turn right onto Main Street and follow it for about 1.5 miles back to your starting point in Sumner.

Variation: If road and weather conditions allow, continue farther up the Carbon River canyon by turning left onto Carbon River Road and following it for about another 5 miles to Mount Rainier National Park's Carbon River Entrance.

MILEAGE LOG

0.0	From the Pierce County Library in Sumner, head south on Fryar Ave. toward Main St.
0.1	Left onto Main St.
0.5	Right onto Wood Ave.
1.2	Left onto Gary St.
1.3	Right onto SR 162. (Valley Ave.).
5.3	Left onto 128th St. E. (Becomes Rhodes Lake Rd. E.)
9.0	Bear left to stay on Rhodes Lake Rd. E.
9.8	Left onto 120th St. E.
11.7	Right onto Elhi Hill Rd./S. Prairie Rd. E.
13.6	Left onto SR 162 E.
14.3	Right onto Lower Burnett Rd. E.
15.6	Bear right to stay on Lower Burnett Rd. E.
16.0	Right onto SR 165 S.
18.1	Wilkeson.
20.4	Carbonado.
23.8	Turnaround; head back toward Carbonado.
30.4	Bear left onto Johns Rd. E.
33.9	Right onto Emery Ave. S. Enter South Prairie.
34.0	Left onto Pioneer Wy. E. (SR 162).
40.5	Left onto Orville Rd. E.
49.7	Right onto Orting–Kapowsin Hwy E.
58.7	Enter Orting.
59.4	Left onto Washington Ave. N. (SR 162).
63.6	Left onto Military Rd. E. (Becomes 122nd St. E.).
65.1	Right onto Shaw Rd. E.
68.5	Right onto E. Main Ave. (Becomes Traffic Ave.; Fryar Ave. in Sumner.)
69.7	Return to start.

22 ORTING–EATONVILLE (DAFFODIL METRIC CENTURY)

Difficulty	Strenuous
Time	3 to 5½ hours
Distance	61.9 miles
Elevation Gain	2735 feet

ROAD CONDITIONS: Low-traffic rural roads with varying shoulders widths (sometimes none) and varying chip-seal roughness; one stretch of state highway with wide shoulder.

GETTING THERE: From I-5 near Des Moines, take exit 149. Head east on SR 516 for 3 miles to SR 167. Turn right and head south for 12.6 miles toward Sumner and the SR 410 E exit. Follow SR 410 E. for 2 miles to SR 162 E. and turn right (south). Follow SR 162 for 7 miles to Orting. Park at the grocery store parking lot at the corner of Whitesell St. NE and Washington Ave. N. (SR 162).

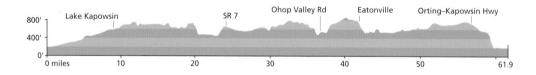

This terrific Pierce County rural ride follows the route of the Tacoma Wheelmens' Daffodil Metric Century and leads riders through farmland and forest in the shadow of Mount Rainier. It includes a couple of climbs but nothing *hors categorie*, that's for sure. Plus, it has a lively return run along Ohop Lake and Lake Kapowsin.

Begin in Orting, known for its terrific Mount Rainier views—the big guy is just 30 miles away—and for being one of the first cities in the state to allow folks to drive golf carts on city streets (thus, the "Golf Cart Zone" signs). Head south out of town on Orville Road, following the sign for the sci-fi-sounding town of Electron. You are following the Puyallup River as it drains Rainier's glaciers. This open-road stretch through pastureland and horse farms climbs ever so slightly (about 50 feet per mile

for the first 10 miles) before entering forest and eventually meeting up with the northern shoreline of Lake Kapowsin.

Head north away from the lake and commence a 12-mile stretch through rolling farmland on lightly traveled rural roads—low speed limit (35 mph, maybe a few stretches of 45), not much shoulder, a little chip-sealy, but scenic, bucolic, mellow. After a sweeping descent, go left onto State Route 7, which leaves a bit of the mellow behind. It's a high-speed roadway but for the most past offers a wide, smooth shoulder as the road beelines you south toward the Eatonville end of world. Big Rainier views are on offer, as are potential headwinds. A couple hills will have you standing to pedal a turn or two. The road passes farms and the various rural commercial concerns that show up in the outlying

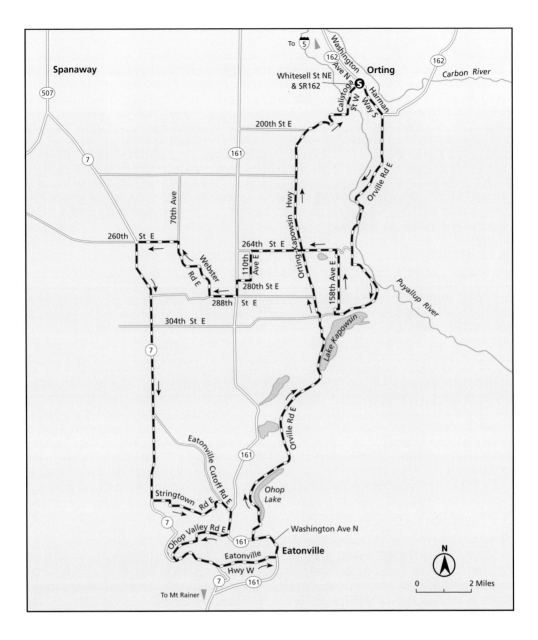

hinterlands—trucking, hauling, digging, drilling, and so forth. An occasional gas station mini-mart shows up as well, offering opportunities to resupply.

At 31.5 miles (after about 9 miles on State Route 7), turn left onto Stringtown Road, a mostly forested meander that after a few twists and turns leads to Ohop Valley Road

and more rural, more forested meanderings. Upon dropping down into then climbing up out of said valley, pass the Pioneer Farm Museum and Ohop Indian Village, which promises "Over 100 Activities to Do." There's a hill or two along this stretch—including a 2-miler that climbs 340 feet—nothing too killer, but probably enough to have you

A forested meander through the Ohop Valley

looking forward to break time in Eatonville, which you reach after a lively descent at the 42-mile mark.

As the eagle flies, Eatonville—which RAMROD (Ride Around Mount Rainier in One Day) veterans will recognize as the site of the first aid stop—is 20 miles due west of Mount Rainier and offers many options in the food and drink department. From here, head north for about 10 miles on Orville Road, an undulating low-traffic road above the shores of Ohop Lake and Lake Kapowsin. Turning north away from the latter lake onto Orting–Kapowsin Highway—which isn't so much a highway as just more rural riding—pedal the homestretch to Orting, which includes a fast, sweeping 4-mile descent back into town.

Note: You reenter town via a different street than you left it; thus, though it might seem odd, you will have to turn left to return to where you started.

MILEAGE LOG

0.0	From the coner of Whitesell St. NE and Washington Ave. in Orting, turn right onto Washington Ave. N.
0.4	Bear right onto Bridge St.
0.5	Left onto Harman Wy. S.
1.7	Right onto Orville Rd. E.
10.3	Right onto Griggs Rd. E.
10.5	Right onto Brownie Rd.

10.5	Bear right onto 296th St. E.
10.6	Left onto 158th Ave. E.
12.7	Left onto 264th St. E.
15.6	Left onto 110th Ave. E.
16.7	Right onto 280th St. E.
17.2	Left onto SR 161.
17.7	Right onto 288th St. E.
18.6	Right onto Webster Rd. E.
21.1	Left onto 260th St. E.
22.6	Left onto SR 7.
31.5	Left onto Stringtown Rd. E.
34.3	Right onto Eatonville Cutoff Rd. E.
34.8	Right onto SR 161.
35.4	Right onto Ohop Valley Rd. E.
35.6	Right to stay on Ohop Valley Rd. E.
37.6	Left onto Peterson Rd. E.
37.7	Left onto SR 7.
39.3	Bear left onto Eatonville Hwy. W. (Becomes Center St. W. in Eatonville.)
41.6	Left onto Mashell Ave.
41.9	Left onto Washington Ave. N. (SR 161).
42.8	Right onto Orville Rd. E. (Becomes Orting–Kapowsin Hwy., then Calistoga St. W. in Orting.)
61.7	Left onto Washington Ave. N.
61.9	Return to grocery store parking lot.

23 GIG HARBOR–PORT ORCHARD LOOP

Difficulty	Strenuous
Time	3 to 5 hours
Distance	56.1 miles
Elevation Gain	3620 feet

ROAD CONDITIONS: Mostly low-traffic rural roads with varying shoulder widths; city and small-town riding with stretches of bike lanes.

GETTING THERE: From I-5 in Tacoma, take exit 132 and head west on SR 16 for 10 miles. Take the Wollochet Dr. NW exit and turn right (east) onto Pioneer Wy. Follow for 0.7 mile into Gig Harbor. Turn left onto Harborview Dr. and look for street parking. (***Note:*** Eastbound traffic must pay a toll to cross the Tacoma Narrows Bridge.)

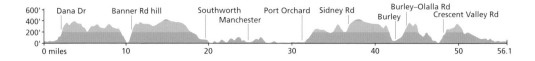

600'
400'
200'
0'

| Dana Dr | Banner Rd hill | Southworth | Port Orchard | Sidney Rd | Burley–Olalla Rd |
| | | Manchester | | Burley | Crescent Valley Rd |

0 miles   10   20   30   40   50   56.1

"Every rose has its thorn," sang some spandex-clad dude in a terrible '80s hair band. And he could have been describing this ride. With its low-traffic roads, otherworldly forests, historic harbor towns, and Puget Sound's glistening waters, the northern Kitsap Peninsula is truly roselike in its beauty. But it's also infested with short, steep, thornlike climbs that'll more than put a sting in your legs.

If hilly challenges are your thing, you'll love this ride. And if you don't love hills, keep in mind that the highest point on the ride is below 450 feet. We're not talking Hurricane Ridge–size hills here—just some very steep ones, with as much as a 16 percent grade in spots.

All that said, get pedaling. After a pleasant warm-up through charming Gig Harbor, with its almost surreal Mount Rainier backdrop—trend north and east along the water on winding roads that meander through dense, moss-hung forest. Expect some steep ups and downs in this section.

The route drops down to the Colvos Passage shoreline, where you'll be lulled by a peaceful stretch of smooth pavement, with rat-tat-tat-ing kingfishers offering in-air entertainment. At 10 miles, turn right onto Banner

A peaceful flat stretch along Colvos Passage; Vashon Island in the distance

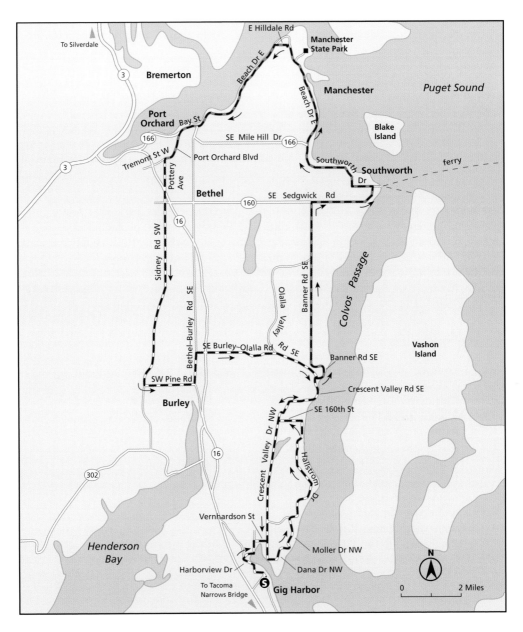

Road, where you'll be rudely shaken from your reverie by a winding, curvy road that appears to go straight up. This is the pointiest of the peninsula's prickers; the first half mile climbs 260 feet and the entire hill is about a mile long.

At the top, Banner turns right and straight-arrows north toward Southworth, up and down lumps and bumps, past farms, forests, and homes with expansive, perfectly manicured lawns. Shoulder width varies as does the road surface, but for the most part it's smooth enough and traffic is not bad.

Reach the ferry terminal town of Southworth at 20 miles (eats and drinks available here) and just ahead begin a scenic 10-mile stretch, mostly tracing the shorelines of Yukon Harbor and Rich Passage on the way to Port Orchard. Along the way, pass through seaside Manchester and encounter a short, steep pitch or two. (Or three. Or six.)

At 31 miles, reach Port Orchard, the busiest town on the route with food marts and fast-food chains galore. (You may want to stock up, since the second half of this route doesn't offer many opportunities.) Check out the huge ships across Sinclair Inlet at the Bremerton Naval Base, and then head inland and up, enjoying a smooth wide bike lane as you work your way south and into the heart of Kitsap County. Inland means—you guessed it—hills, so expect some climbs over the next 7 miles or so. But the roads are good, the shoulders for the most part decent, and the speed limit is usually 35 and 45 miles per hour.

At Pine Road, turn left to head east on wide-shouldered, forested roads, some sporting "Bikes on Road" signs (and even the occasional bike lane). And, to be frank, quite a few sporting some steep ups and downs. Burley–Olalla Road is a roller coaster as are the first few miles of Crescent Valley Road; both have pitches, up *and* down, of more than 10 percent.

The last 4 miles back into Gig Harbor are slightly downhill or flat, allowing you to recover and enjoy the Kitsap landscape while rolling back into Gig Harbor.

Variation: Combine this with Burly Burley–Key Peninsula Route (Tour 58) for a super strenuous 100-miler.

MILEAGE LOG

0.0	From on-street parking on Harborview Dr. in Gig Harbor, head north on Harborview Dr.
0.5	Bear right to stay on Harborview Dr.
0.8	Right onto N. Harborview Dr.
1.6	Right onto Vernhardson St.
1.9	Right onto Crescent Valley Dr. NW.
2.2	Left onto Dana Dr. NW. (Becomes 94th St. NW, then Moller Dr. NW.)
4.2	Left onto Hallstrom Dr. NW.
7.7	Left onto SE 160th St.
8.3	Right onto Crescent Valley Rd. SE.
10.6	Right onto Banner Rd. SE. Steep hill.
17.0	Right onto SR 160 (SE Sedgwick Rd.).
19.5	Enter Southworth. Left onto SE Southworth Dr.
20.2	Right to stay on SE Southworth Dr.
20.9	Left to stay on SE Southworth Dr.
22.3	Right onto Yukon Harbor Rd. SE.
23.1	Right onto Colchester Dr. SE.
24.5	Enter Manchester. Left onto E. Main St.
24.6	Right onto Beach Dr. E.
26.5	Left onto E. Hilldale Rd.
27.1	Left onto Beach Dr. E. (Becomes Bay St.)
31.0	Enter Port Orchard. Bear right to stay on Bay St. (SR 166.)
31.8	Left onto Port Orchard Blvd.
32.9	Right onto Tremont St. W.
33.1	Left onto Pottery Ave. (Becomes Sidney Rd. SW.)

40.7	Left onto SW Pine Rd.
42.4	Left onto Bethel–Burley Rd. SE.
43.4	Right onto SE Burley–Olalla Rd.
46.2	Right onto Olalla Valley Rd. SE.
47.8	Right onto Crescent Valley Rd. SE.
54.2	Right onto 96th St. NW (Vernhardson St.).
54.5	Left onto N. Harborview Dr.
55.3	Left to stay on Harborview Dr.
56.1	Return to start.

24 OLYMPIA–ROCHESTER–RAINIER

Difficulty	Strenuous
Time	3 to 6 hours
Distance	66.2 miles
Elevation Gain	1930 feet

ROAD CONDITIONS: Urban streets and roadways, many with bike lanes and/or "Share the Road" signs; low-traffic rural roads with varying shoulder widths and chip-seal surface; paved and crushed gravel regional trail.

GETTING THERE: From I-5 in Olympia, take exit 105. Head north on Plum St. SE for 0.2 mile to Union Ave. SE and turn left. In 0.4 mile, turn right onto Capitol Wy. S. and follow for 0.3 mile to Sylvester Park. Look for parking here or at Capitol Lake Park, 2 blocks west.

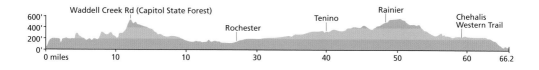

From the state's capitol, head south for a delightful, not too hilly Thurston County exploration. Along the way, pedal past the lower flanks of the off-road playground that is Capitol State Forest (almost 200 miles of trails), ride through several small towns, and pedal a trio of paved pathways, the Yelm–Tenino Trail, the Chehalis Western Trail, and the Olympia Woodland Trail.

Begin by making your way south out of Olympia via Capitol Way and Capitol Boulevard. Pass through Tumwater and eventually head west toward Capitol State Forest, skirting the shores of Black Lake on the wide

The Chehalis Western Trail is one of three terrific paved regional trails featured on this route.

shoulder of a boulevard of the same name. Leaving the lakeshore, follow rolling Delphi and Waddell Creek roads toward the deep, dark lower reaches of the Black Hills and 90,000-plus-acre Capitol State Forest. The road is a bit chip-sealy here and the shoulder not very wide, but traffic is low and you'll feel as though you have the road all to yourself.

Views of Mount Rainier open up and you pass by the Mima Mounds Natural Area—truly a geologic wonder with its dozens of mounds, six- to eight-feet high, dotting the landscape. Continuing south, pedal through a prairieland of llama and alpaca ranches, wide-open fields, Christmas tree farms, and not a whole lot of traffic.

Near Rochester, which at the 28-mile mark offers plenty of places to refuel, begin heading east, first via US Highway 12 (which can be busy but boasts a wide shoulder), then 183rd Avenue and Old Highway 99. In Tenino begins the first regional trail section along this route. The 14.5-mile paved Yelm–Tenino Trail parallels State Route 507 between the two small Thurston County burgs, passing farms, creeks, and wetlands. Jump on it here and follow for 8-plus bucolic miles—very gradually gaining elevation along the way. At about the 50-mile mark, enter Rainier, yet another small town that offers opportunities for refreshment.

Back on road, climb steeply, if only briefly, north out of Rainier via Rainier Road for about 9 miles to the southern reaches of Lacey where—ta da!—you jump onto two more paved bike trails. First is the Chehalis Western Trail, which takes you toward downtown Lacey (passing through Chambers Lake Park along the way), and then the Olympia Woodland Trail, which skirts the Lacey franchise-big-box-traffic-light mess and drops you off a little more than a mile from your starting point in Olympia.

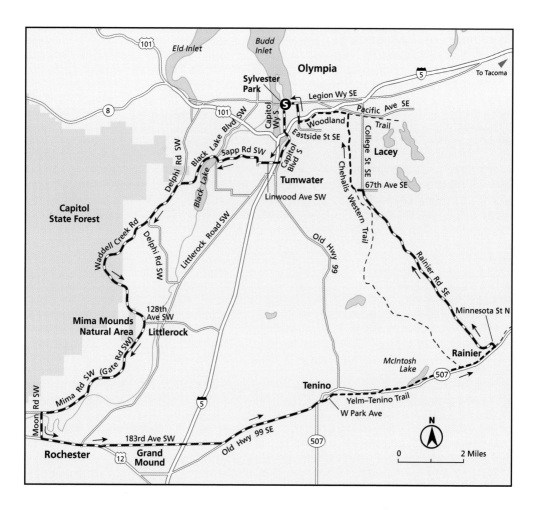

0.0   From Sylvester Park in Olympia, head south on Capitol Wy. S.
1.2   Bear left to stay on Capitol Wy. S. (Becomes Capitol Blvd. S.)
2.8   Right onto Linwood Ave. SW.
3.7   Right onto Sapp Rd. SW.
5.9   Right onto Black Lake–Belmore Rd. SW. (Might not be a sign there.)
6.2   Left onto Black Lake Blvd. SW. (Becomes 62nd Ave. SW.)
8.5   Left onto Delphi Rd. SW.
10.6   Right onto Waddell Creek Rd. SW.
13.4   Left to stay on Waddell Creek Rd. SW. (Becomes Mima Rd. SW, then Gate Rd. SW.)
21.3   Bear left to stay on Gate Rd. SW.
24.8   Left onto Moon Rd. SW.
26.0   Left onto US Hwy 12.
28.0   Rochester
29.0   Left onto 183rd Ave. SW.

34.6	Left onto Old Hwy 99 SE.
40.0	Tenino. Left onto W. Park Ave.
40.4	Right onto S. Olympia St.
40.4	Left onto Yelm–Tenino Trail.
42.8	Trail crosses to north side of SR 507.
48.5	Rainier. Left onto Minnesota St. N. (Becomes Rainier Rd. SE.)
58.4	Lacey. Left onto 67th Ave. SE.
58.7	Right onto Chehalis Western Trail.
62.4	Left onto Olympia Woodland Trail.
64.9	Right onto Eastside St. SE.
65.6	Left onto Legion Wy. SE.
66.2	Left onto Capitol Wy. S. where route started.

MOUNT RAINIER AND SOUTHWEST WASHINGTON

Routes here run the gamut: from the alpine heights and panoramic sights of the state's highest mountain—14,410-foot Mount Rainier—to the rural prairieland roads of Lewis and Clark counties. Routes explore Vancouver too (Washington's Vancouver), as well the Columbia River, the Northwest's great waterway.

25 SUNRISE–CAYUSE–CHINOOK

Difficulty	Very Strenuous
Time	4 to 7 hours
Distance	54.4 miles
Elevation Gain	5850 feet

ROAD CONDITIONS: At-times busy state highway with narrow shoulder (though "Bikes on Road" signs); winding mountain road in national park, which can be busy on summer weekends. *Note:* Because of snowfall, the upper reaches of the road to Sunrise are closed most years from sometime in October until sometime in July. Check the Mount Rainier National Park website for latest conditions (www.nps.gov/mora/planyourvisit/road-status.htm).

GETTING THERE: From Enumclaw, head south on SR 410 for 33 miles to Crystal Mountain Blvd. Turn left and in about 50 yards, turn right into a large gravel parking lot that in winter is Silver Springs Sno-Park. (Or, if you feel that's asking for someone to break into your car, park on the ample roadside pullout on Crystal Mountain Blvd.)

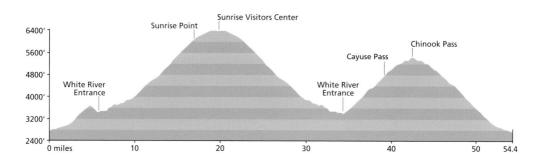

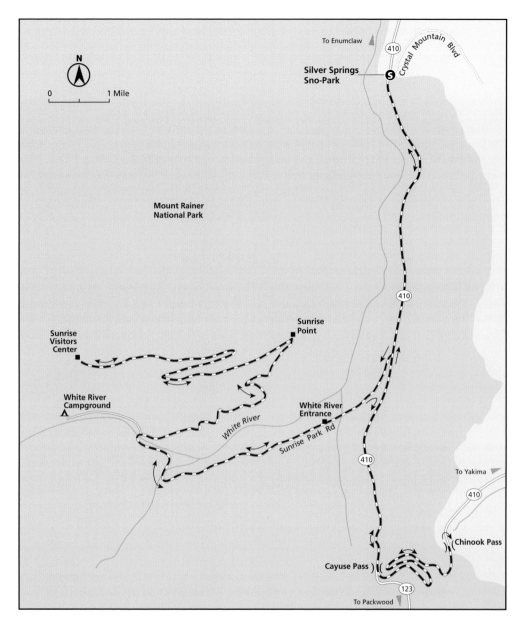

No huge surprise that Washington's most epic mountain offers some of the state's most epic riding. Sure, anytime you ride near Rainier you have to climb a bit—actually a lot of bits—but the out-of-this world alpine vistas make it more than worth it. The trek to Sunrise is a consistent, but not outrageously steep, 14-mile climb. (Your reward, of course, is a 14-mile descent, where you'll feel like you're flying.) The climb to Cayuse and Chinook passes is more than 8 miles long, again with no letup. (But again, followed by a thrilling descent.)

From Crystal Mountain Boulevard, head left (south) onto State Route 410 and get

< The climb to Chinook Pass isn't as long as the one to Sunrise, but it's no less spectacular.

those quads and hamstrings loosened up on the 5-mile uphill ride to Mount Rainier National Park. You'll likely loosen up your bike-handling skills too. Although there is a shoulder and signs alerting drivers to bikes on the roadway, this section can be busy, especially on summer weekends.

Turn right onto Sunrise Park Road, heading toward the White River Entrance to the park, and say good-bye to high-speed traffic for a while. After paying your entry fee (keep your receipt in case you want to experience this or the Paradise climb again over the next week), resume climbing for about 3 miles— with a few rollers thrown in to keep things interesting—before crossing the glacially silted White River. Once across, bear right, lest you end up in the White River Campground, and climb some more, this time with no letup for about 8 miles. Just find your rhythm and enjoy your surroundings—the forest smell, tumbling waterfalls, columnar basalt, and ever-expanding vistas.

At Sunrise Point, the grade lessens, and if you want to shoot some photos, do so here. At over 6000 feet, you're in true mountain heaven, with views all the way from Mount Baker to the north, Mount Stuart in the Enchantments to the east, and Mount Adams to the south— all dominated by massive Mount Rainier, which, as you continue over the final 2.5-mile stretch to the Sunrise Visitors Center, seems to expand with every pedal stroke. The mountain is so close you feel as though you're going to ride right up the Emmons Glacier. It's fast here, too; the final stretch is mostly flat with a slight downhill section.

Sunrise is at the end of the highest paved road in the state and, along with incredible wildflower meadows, boasts a day lodge with food concession, gift shop, water, and restrooms. But you've got more riding to do. So zip up your jacket or vest for the descent and fly back down the hill and out to State Route 410. (Note that the 2.5-mile stretch from Sunrise to Sunrise Point has quite a narrow shoulder on the downhill (right) side and a fall could be deadly. Best to skootch out a bit.)

Once out on State Route 410, turn right and climb steeply for 3.5 miles to Cayuse Pass. Bear left, following 410 and the sign for Chinook Pass and Yakima. Ride under sheer rocky cliffs with a vast mountain vista to the south. After switchbacking steeply a few times for another 3.5 miles, reach the pass. The best views are just before you reach the pass, where Tipsoo Lake sits nestled in an alpine bowl with Mount Rainier as a backdrop. Pose for photos here. Restrooms are just a couple hundred yards down the other (north) side of the pass.

Return the way you came, following State Route 410 back to Crystal Mountain Boulevard. Twelve-plus miles, all of it downhill— Yee-haw!

MILEAGE LOG

0.0	Depart sno-park at Crystal Mountain Blvd., turn left onto SR 410.
4.6	Right on Sunrise Park Rd. to enter Mountain Rainier National Park.
6.1	Pay entry fee at White River Entrance.
9.9	Bear right at sign for White River Campground.
17.5	Sunrise Point.
20.1	Turnaround point at Sunrise Visitors Center.
35.6	Right onto SR 410.
39.1	Cayuse Pass; bear left following SR 410.
42.8	Chinook Pass turnaround.
46.5	Cayuse Pass; bear right continuing on SR 410.
54.4	Right onto Crystal Mountain Blvd. and back to starting place.

26 PARADISE FROM STEVENS CANYON

Difficulty	Strenuous
Time	3 to 5 hours
Distance	42.3 miles
Elevation Gain	4950 feet

ROAD CONDITIONS: Winding mountain road in national park; potential for rough patches and delays for road repair. ***Note:*** Because of snowfall, the upper reaches of Stevens Canyon Rd. are closed most years from sometime in October until sometime in June. Check the Mount Rainier National Park website for latest conditions (www.nps.gov/mora/planyourvisit/road-status.htm).

GETTING THERE: From Enumclaw, head south on SR 410 for 50 miles to Mount Rainier National Park's Stevens Canyon Entrance parking lot.

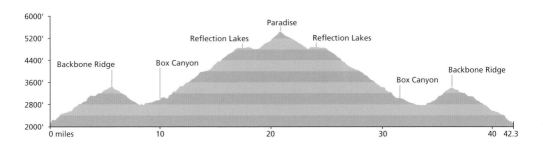

Each year some 800 folks pedal Redmond Cycling Club's classic RAMROD (Ride Around Mount Rainier in One Day). The ride's 154-mile route includes as its highpoint—both literally and figuratively—an ascent to Paradise, the aptly named 5400-foot meadow and mountain playground that boasts some of the most breathtaking scenery in the country. That ride approaches Paradise from the west, the Nisqually–Longmire side; this one gets there from the east, the Stevens Canyon–Ohanapecosh Visitors Center side.

What's the difference? Along with there being less car and RV traffic on this eastern approach, some say the views are even more dramatic. And in riding more slowly, as you're apt to do during a nearly 13-mile climb, you've got more time to enjoy incredible vistas to far-off Mount Adams or into Reflection Lakes, where Mount Rainier's awesome visage is doubled.

Climb-wise, what's the difference? The ride up and back to Paradise from the Stevens Canyon side involves three climbs, totaling nearly 5000 feet of elevation gain over 42 miles. Riding to Paradise and back from the Nisqually-Longmire side requires just one sustained 3500-foot climb spread out over 20 miles. Want more details? This Stevens Canyon route first climbs Backbone Ridge, ascending 1225 feet in 5.7 miles, and then, after a 3-mile descent, climbs 12.4 miles to Paradise, gaining over 2600 feet. On the descent, Backbone Ridge has to be climbed again—about 600 feet in 3 miles.

For this eastern approach to Paradise, start at the Stevens Canyon entrance to Mount Rainier National Park. After you pay your entrance fee (good for one week), head up to Backbone Ridge through heavy timber, switchbacking pretty much from the start. Along the way, pass the trailhead to the Grove of the Patriarchs, an old-growth forest with trees some 50 feet in circumference and a thousand years old. Ease into this climb—parts of it are steeper than the longer climb to come—and given that you're just getting started, chances are you're not warmed up.

Reach the ridge top just before 6 miles and commence a 3-mile descent before the uphill pedaling resumes. The climb begins gently at

Mount Rainier appears to grow before your very eyes on this eastside approach to Paradise. (David Longdon)

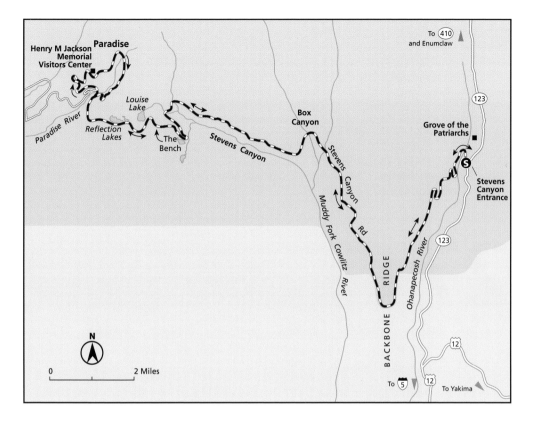

first, but when it becomes more rude, you've emerged from the forest into wide-open Stevens Canyon, where big-time views will lessen the suffering. Mountains, meadows, cliffs, and ridges seem to extend forever in all directions. Several pullout areas and picnic spots offer places to take a breather and a photo or two; the Bench, at about mile 15, is a good one, or just ahead at Reflection Lakes, where the road flattens for a bit and Mount Rainier—her glaciers and meadows and all her finery—are reflected in the mellow pools.

Reach the Paradise complex at mile 19, follow the one-way signs around for the final 2-mile, 600-foot climb to the large Paradise parking lot, Henry M. Jackson Memorial Visitors Center (with restrooms and restaurant), and gigantic Rainier views. Sated with food, drink, and mountain vistas, continue following the one-way signs back to Stevens

Canyon Road and return the same way you came, enjoying what is this author's favorite mountain descent. You'll encounter an uphill climb at Backbone Ridge, but it really isn't all that bad.

Variations: Some cyclists put together informal routes called BOMROD (Best Of Mount Rainier in One Day), which is basically just Mount Rainier National Park road climbs with as little flat riding as possible. For example, after riding from Stevens Canyon to Paradise and back, one can add a ride up to Cayuse Pass and back down for a 64-miler that climbs 8200 feet. And since it's so close, why not throw in Chinook Pass (74 miles and 9100 feet). The ultimate BOMROD would be ups and backs to Paradise, Cayuse, Chinook, and Sunrise, for a 110-miler that climbs about 15,000 feet! These BOMROD routes can start from the Sunrise entrance as well.

0.0   From the Stevens Canyon Entrance, head up Stevens Canyon Rd.
5.7   Backbone Ridge.
10.4 Box Canyon.
17.4 Reflection Lakes.
19.0 Left onto Paradise–Longmire Rd.
20.9 Paradise. Henry M. Jackson Memorial Visitors Center.
23.4 Left onto Stevens Canyon Rd.
36.6 Backbone Ridge.
42.3 Return to starting point.

27 PACKWOOD–PARADISE–STEVENS CANYON LOOP

Difficulty	Very Strenuous
Time	4½ to 7 hours
Distance	78.2 miles
Elevation Gain	6030 feet

ROAD CONDITIONS: Chip-seal surface on Skate Creek Rd. Potential for rough patches and road repair delays once in Mount Rainier National Park. Wide shoulders (though big trucks) on US Hwy 12. Because of national park traffic, weekdays are better than weekends. ***Note:*** Because of snowfall, the upper reaches of Stevens Canyon Rd.—the road from Paradise east to SR 123—is closed most years from sometime in October until sometime in June. Check the Mount Rainier National Park website (www.nps.gov/mora/planyourvisit/road-status.htm) for latest conditions. Snowfall also closes Skate Creek Rd. (FR 52) from sometime in November until sometime in May.

GETTING THERE: From Enumclaw, head south on SR 410 for 40 miles to Cayuse Pass. Continue straight as the road becomes SR 123 and in 16 miles, turn right onto US Hwy 12. Packwood and Skate Creek Rd. (FR 52), where this route starts, are 8 miles ahead. Park in one of the market or gas station parking lots near the intersection of US Hwy 12 and Skate Creek Rd., which is the main intersection in town.

There really aren't enough superlatives to describe Mount Rainier National Park. And since 40-plus miles of this route pass right through some of the park's most incredible natural splendors, it stands to reason that words will have a hard time doing this route justice. Still, we'll try.

This route is a kind-of RAMROD Jr. (Ride Around Mount Rainier in One Day). About half the length of RAMROD, it includes the

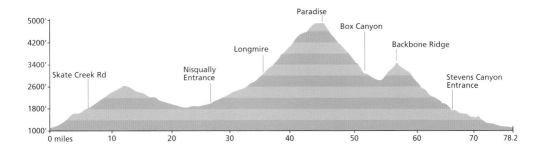

long climb to Paradise and the 3-mile ascent of Backbone Ridge, but not the 9-mile climb to Cayuse Pass.

Starting in Packwood, a tiny mountain burg of about a thousand located due south of the park, head northwest on Skate Creek Road, also called Forest Road 52. Though paved the whole way, heavy snowfall usually closes this road from sometime in November until sometime in May. Keeping an eye out for elk, climb gradually through dense forest as you follow Skate Creek, gaining about 100 feet per mile for the first 13 miles. (Not quite yet warmed up, you may feel like you're pedaling through glue.) The road then crests a hill and, with Skate Creek no longer roadside, flattens out, and then descends at about the same rate for the next 8 miles.

After swinging north and then intersecting State Route 706, where you turn right, begin the initially very gradual 21-mile climb to Paradise, elevation 5400 feet. (You're at about 1800 feet here.) Take advantage along this stretch for any last-minute restroom breaks or espresso needs. After 3 miles on State Route 706, enter Mount Rainier National Park at the Nisqually Entrance, paying your entry fee (good for one week). Resume climbing, now a bit more steadily, on a narrow national park road, winding through forest with occasional sweeping views of the Nisqually River to the right.

About 6 miles into the park, you reach Longmire, which along with an inn, offers restrooms and food concessions. From here

on, the climb stiffens a bit and remains fairly consistent in the 5 to 7 percent range the remaining 11 miles to Paradise. But if you'd ridden in the mountains before, you know that's how it works: you climb for pain, to be repaid in visual gain. Everything gets bigger, closer, and more impressive the higher you go. Rampart Ridge, Christine Falls, and Narada Falls garner attention, as does the ever-more massive 14,410-foot stratovolcano herself.

Follow signs for Paradise—it's a one-way loop near the top, which can be a little confusing. It's stunning at the top, with expansive views and more than likely, too many people. Restrooms, a food concession, and a place to fill your bottles are available. Once you've had your fill of the views, climb back on your bike for a couple of the author's all-time favorite descents, one that's 13-miles long, the other, about 10.

Just below Paradise, as the one-way road swings south, steal a couple glances to the right, down into the Paradise Valley meadow where bears are often spotted. Just ahead, the road flattens out for about a mile-and-a-half, right where the Reflection Lakes' reflection of Mount Rainier pretty much begs for a photo to be taken. Continue down through Stevens Canyon, a long fast straightaway on which you'll swear that this must be what flying is like. Down, down, down you go, swooping to the right through Box Canyon for another couple miles until the party pooper that is Backbone Ridge rears its head with its roughly 600-foot climb over 3 miles. Once

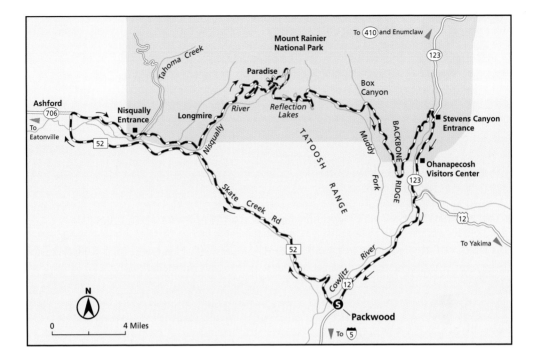

over the top, you're flying downhill again for another 10 miles, with momentary slow-downs and stops to exit the park through the Stevens Canyon Entrance and pass through the Ohanapecosh Visitor Center.

Turn right on US Highway 12 and follow the wide-shoulder roadway for about 8 miles into Packwood where you started.

Variation: To make this route an even century, at the Stevens Canyon Entrance, go left onto Highway 123 and climb 11 miles to Cayuse Pass, gaining 2300 feet along the way. Once at the top, turn around and head back down to the Stevens Canyon Entrance. From there, follow the route back to Packwood.

MILEAGE LOG

0.0	Start in Packwood at Skate Creek Rd. (at the intersection of FR 52 and US 12).
21.5	Follow Skate Creek Rd. as it heads north toward SR 706.
23.0	Right onto SR 706.
26.5	Enter Mount Rainier National Park at Nisqually Entrance.
32.8	Longmire.
43.8	Paradise, elevation 5400 feet.
47.5	Reflection Lakes.
59.2	Backbone Ridge.
65.4	Stevens Canyon Entrance; right onto SR 123.
70.5	Right onto US Hwy 12.
78.2	End route back at Packwood.

< *Just below Paradise, Reflection Lake invites cyclists to stop, take a break, and gaze in wonder at majestic Mount Rainier.*

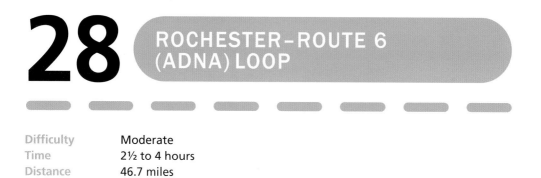

28 ROCHESTER–ROUTE 6 (ADNA) LOOP

Difficulty	Moderate
Time	2½ to 4 hours
Distance	46.7 miles
Elevation Gain	1470 feet

ROAD CONDITIONS: Rural, low-traffic chip-seal roads with narrow or nil shoulder.

GETTING THERE: From I-5 in Grand Mound, take exit 88. Head west on US Hwy 12 for about 5 miles to Rochester and the grocery store parking lot on the left.

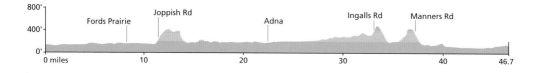

This is a fun, rural route exploring the low-traffic roads of north Lewis County. (And a tiny bit of Thurston County as well; in fact, parts of this route often show up on the Capital Bicycling Club of Olympia's Two County Double Metric Century ride.) Fields, farmland, and ranches—not to mention mountain vistas—are all yours. Bustling metropolises too (he wrote facetiously), such as Fords Prairie, Galvin, Littell, and Adna—most of which are small enough that you can roll through with nary a delay but large enough to have a mini-grocery store for refueling. While this route isn't a major elevation gobbler, it offers a few short, steep stingers to keep your climbing legs from taking the day off.

Start the route with 10-plus miles of flat country roads and old state highway with ample shoulder, past farms, hayfields, and ranches. Turning west at Fords Prairie, follow the rural Lewis County road toward Galvin, just across the Chehalis River. Here, on Joppish

Road, is the first other-than-flat stretch of rural chip seal: a 1.2-miler that climbs 250 feet. No biggie. Not far past the top, drop back down into the Chehalis River valley and the outskirts of Centralia via a screaming fast descent. Turn right onto Scheuber Road and continue more flat country-road riding through the Chehalis River valley. Enjoy a field-and-farm landscape punctuated with barns and silos, sheep and llamas, and long stretches of white rail fence. (Much of this route—especially the first half—lacks protection and shade from trees, so winds and/or heat can be an issue.)

At about mile 20, go right on State Route 6 (busy, but with a wide shoulder) for 3 miles to Adna and Bunker Creek Road. Along this stretch and in tiny Adna, a mini-mart or two offers the last opportunity for restrooms and supplies.

This western and second half of the loop continues the rural-riding theme but with more hills (in particular, two challenging ones that aren't overlong but that do have pitches to 8 percent), and more forest (much of it working forestland, which means you need to watch for logging trucks). But there's even less traffic and fewer (as in zero) towns.

The last 5 miles to Rochester is a winding, forested frolic along the Chehalis River.

Variation: Combine this with the Adna (Chehalis)–Vader Loop, Tour 30, for a challenging, 95-miler that climbs about 3300 feet.

MILEAGE LOG

0.0	From the grocery store parking lot in Rochester, turn right onto US Hwy 12.
0.2	Right onto Albany St. SW. (Becomes James Rd.)
4.6	Right onto Old Hwy 9.
5.9	Right onto Old Hwy 99.
8.6	Right onto Sandra Ave.
9.3	Right onto Galvin Rd.
10.9	Left onto Joppish Rd.
12.7	Left onto Cooks Hill Rd.
14.9	Right onto S. Scheuber Rd.

Wheel through the rural countryside of Lewis and Thurston counties where barns, silos, and long stretches of rail fence are common sights.

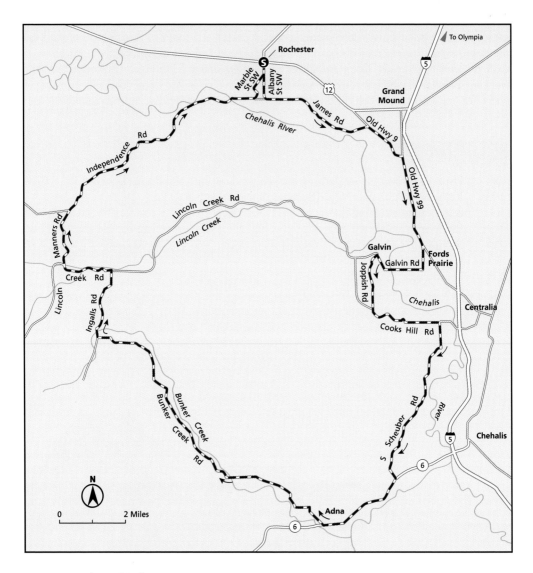

20.1	Right at SR 6 W.
22.5	Right onto Bunker Creek Rd.
32.6	Right at Ingalls Rd.
34.8	Left at Lincoln Creek Rd.
36.3	Right at Manners Rd. (Becomes Independence Rd.)
45.4	Left onto Marble St. SW.
46.3	Left onto Albany St. SW.
46.5	Left onto US Hwy 12.
46.7	Left to return to parking lot and starting point.

29 CENTRALIA–RAINIER–LITTLEROCK LOOP

Difficulty	Strenuous
Time	3 to 6 hours
Distance	66.9 miles
Elevation Gain	1620 feet

ROAD CONDITIONS: Rural, low-traffic county roadways with varying shoulder widths (and frequent chip-seal surfaces); some state and US highway, mostly with ample shoulders; paved bike path.

GETTING THERE: From I-5 in Centralia, take exit 82. Head west on Harrison Ave. for about 0.5 mile to a large grocery store on the left. Park there.

This rural route south of Puget Sound treats riders to hours of wide-open country-road riding through flatland prairie, rolling fields, and open farmland, much of it under the watchful gaze of Mount Rainier. A few forested hills offer challenging climbs, thrilling descents, and the opportunity to shout "Wheeeee!" A number of small towns—Bucoda, Rainier, Littlerock, etc.—add a nice roadside Americana touch to this ride.

Begin by heading north and east out of the Chehalis River Valley through a few miles of residential and light industry before turning right onto Big Hanaford Road. What follows is a sort of cloverleaf loop (the first of two in this route) that takes you through and across Hanaford Creek Valley. Along the way, pass farms and fields (as well one or two unique residential compounds whose lawns are adorned with seemingly dozens of junker

cars) on smooth rural roads that offer stunning visuals of Mount Rainier. After a close ride-by of the Transalta steam power plant, whose sheer size makes it appear almost otherworldly, cross the valley and at about the 10-mile mark, reach the roller coaster that is Tono Road.

If you like challenges—that is, steep rolling hills that yank you way up, up, up, only to quickly toss you down the other side, then do it all over again—you'll find Tono Road incredibly fun. If not ... did I mention the Mount Rainier views earlier in the ride? They're really pretty. (Kidding aside, the truly hilly section is only 3 miles long.)

At 14 miles, after a steep descent, you fairly fly into Bucoda, a small quiet burg where you'd half expect to see an old lazy dog walking right down the middle of Main Street, causing inconvenience to no one. Though it's small,

Small towns, rural roadways, and spectacular fall foliage greet riders along this route.

Bucoda does have a country store should you need to resupply. Back on the bike, begin the cloverleaf through the farms and ranches along the Skookumchuck River. It's terrific rural riding—mostly smooth road, not much traffic, and enough twists and turns and mini ups and downs to keep it interesting. Head north on Johnson Creek Road, where just beyond State Route 507, a paved (and car-free!) trail awaits: the Yelm–Tenino Trail. Hop on board and ride it for 2.5 miles to Rainier, a small town named after a big mountain, where eats and drinks can be had.

Just north of Rainier, a steep little pitch awaits, but aside from that it's mostly flat (even slightly downhill) rural riding as you work your way north and west across Thurston County. At about mile 49, shortly after crossing over Interstate 5, turn left onto Littlerock Road and begin making the return run south through Mima Prairie toward Centralia. Three miles ahead, the small town of Littlerock offers a grocery store and mini-mart.

In Grand Mound, where you pass the Great Wolf Lodge, a giant indoor waterslide park, hop on Old Highway 99 for the homestretch. The shoulder and surface smoothness vary, but since it parallels nearby Interstate 5, most of the high-speed traffic is over there. Eventually the road becomes Harrison Avenue, which takes you to the grocery store parking lot where you started.

0.0 From the grocery store parking lot in Centralia, cross Harrison Ave. and head north on Belmont Ave.

0.1 Right onto Haviland St.

0.2 Left onto Lum Rd.

0.6 Right onto W. Reynolds Ave.

1.7 Left onto N. Pearl St. (SR 507).

3.0 Bear right to stay on SR 507 (Downing Rd).

3.6 Right onto Big Hanaford Rd.

10.3 Left onto Tono Rd.

14.2 Enter Bucoda. Right onto S. River St.

14.3 Left onto E. 6th St.

14.5 Right onto Front St. (SR 507). (Might not be a sign here.)

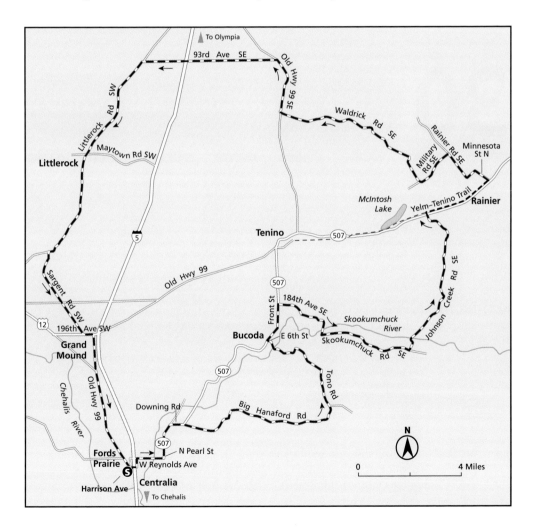

15.9	Right onto 184th Ave. SE. (Becomes Skookumchuck Rd. SE.)
18.4	Bear left to stay on Skookumchuck Rd. SE.
22.1	Left onto Johnson Creek Rd. SE.
28.5	Cross SR 507, go right onto Yelm–Tenino Trail.
31.0	Enter Rainier. Turn left at Minnesota St. N. (Becomes Rainier Rd. SE.)
33.1	Left onto Military Rd. SE.
34.7	Right onto Waldrick Rd. SE.
41.4	Right onto Old Hwy 99 SE.
43.5	Left onto 93rd Ave. SE.
48.7	Left onto Littlerock Rd. SW.
52.9	Enter Littlerock. Right onto Maytown Rd. SW.
53.0	Left onto Littlerock Rd. SW.
57.3	Left onto Sargent Rd. SW.
60.9	Grand Mound. Left onto 196th Ave. SW.
61.3	Right onto Elderberry St. SW. (Becomes Old Hwy 99, then Harrison Ave.)
66.9	Return to parking lot and starting point.

30 ADNA (CHEHALIS)–VADER LOOP

Difficulty	Moderate
Time	2½ to 4 hours
Distance	48.3 miles
Elevation Gain	1800 feet

ROAD CONDITIONS: Rural, low-traffic chip-seal roads with narrow or nil shoulder.

GETTING THERE: From I-5 in Chehalis, take exit 77. Head west on SR 6 for 2.2 miles to the intersection with SR 603. Park at the small grocery store parking lot on the corner.

Like the Rochester–Route 6 (Adna) Loop (Tour 28), this is a wonderful exploration of rural Lewis County—its farms, fields, forests, and tiny towns (Evaline, Vader, Boistfort, and, of course, Winlock, world-famous for having the world's largest—albeit fake—egg). The route's western half features a couple steep climbs likely to have you searching for one tinier gear. But that just means you've earned a healthy descent, right?

Begin by heading south through fields and rural farmland on country roads that may lack a wide shoulder, but also lack traffic. At about mile 3, turn left onto Pleasant Valley Road and commence a terrific 7-mile stretch along Stearns Creek. This section couldn't be more aptly named, bringing together the elements that make road riding special: a winding ribbon of pavement through forest and farmland, some rollers to keep you honest, a water feature (Stearns Creek), and not much traffic.

The last 2 miles do kick up a bit before dropping down and delivering you to tiny Evaline. Not much here to be quite honest, so head 3 miles south on State Route 603 (some traffic but ample shoulder) to Winlock for a gander at the mega-egg. Twelve feet long and weighing 1200 pounds, the egg sits atop a 10-foot pole and pays homage to a time when Winlock was the nation's second-largest egg producer. (Kinda makes you wonder how big they'd have made the egg if they were number one.) Along with the big egg, Winlock offers plenty of refueling and restroom opportunities.

Continuing south, reach State Route 506 on the outskirts of tiny Vader and turn right. A pleasant, winding 4-mile stretch past tree farms and llama farms and horse farms (oh my!) follows, upon which you turn right onto Wildwood Road and begin the hilly half of this route. And really, there are just two: Wildwood Road climbs almost 500 feet in a little more than 2 miles; Curtis Hill Road, at about the 42-mile mark, climbs 400 in just over a mile. Ouch!

There's more to this Lewis County route than just Winlock's world's largest egg; miles and miles of terrific low-traffic roads await you, too.

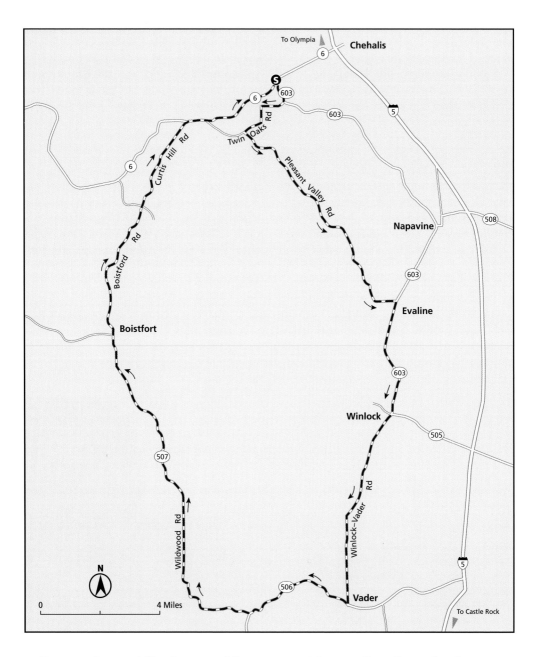

Between the two hills, the route follows pleasant rural roads through farms and horse country. Boistfort, at the 38-mile mark, offers the Boistfort Store, should you need food and drink.

At the bottom of the screaming-fast Curtis Hill Road descent (14 percent, the sign says),

turn right onto State Route 6 and return to your starting point, about 3 miles ahead.

Variation: Combine this with the Rochester–Route 6 (Adna) Loop (Tour 28) for a challenging 95-miler that climbs about 3300 feet.

0.0   From grocery store parking lot at the intersection of SR 603 and SR 6, turn right onto SR 603.
0.7   Right onto Twin Oaks Rd.
2.7   Left onto Pleasant Valley Rd.
10.8   Right onto SR 603. (Becomes Kenton Ave. in Winlock, then Winlock–Vader Rd.)
21.3   Right onto SR 506.
25.2   Right onto Wildwood Rd.
37.8   Boistfort. (Wildwood Rd. becomes Boistfort Rd.)
41.7   Right onto Curtis Hill Rd.
45.1   Right onto SR 6.
48.3   Return to grocery store parking lot and starting point.

31 NORTH CLARK COUNTY– TUMTUM MOUNTAIN

Difficulty	Very strenuous
Time	4 to 7 hours
Distance	73.9 miles
Elevation Gain	6025 feet

ROAD CONDITIONS: Rural, low-traffic roads with narrow or no shoulders. Chip-seal surfaces on some outlying roads. Paved forest service road that can be downright rough.

GETTING THERE: From I-5 between Kalama and Vancouver, take exit 14. Go east on NW 269th St. (Pioneer St.) and just ahead in quick succession turn right onto S. 65th Ave., left onto NW 264th St., and right onto NE 259th St. (S. Union Ridge Pkwy.). Follow NE 259th St. east for 4 miles to NE 82nd Ave. Turn left and park at Daybreak Park, which is 0.3 mile ahead on the right.

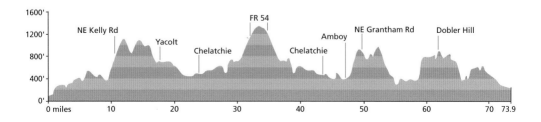

This rural north and east Clark County route explores numerous tiny towns and unincorporated areas—as well as passing through countless acres of field and farmland, before plunging into Gifford Pinchot National Forest, in the shadows of Mount St. Helens. Plus, you ride right by Tumtum Mountain, which is always fun to say. Also nice, at various points, riders are treated to terrific views of Mount Hood, Mount St. Helens, and sundry surrounding peaks.

Not a route for your heavy aero wheels, this ride features plenty of climbing—over 6000 feet in all—including a couple 2- to 5-milers, one of which is on rough (though paved) forest service road. That climb can easily be skipped, however. Just turn around when you reach Tumtum Mountain. (A shout-out to Lap Lai of the Vancouver Bicycle Club, who devised this route.)

From Daybreak Park near Battle Ground, make your way east via a series of mostly straight-arrow roads at 90-degree angles to one another, reaching the outskirts of town and Battle Ground Lake State Park. (Battle Ground is named in honor of a battle between US Army soldiers and Klickitat Indians that never actually took place.) A couple miles north of the park, after a fast smooth descent to cross the East Fork of the Lewis River, go left onto Kelly Road and get started on the first sustained climb of the day—a 2.5-miler that ascends more than 700 feet, with the toughest pitches being about 8 percent. Some rollers follow, on sometimes smooth, sometimes chip-sealy surfaces. There is no shoulder, but also little traffic. The road gradually descends, passing through tiny Yacolt, which at the 17.5-mile mark offers a grocery store, mini-mart, and the like. (In the early twentieth century, this town was nearly destroyed by the Yacolt Burn, the state's worst forest fire, which burned more than a quarter-million acres of forest.)

After Yacolt, head north and east via more rural roadways—including State Route 503—

Pedal past Tumtum Mountain where, according to legend, a Native American chief is buried at the summit.

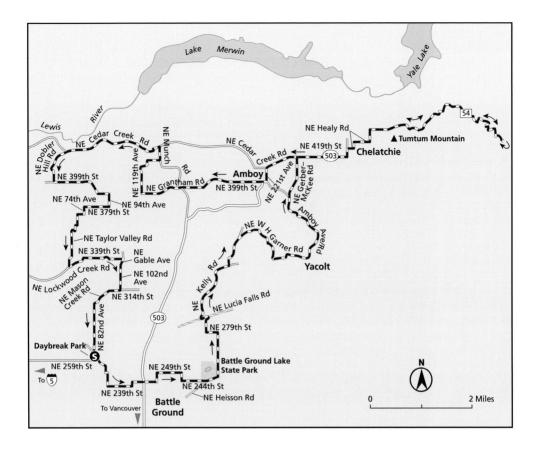

for Chelatchie and Tumtum, which sound like a dynamic duo in a kids' TV show. If you like, stop at the Chelatchie Prairie General Store and City Center. (I'd wager there are more letters in those words than there are residents in the town.) Otherwise, turn right onto Healy and make for that giant tree-covered Hershey's Kiss in the near distance, Tumtum Mountain. Legend has it that a Native American chief is buried at the summit of this perfectly symmetrical, extinct volcano. (Apparently, Tumtum means "heart.")

From here, it's up to you how far you want to go. Healy becomes Forest Road 54, rough and tumble chip seal that climbs up and up before eventually turning to gravel. This route suggests a roughly 9-mile (one-way) foray from the Chelatchie store before turning around—which includes a 5.5-mile sustained

climb that rises about 800 feet—but as mentioned above, the climb can easily be skipped.

Either way, back at the Chelatchie store, retrace your pedal strokes on State Route 503 but this time continue straight to Amboy, another quaint town of about 2000. Turning right onto NE 399th Street, begin a challenging 5-mile stretch that starts with a tough 2-mile climb, further challenges with some rollers, and ends with a fast descent to Cedar Creek. More rural roads follow before the steepest climb of the day, Dobler Hill Road, which ascends 400 feet in 1.3 miles, with stretches of 17 percent grade (yes, 17!). I'm so sorry.

From here, the remaining 14 miles of the route follow more of Clark County's rural roads, the last 4 miles offering a gradual descent to Daybreak Park and your starting point.

0.0	From Daybreak Park near Battle Ground, go south on NE 82nd Ave.
0.3	Left onto NE 259th St. (Becomes NE Manley Rd.)
1.6	Left onto NE 239th St.
2.6	Left onto NE 112th Ave. (Becomes NE 244th St.)
3.8	Left onto NE 132nd Ave.
4.1	Right onto NE 249th St.
5.1	Right onto NE 152nd Ave. (Becomes NE 244th St.)
5.8	Left at NE Heisson Rd. intersection to stay on NE 244th St. (Becomes NE Palmer Rd., then NE 182nd Ave.)
6.8	Battle Ground Lake State Park.
8.3	Left onto NE 279th St.
8.8	Right onto NE 172nd Ave.
9.5	Left onto NE Lucia Falls Rd.
9.8	Right onto NE Kelly Rd.
13.7	Right onto NE W. H. Garner Rd.
17.5	Enter Yacolt.
17.7	Left onto N. Amboy Ave. (Becomes NE Amboy Rd.)
20.8	Right onto NE Gerber–McKee Rd.
22.5	Bear right onto NE 419th St. (SR 503).
24.7	Enter Chelatchie. Right onto NE Healy Rd. (Becomes FR 54.)
33.7	Gravel road turnaround point.
43.0	Left onto SR 503 S./NE Yale Bridge Rd. (Becomes NE 419th St.)
45.2	Continue straight on NE 419th St. (Becomes NE Cedar Creek Rd.)
46.6	Left onto NE 221st Ave.
47.1	Enter Amboy. Left onto NE 399th St. (Becomes NE Grantham Rd.)
52.3	Right onto NE 119th Ave. (Becomes NE Hoff Rd. and NE 414th St.)
54.2	Left onto NE Munch Rd.
54.7	Left onto NE Cedar Creek Rd.
58.8	Left onto NE Dobler Hill Rd.
60.2	Left onto NE 399th St. (Becomes NE Sorenson Wy.)
62.7	Right onto NE 94th Ave.
63.2	Right onto NE 379th St.
64.2	Left onto NE 74th Ave. (Becomes NE 374th St. NE 68th Ave., NE Taylor Valley Rd.)
66.7	Bear right onto NE 339th St.
66.8	Left onto NE 60th Ave.
67.0	Left onto NE Lockwood Creek Rd. (Becomes NE 339th St.)
69.3	Right onto NE Gable Ave. (Becomes NE 102nd Ave.)
70.5	Bear right onto NE 314th St. (Becomes NE Mason Creek Rd., NE 82nd Ave., NE Hyatt Rd.)
73.7	Bear left onto NE Daybreak Rd.
73.9	Return to Daybreak Park.

32 RIDE AROUND CLARK COUNTY

Difficulty	Strenuous
Time	3 to 6 hours
Distance	65 miles
Elevation Gain	3010 feet

ROAD CONDITIONS: Urban riding on busy roads with bike lanes, rural low-traffic roads with narrow or no shoulder but low speed limits. Chip-seal surface on some outlying roads.

GETTING THERE: From I-5 in Vancouver, take exit 1C. Head east on E. Mill Plain Blvd. for 2.6 miles to N. Divine Rd. Turn right and look for street parking or park in the middle school lot 0.3 mile ahead on the left.

This is essentially the 65-mile route of the annual Ride Around Clark County, a popular annual event put on by the Vancouver Bicycle Club. However, this ride goes in the opposite direction. Bookended with an urban start and finish—mostly on smooth roads offering bike lanes and bike-friendly signs—the middle 40-plus miles feature terrific low-traffic country roads through seemingly endless fields and farmland, scenic stretches along the mighty Columbia River, and giant look-sees of snow-clad volcanoes. Certainly not flat, the route boasts several hills that'll get the blood rushing—but nothing that thrusts one into the pain cave with no hope of being let out.

Begin by making your way through bike-friendly downtown Vancouver, passing Clark College along the way. Many streets and roadways offer bike lanes, bike signs, and bike-friendly speed bumps (little cut-outs on

the far right so cyclists don't suffer involuntary end-oes). Upon making your way out of town via NW Bernie Drive, pedal north along Vancouver Lake and after a series of rolling lumps—as well as the small town of Felida—head west toward the Columbia River. The next 7 miles or so are every reason why you ride a road bike—gentle rollers on low-traffic roads through orchards, berry fields, and farms, following the mighty wonder that is the Columbia River, backed by Pumpkin Ridge on the Oregon side. When the route swings east, you're treated to Cascade views, punctuated by snowy stratovolcanoes.

Continue east into the heart of Clark County (Washington's first county) and enjoy miles of rolling countryside. Admittedly, some of the "rolling" might be interpreted as "hilly," especially an upward trending 7 miles just north of Battle Ground. But a couple of

Clark County offers everything from bike-friendly urban roadways to wide open countryside with rolling hills and scenic vistas. (Jeff Beilfuss)

parks—Daybreak Park (at about mile 26) and Battle Ground Lake State Park (mile 32)—as well as the town of Hockinson (mile 38)—offer potential rest and/or restroom breaks. The route's highest point is less than 600 feet, so the climbs are relatively short. Be aware, however, that much of this route lacks tree protection, so wind and potentially heat can be an issue.

Eventually making your way south, enjoy Every Reason to Ride a Road Bike Redux: a mile-long stretch of smooth, swooshing riding on Leadbetter Road, by Lacamas Lake. After swinging around to the right at the south end of the lake onto NW Lake Road (Heritage Park on the right offers restrooms),

begin your last real climb of the day. A half mile gets you high above the lake and into the midst of the tony homes you likely spotted earlier from Leadbetter. It's a busy roadway, but bike lane and/or ample shoulder make it fairly painless.

From here, much of the rest of the way is commercial and residential roadways, but almost all of it offers dedicated bike lanes. Good on ya', Vancouver!

Variation: This is the Ride Around Clark County route (65-mile option) ridden in reverse. To match what's done on the May ride day, ride the opposite direction from what's described above.

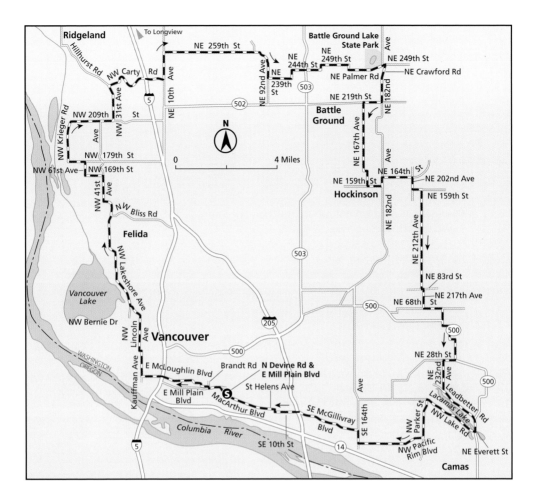

0.0   From the middle school parking lot on Vancouver's N. Devine Rd., head south on Devine.

0.1   Right onto MacArthur Blvd.

0.5   Left onto E. Mill Plain Blvd.

1.0   Right onto Brandt Rd.

1.1   Left onto E. McLoughlin Blvd.

3.5   Left onto Franklin St.

3.5   Right onto W. McLoughlin Blvd.

3.7   Right onto Kauffman Ave.

4.8   Left onto W. 39th St.

4.9   Right onto NW Lincoln Ave.

6.1   Left onto NW Bernie Dr.

6.2   Bear right to stay on NW Bernie Dr.

6.7   Right onto NW Fruit Valley Rd. (Becomes NW Lakeshore Ave., NW 41st Ave.)

12.0	Left onto NW 169th St.
13.0	Right onto NW 61st Ave.
13.6	Left onto NW 179th St. (Becomes NW Krieger Rd.)
15.5	Right onto NW 209th St.
17.5	Left onto NW 31st Ave.
18.9	Right onto NW Carty Rd.
21.3	Left onto NE 10th Ave.
22.1	Right onto NE 259th St.
25.1	Left to stay on NE 259th St. (Becomes NE Manley Rd., then NE 92nd Ave.)
27.0	Left onto NE 239th St.
27.9	Left onto NE 112th Ave.
28.2	Bear right as road becomes NE 244th St. (Becomes NW 25th St.)
29.2	Left onto NE 132nd Ave.
29.4	Right onto NE 249th St.
30.4	Right onto NE 152nd Ave.
30.7	Left onto NE 244th St.
31.1	Left to stay on NE 244th St.; sign says NE Heisson Rd. (Becomes NE Palmer Rd.) Battle Ground Lake State Park is on your left.
32.2	Right onto NE 249th St.
32.3	Right onto NE Crawford Rd. (Becomes NE 182nd Ave.)
33.8	Right onto NE 219th St.
34.5	Left onto NE 167th Ave. (Becomes NE 169th St., then NE 170th Ave.)
37.7	Left onto NE 159th St.
38.2	Hockinson. Left onto NE 182nd Ave.
38.5	Right onto NE 164th St.
39.5	Right onto NE 202nd Ave.
39.7	Left onto NE 159th St.
40.2	Right onto NE 212th Ave.
44.0	Left onto NE 83rd St.
44.2	Right onto NE 217th Ave.
45.0	Left onto NE 68th St.
45.7	Right onto NE 232nd Ave. (Becomes SR 500.)
48.1	Right onto NE 28th St.
48.6	Left onto NE 232nd Ave. (Becomes Leadbetter Rd.)
51.5	Right onto NE Everett St.
52.1	Right onto NW Lake Rd.
54.5	Left onto NW Parker St.
56.0	Right onto NW Pacific Rim Blvd. (Becomes SE 34th St.)
58.1	Right onto SE 164th Ave.
59.5	Left onto SE McGillivray Blvd. (Becomes SE 10th St.)
62.8	Right onto SE 98th Ave.
62.9	Left onto St. Helens Ave. (Becomes MacArthur Blvd.)
65.0	Right onto N. Devine Rd. and back to your starting point.

WASHOUGAL AND EAST, HILLZ 'N' MORE

Difficulty	Very Strenuous
Time	3½ to 6 hours
Distance	63.5 miles
Elevation Gain	5225 feet

ROAD CONDITIONS: Urban riding on busy roads with bike lanes, rural low-traffic roads with narrow or no shoulder. Chip-seal surface on some outlying roads.

GETTING THERE: From I-205 in Vancouver, take exit 28. Head east on SE Mill Plain Blvd. for 2.8 miles to SE 164th Ave. Turn right and follow for 0.4 mile to SE 15th St. Park in the shopping center lot on the left.

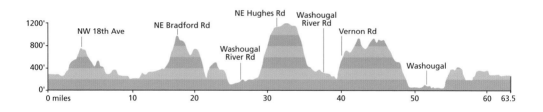

Sure, this mostly rural, hilly-as-heck route features a few spots of bother, but routes like these build character, making us stronger, wiser, and even better looking. (OK, I can't guarantee *all* of those, but they will make you stronger.) A couple swervy-curvy descents will test your bike-handling skills as well.

But don't let these challenges scare you off, for the scenery on this route is tops—stunning mountain vistas as well as a couple stretches along the sparkling Washougal River. And besides, the two biggest climbs can easily be skipped (see Variations, below). This is another fun, challenging route devised by Vancouver Bicycle Club's Lap Lai.

From the sprawling shopping center in Vancouver, head east on SE 15th Street (bike lane provided), where the sprawl thins

out rather quickly. Following the Mileage Log directions, you'll soon find yourself on SE Payne Road (aptly named), undertaking a stiff 2.5-mile climb with pitches at 12 percent. The views at the top are amazing—mountains galore, the Columbia River, and the eastern reaches of the Vancouver-Portland metro area.

Quads and hammys warmed up, begin making your way north via smooth roads with ample shoulders and/or bike lanes toward the more rural reaches of Clark County. Ride through rolling hills, past golf courses and farmland. Eventually, at the 16-mile mark, reach the second significant climb of the day: a well-shaded 2-miler that climbs 600 feet in about three stages. The last two, at about 13 percent, are the toughest.

Waterfall tumbling down the hillside into the Washougal River

The next 7 miles offer a series of rural rollers, some wooded, some not (thus, wind can be a factor), with occasional views of the surrounding mountains. Near the 20-mile mark, the Fern Prairie Market offers eats, drinks, and restrooms. Continue the ups and downs until you reach Washougal River Road. Go left and commence a terrific 4-mile, slightly uphill stretch of riverside riding, deep in the woods. Roadside pullouts offer opportunities for contemplative river-gazing and/or oohing and ahhing at various waterfalls streaking down the hillside. Enjoy it because once you turn left onto NE Hughes Road and undertake a 4-mile climb that gains about 1000 feet, you might find yourself wondering why you didn't take up tennis instead of cycling. Some stretches have an 11 and 12 percent

grade, but if you're a climber, you'll love the challenge. (If you're not a climber, see Variations, below.)

After a brief breather through the rolling farmland up top, take a wild and winding descent back down to Washougal River Road. Turn right at the bottom and enjoy a gradual 4-mile descent along the scenic river—throw in a stop at roadside Washougal River Mercantile if you like—before heading to NE Vernon Road and the route's next big climb.

Though it's not as relentlessly steep as Hughes Road—Vernon Road climbs about 700 feet in 3.2 miles, with pitches at 12 percent—this climb offers its own charms. For one, your reward at the top is a series of challenging rollers, but through a rural countryside that is stunning. At about the 45-mile

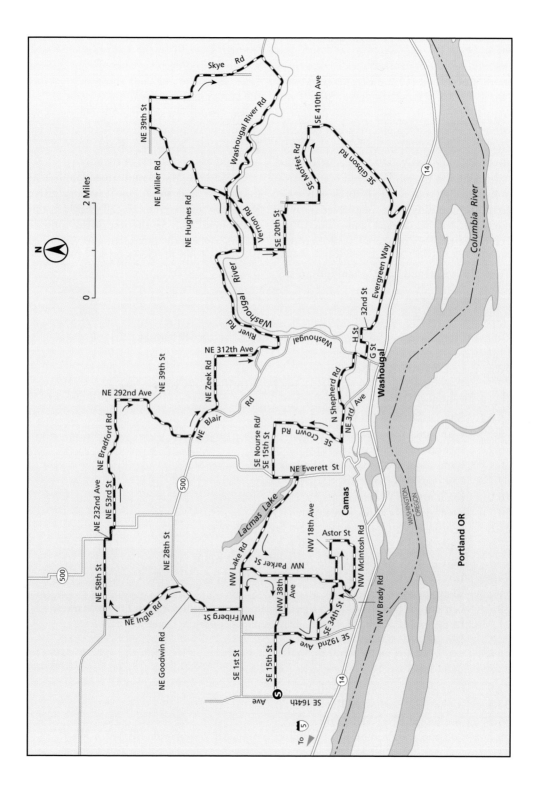

mark, begin a long, sweeping, and very fast descent on smooth road with wide open views south toward the Columbia River, Mount Hood, and her Cascade brethren. Stop if you want to admire the view, for the descent is curvy as well as steep and requires not only excellent bike-handling skills, but all your attention too. (See Variations below if you'd rather skip the Vernon Road hill.)

Eventually, you make it back down to earth and, heading west, maneuver through the streets of Washougal and Camas (the "Home of the Papermakers"), and then take the last climb of the day—an ascending ride-by of scenic Lacamas Lake. Thankfully, many (though not all) of the roadways offer wide shoulders and/or bike lanes. From Lacamas Lake, return to the start using pretty much the same roads you began the route with.

Variations: To skip the NE Hughes Road climb, just continue east on Washougal River Road for 4 miles to Skye Road. Turn around here and follow the rest of the route.

To skip the NE Vernon Road climb, continue west and south on Washougal River Road for about 6 miles, all the way into Washougal. Pick up the rest of the route by turning right at the intersection of Washougal River Road and N. Shepherd Road.

MILEAGE LOG

0.0	From the shopping center in Vancouver, go east on SE 15th St.
1.3	Right onto SE 192nd Ave.
2.3	Left onto SE 34th St.
2.7	Right onto SE Payne Rd. (Becomes NW 18th Ave., NW 16th Ave.)
4.4	Left onto NW Hood St.
4.6	Right onto NW 18th Ave.
4.8	Right onto NW Astor St.
5.2	Left onto NW McIntosh Rd.
6.4	Right onto NW Brady Rd. (Becomes NW Parker St.)
9.1	Left onto NW Lake Rd.
10.0	Right onto NW Friberg St.
10.7	Right onto NE Goodwin Rd.
11.6	Left onto NE Ingle Rd. (Becomes NE 199th Ave.)
13.5	Right onto NE 58th St (SR 500 E.)
15.1	Bear right to stay on SR 500 (now NE 232nd Ave.).
15.6	Left onto NE 53rd St. (Becomes NE Bradford Rd., NE 292nd Ave.)
19.2	Right onto NE 39th St.
20.7	Left onto NE Blair Rd. (Go right on 19th for 0.4 mile for Fern Prairie Market.)
21.5	Left onto NE Zeek Rd. (Road changes names multiple times.)
24.5	Left onto SE Washougal River Rd.
28.6	Left onto NE Hughes Rd. Big hill. (Road changes names multiple times.)
31.6	Right onto NE 39th St. (Becomes Skye Rd.)
33.9	Bear left to stay on Skye Rd.
35.4	Right onto Washougal River Rd.
35.9	Washougal River Mercantile.
39.2	Left onto NE Vernon Rd. Big hill. (Becomes SE Vernon Rd., SE 357th Ave.)
41.2	Left onto SE 20th St.
42.4	Right onto SE 377th Ave.

43.5	Bear left onto SE Moffet Rd.
45.0	Right onto SE 410th Ave. (Becomes SE Turner Rd.)
45.5	Right onto SE Gibson Rd. (Becomes SE Evergreen Blvd. and Evergreen Way)
50.7	Right onto 32nd St.
50.9	Left onto H St.
51.3	Left onto 25th St.
51.4	Right onto G St.
51.8	Right onto Washougal River Rd.
52.1	Left onto N. Shepherd Rd.
53.2	Right onto NE 3rd Ave. (E St.).
53.9	Right onto SE Crown Rd. (Becomes SE 283rd Ave.)
55.6	Left onto SE 15th St. (SE Nourse Rd.)
56.8	Left onto NE Everett St.
57.3	Right onto NE Lake Rd.
59.7	Left onto NW Parker St.
60.8	Right onto NW 38th Ave. (Road changes names multiple times; eventually becomes SE 15th St.)
63.5	Return to shopping center parking lot.

NORTH CASCADES

Here you'll find big climbs (and accompanying big big views) on roads that spend much of the year under multiple feet of snow. So take advantage of them during the few months that they're open. Also included are heavenly routes through the beloved Methow Valley on the high, dry eastern flank of the Cascades.

34 EVERSON TO MOUNT BAKER

Difficulty	Very Strenuous
Time	5½ to 8 hours
Distance	99 miles
Elevation Gain	7210 feet

ROAD CONDITIONS: Rural farm roads with chip-seal surfaces and steep, winding mountain road with varying shoulder widths. ***Note:*** Because of the area's prodigious annual snowfall, the road is clear to Artist Point for only about two months each year, usually starting in mid-July. The road is usually clear of snow to just above the Mount Baker Ski Area, about 2.5 miles and 800 feet below Artist Point.

GETTING THERE: From Bellingham, head east on SR 542 (Mount Baker Hwy.) for about 5 miles and turn left onto Everson–Goshen Rd. Follow for about 8 miles into Everson. (Along the way, the road becomes SR 544.) In town, the road becomes Main St.; park in the grocery store parking lot in the center of town or on Main St. itself.

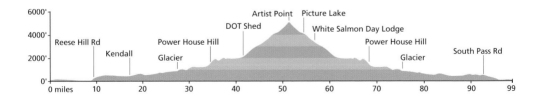

Here's a challenging century that takes in three of Whatcom County's most notorious climbs: Reese Hill, the Power House Hill past Nooksack Falls, and the 10.5-mile, 3000-foot ascent to Artist Point. The return ride on this mostly out-and-back route includes the road bike leg of the long-running Ski to Sea relay race. Ride this and consider yourself an honorary Whatcom County resident.

Begin by rolling east down Main Street in Everson, passing through the town and out into flat farmland, making your way in a northeasterly direction toward Sumas, last stop before Canada. A mile south of the border, about 8 miles into the ride, hang a right onto Reese Hill Road and after about a mile of eyeing the forested hilly hump ahead of you, get to it. Though not the longest climb of the day, it's the steepest, with a 0.8-mile stretch that climbs 350 feet, including upward tilts at 15 percent. The whole thing—which also includes a roller coaster down 'n' up stretch—is about 2.5 miles long.

Reese Hill now in your rear-view mirror, continue south past a forested community called Paradise and at 17 miles (now on Kendall Road), reach the Mount Baker Highway (State Route 542) and the small town of Kendall. A couple gas station mini-marts offer places to resupply.

Continue east, now on Mount Baker Highway, which is likely to have the most vehicle traffic and not a very wide shoulder. The highway climbs gradually for the next 10 miles, passing through Maple Falls. Reach Glacier at about 27 miles; its general store is the last chance for food and drink until you

pass this way again at the 75-mile mark, so take advantage of it. Back on the bike, enter the Mount Baker–Snoqualmie National Forest. After crossing the Nooksack River, begin one of a number of short steep pitches the route throws at you in order to get you up to the 2000-foot level, where the culminating climb to Artist Point begins. One of those pitches isn't all that short—the Power House Hill is 1.8 miles long and climbs 600 feet, and some riders think it's the toughest climb of the route.

At 41 miles, just after passing the DOT shed, cross over the Nooksack River one last time and begin the 10.5-mile, 3000-foot climb to Artist Point. Stunning straight-on views of Mount Shuksan tend to pull you up the hill and soon enough (or maybe not so soon if climbing isn't your forte), you're passing below the unoccupied chair lifts of Mount Baker Ski Area, where giant sculpted ravens stand guard.

Views (and, to be honest, steepness quotient) are ratcheted up even higher on the second half of the climb—lovely heathery meadows, the icy craggy peaks of the Nooksack Ridge, the bluish glaciers adorning Mount Shuksan, which appears close enough to touch. Reach Artist Point, the great big parking lot in the sky, at about the 51-mile mark. Whew! More than halfway done.

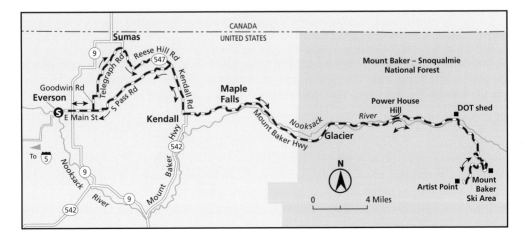

A lone cyclist nears the final switchback on the long and hard—but stunningly beautiful—climb to Artist Point.

Return the same way—watching for falling rocks on the mountain descent—following the route to Kendall Road. (You probably won't be happy about the short, steep climb before Maple Falls at mile 82.) At mile 89, instead of continuing straight to Reece Hill, turn left onto South Pass Road. As well as being a nice alternative return to Everson, this keeps you on the Ski to Sea road bike route, which you've been following since you passed the DOT shed (mile 62 on the way back), at the bottom of the Artist Point climb.

Passing through forest, fields, and farmland, the rural, low-traffic road presents about 3 miles of rolling hills but then rewards with a 3-mile descent that drops into a flatland run into Everson. Keep your eyes open for the town limits sign and go for it. The start/finish parking lot is about a mile ahead.

0.0	From the grocery store parking lot in Everson, head east on E. Main St.
2.4	Left onto Goodwin Rd.
3.4	Right onto Sorenson Rd.
3.7	Left onto N. Telegraph Rd.
6.8	Bear right to stay on Telegraph Rd.
9.3	Right onto Reese Hill Rd. (SR 547).
12.2	Right onto Kendall Rd. (SR 547).
17.2	Kendall; continue straight onto SR 542 (Mount Baker Hwy.).
20.2	Maple Falls.
27.6	Glacier.
33.8	Power House Hill.
41.1	DOT shed and start of Artist Point climb.
46.4	White Salmon Day Lodge, Mount Baker Ski Area.
48.9	Upper Ski Lodge.
51.6	Artist Point. Turn around.
62.2	DOT shed. (Start of Ski to Sea road bike course.)
75.3	Glacier.
82.6	Maple Falls.
85.6	Straight onto Kendall Rd. (SR 547).
89.5	Left onto S. Pass Rd.
97.9	Everson town limits.
99.0	Return to parking lot starting point.

35 MOUNT BAKER HILL CLIMB

Difficulty	Strenuous
Time	3 to 4½ hours
Distance	47.8 miles
Elevation Gain	4850 feet

ROAD CONDITIONS: Winding mountain road with rolling steep hills including one that's 10.5 miles long. No bike lanes and the road has narrow shoulders. Can be busy on summer weekends, so best to ride during weekdays or early on weekend mornings. *Note:* Because of heavy snowfall, the last 3 miles of SR 542 to Artist Point are open only from about mid-July to early October.

GETTING THERE: From I-5 in Bellingham, head east on SR 542 (Mount Baker Hwy.) for 33 miles to the tiny town of Glacier, located just past milepost 33. Turn right just past the post office and park at the public restrooms and parking lot about 25 yards ahead. (Parking is also available at the Glacier Public Service Center 0.3 mile east on SR 542.)

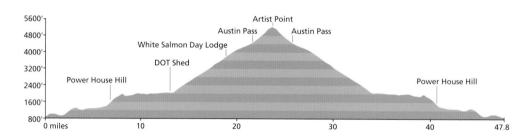

Popular as one of the birthplaces of snowboarding, Mount Baker is popular also with road cyclists, especially those who love spectacular alpine vistas and consider a relentless 10.5-mile-long uphill push a good time. Each fall, close to a 1000 cyclists (including a unicyclist or two) head here for the annual Ride 542 Festival, wherein some girl and guy can win a couple thousand dollars in prize money for being the first one to Artist Point, the viewpoint at the end of the highway. (***Note:*** The parking lot by the start/finish of this ride is next to a country store and a couple restaurants that offer pre- and post-ride eat-'n'-drink refreshment.)

Along with the stunning views, and usually primo road conditions, that end-of-the-highway aspect is one of this ride's calling cards. Because the road is not a cross-state highway, there's often not a lot of traffic and on a weekday morn, one can make it to the top seeing fewer than ten cars. Conversely, busy good-weather weekends can mean a lot of cars, which on a narrow mountain road sans guardrails, can be scary for some. That said, the Mount Baker Highway is certainly one of the state's—perhaps the country's—most spectacular road rides. As with all Cascade climbs, be sure to pack a jacket or other wind-stopper for the ride down—a long

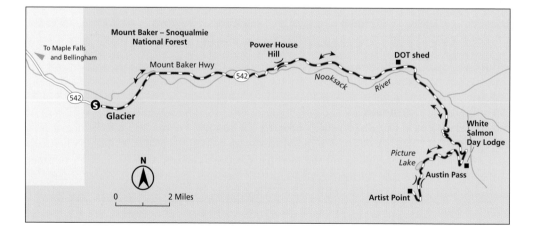

With Table Mountain in the background, two riders grind out the final pedal strokes of the 3,000-foot climb to Artist Point.

descent at 30- to 40-plus miles per hour can chill one's bones.

This route, most of which is Mount Baker–Snoqualmie National Forest, starts with a number of short, steep pitches. At mile 7, you encounter the first big climb—Power House Hill (also known as the Nooksack Falls Hill). Many riders think it is the harder of the two climbs on this route. It's certainly steeper, gaining 600 feet in little more than 1.5 miles. However, at the top, it rewards riders with a short, fast descent, then gives them about 5 miles to catch their breath before the next long, winding climb—a 10-miler to the top.

About 13 miles from the start, the road passes a prominent DOT shed, crosses the Nooksack River, and starts climbing. Find a gear you're comfortable with and get used to it; you're going to be in it for a while. Of course, the higher you go, the better the views become. Mount Shuksan (9127 feet), one of the most photographed mountains in the world, lures you along as the road winds higher beneath steep cliffs of columnar basalt and alongside deep drop-offs with no guardrails.

About halfway up the 10.5-mile climb, you pass the giant sculpted ravens that guard the entrance to the Mount Baker Ski Area's White Salmon Day Lodge. (The Heather Meadows Day Lodge entrance is 3 miles up the road.) From here, the views get kicked up a notch: the jagged ridgeline and alpine meadows near the US-Canada border just 10 miles north;

ever-expanding Mount Shuksan against a backdrop of countless North Cascade peaks, and finally, once you've made it all the way to Artist Point, straight-on views of the giant white volcano that is Mount Baker.

That is, if you're able to ride that far. This area averages 600 inches of snow each season and thus the last 3 miles—from the Heather Meadows Day Lodge to Artist Point—are usually snow-free for only about two months each year.

Once at the top, or wherever the wall of snow turns you around, take in the views, snap some pics, and return the way you came. It's a fast, potentially chilly descent, so ride safely and dress accordingly.

Variation: Some riders start at Maple Falls, 7 miles west of Glacier, for a 62-mile ride.

MILEAGE LOG

0.0	Take a right out of parking lot near the post office in Glacier onto Mount Baker Hwy. (SR 542).
6.7	Begin Power House Hill.
13.1	Pass DOT shed.
13.8	Begin long climb.
19.0	White Salmon Day Lodge (Mount Baker Ski Area).
21.0	Right at loop around Picture Lake.
22.2	Austin Pass, a turnaround spot when road is still snow-covered.
23.9	Artist Point turnaround point; return the same way.
47.8	Arrive back at parking lot in Glacier.

36 NEWHALEM TO WINTHROP (ONE-WAY)

Difficulty	Very Strenuous
Time	4½ to 7 hours (one-way)
Distance	73 miles
Elevation Gain	6425 feet

ROAD CONDITIONS: Well-traveled state highway with wide shoulders and "Bikes on Road" signs. Road usually in good shape, though there are always spots undergoing repair from winter's effects. Cell service is sketchy to nonexistent through the entire route, and there are no stores or services for the middle 50 miles, from Diablo to Mazama. Carry extra tubes, spokes, collarbones, or whatever you may need—you're truly on your own. ***Note:*** Because of snowfall, most years SR 20 is closed from near Ross Lake to just below Washington Pass from about November until April.

GETTING THERE: Drive SR 20 to Newhalem at milepost 120, about 55 miles east of Sedro-Woolley. Just before the locomotive, turn right into the Skagit Information Center parking lot. If you want to make this a one-way shuttle trip, park a second car at Winthrop's Methow Cycle and Sport, right on SR 20 as you enter Winthrop (or next door at the town park by the big red barn).

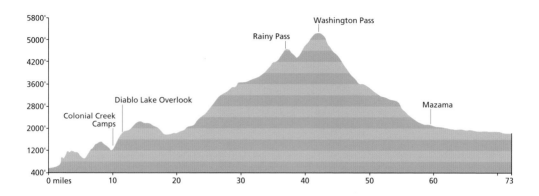

In late spring and early summer, this route attracts the long-long distance set: riders pedaling heavily panniered bikes weighed down with tents, sleeping bags, and cooking gear, inching their way to Colorado or somewhere on the East Coast. The route as described here, however, is as if you're riding the North Cascades Highway as a day trip, focusing on its greatest scenic hits. "Gateway to the American Alps," read signs in Sedro-Woolley,

Marblemount, and elsewhere, and they're not far from the truth. With jagged icy peaks, high alpine meadows, glaciers by the dozens, and the range's eponymous cascading waterfalls, you'll feel as though you're riding through a mountain stage of the Tour de France.

Begin by climbing up the narrow gorge gouged out over the millennia by the mighty Skagit River, now dammed in three places to provide hydroelectric power for Seattle.

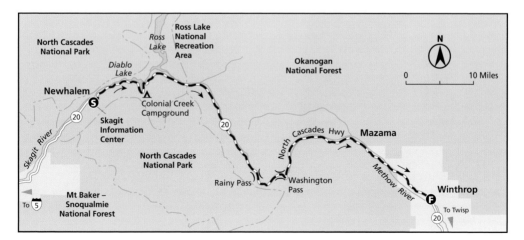

Shortly after starting out, look up and spot the aftereffects of the massive 2003 rockslide, when some 3 million cubic yards of rock let loose from the mountainside, cutting off the tiny town of Diablo from the west side of the state.

After pedaling through a couple tunnels, check out the turquoise-blue of Gorge Lake on your right. It's a color you'll be absolutely floored by in about 5 miles when you cross Thunder Arm and breathtaking Diablo Lake opens up on your left, below daunting Sourdough Mountain. The lake's color is from glacial sediment carried down Thunder Creek from deep in the heart of the North Cascades, one of the most glaciated spots in the Lower 48. If you're going to make only one stop along the route, make it at the well-signed Diablo Lake Overlook. Colonial and Pyramid peaks dominate the sky to the southwest, with Davis Peak to the west, all high above Diablo Dam and its dam-top road to Diablo, another Seattle City Light company town. (Restrooms available here.)

If, like me, you've driven this road countless times, you probably never realized all the sights and sensations you were missing while speeding along at 60 miles per hour. The Indian paintbrush, the rush of chilly air from tiny waterfalls pouring down the rocks, the endless hidden peaks and meadows. Pedaling along this heavenly highway, you will become aware of all that you missed before.

Near Ross Lake and Ruby Arm, the highway levels off for about 5 miles. But at about the 20-mile mark from Newhalem (near milepost 140), the road embarks on a long, consistent climb. If you don't have an altimeter, you might not realize you're climbing—but believe me, you are. After about 15 miles, the climb stiffens for a couple miles before reaching Rainy Pass (elevation 4855 feet). It then descends for a mile-and-a-half before offering up the steepest (and last) climb of the

day—900 feet in 3.4 miles—culminating in Washington Pass (elevation 5477 feet).

If you're going to stop at only two places, stop here at the Washington Pass Overlook. Along with restrooms, it boasts a paved trail to one of the state's top panoramic vistas. To the west is the impressive 1200-foot rock face of the Liberty Bell group, star of more Washington State photo calendars and coffee table books than probably any mountain save Rainier. Below is the wide hairpin turn, the pivot point where Western Washington becomes Eastern Washington and where, back on your bike, you'll enjoy one of the best descents of your life.

It goes on and on, pretty much all the way to Winthrop, and after all the climbing you've done, you'll feel unstoppable. The first 15 miles to the Mazama turnoff (which you pass on the way to Winthrop) are especially fast; the last 15 miles from Mazama to Winthrop, although flat or downhill, might be a little slower due to winds, especially later in the afternoon. No doubt, you'll be amazed by the contrast to the west side of Washington Pass. Here on the dry side, it's ponderosa forests, wide-open fields, and horse ranches, much of it set against a backdrop of dry, craggy peaks.

Once in the Old West–spirited town of Winthrop, grab something to eat, stop at the terrific bike store here, stay the night, and do it all again in the opposite direction tomorrow. Or get a ride home (see shuttle recommendations in "Getting There," above).

Variations: There are myriad variations for this ride. For exactly 100 miles (and about 9000 feet of climbing), park at Colonial Creek Campground (9.7 miles east of Newhalem) and ride to Mazama and back.

Another North Cascades Highway century (actually 96 miles) is to ride Marblemount to Twisp one way. (Though the narrow road shoulder on the 15-mile stretch from Marblemount to Newhalem makes me uncomfortable.)

< *It's (almost) all downhill from here: from Washington Pass, riders enjoy a nearly 20-mile non-stop descent to Mazama.*

0.0	From the Skagit Information Center parking lot in Newhalem, turn right onto US Hwy 20.
9.7	Colonial Creek Campground.
11.4	Diablo Lake Overlook.
37.5	Rainy Pass (elevation 4855 feet).
42.4	Washington Pass (elevation 5477 feet).
59.6	Lost River Road (turnoff for Mazama).
73.0	Arrive at Methow Cycle and Sport/big red barn at entrance to Winthrop.

37 WINTHROP TO ANDREWS CREEK AND BACK

Difficulty	Moderate
Time	2½ to 4 hours
Distance	46.8 miles
Elevation Gain	2260 feet

ROAD CONDITIONS: Rural roads and paved forest roads with chip-seal surface.

GETTING THERE: From Burlington, head east on SR 20 (North Cascades Hwy.) for about 130 miles. Just before entering Winthrop, park at Methow Cycle and Sport, located on the right side of the road.

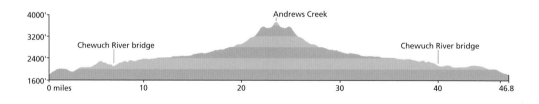

This pleasant, out-and-back route is one of those quintessential Methow rides that makes you feel as though you're out for a hike on your road bike. Winding along the gurgling waters of the Chewuch River, you head farther and farther into the dry conifers of the Okanogan National Forest, likely getting high as a kite from its dry pine-forest smell.

From Winthrop, cross State Route 20 and head up Westside Chewuch Road. The first mile climbs rather rudely, but fret not, my two-wheeled friend, most of this route

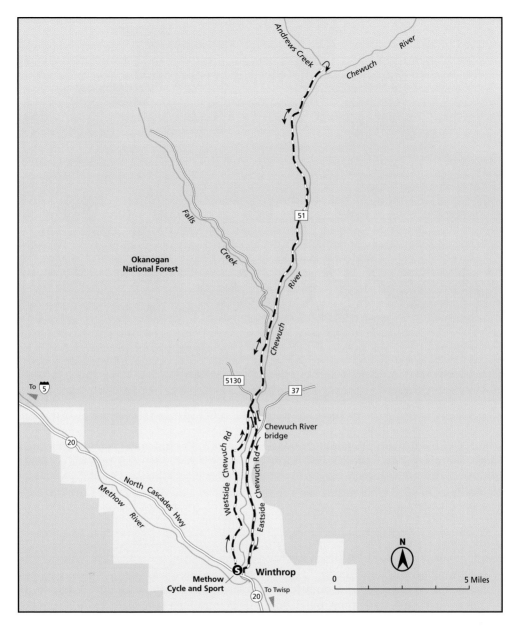

consists of gentle rollers, with only a couple spots as steep as this beginning mile. Overall, it climbs an average of about 80 feet per mile—not too killer on the way out, but just enough to make the return ride feel surprisingly easy.

Follow the rural road north, meandering past open fields, farms, and ranches, spotting the occasional inflatable Godzilla or other nonsensical yard ornament. At about 6.8 miles, continue straight at the Chewuch River bridge. Note this spot because on the way back, you'll cross the Methow River here and return to Winthrop via Eastside Chewuch Road. (*Chewuch* is a Native American word meaning "creek.")

On a clear, crisp autumn morn, tandem cyclists set out from downtown Winthrop.

Just ahead, enter the Okanogan National Forest. The chip-seal road, which wasn't exactly smooth as glass to begin with, can be a tad rougher here, depending on maintenance and Mother Nature's impact. Forest service roads might not be the smoothest, but they offer less traffic as well as scenery that's often out of this world. As for Forest Road 51, which is what you're now riding: check and check.

Follow the road deeper and deeper into the forest—past numerous campgrounds and riverside pullouts, powering up the occasional steep but short pitch. In just over 23 miles, the pavement ends at Andrews Creek bridge, which is your turnaround point. After a quick stop at the Andrews Creek trailhead pit toilet, remount your steed and head back toward Winthrop, aided by the road's downhill pitch.

About 40 miles into your ride—17 miles south of your turnaround point at Andrews Creek—go left and cross the Chewuch River bridge that you passed earlier. Once across, bear right onto Eastside Chewuch Road and follow it for 6 miles back into Winthrop. In town, turn right onto State Route 20 and just after recrossing the Chewuch River, find the bike shop and your starting place ahead on the left.

MILEAGE LOG

0.0   From Methow Cycle and Sport in Winthrop, cross SR 20 onto Westside Chewuch Rd.
6.8   Pass Chewuch River bridge.
23.3 Turn around at Andrews Creek.

39.9   Left onto Eastside Chewuch Rd. (Becomes Bluff St., then Riverside Ave.)
46.6   Right onto SR 20.
46.8   Return to start.

38 WINTHROP TO WASHINGTON PASS VIA MAZAMA

Difficulty	Strenuous
Time	3½ to 5 hours
Distance	61 miles
Elevation Gain	4750 feet

ROAD CONDITIONS: Some chip-seal pavement on rural county road; state highway with varying shoulder widths. *Note:* Because of snowfall, most years SR 20 is closed just east of Washington Pass from about November until April.

GETTING THERE: From Burlington, head east on SR 20 (North Cascades Hwy.) for about 130 miles. Just before entering Winthrop, park at Methow Cycle and Sport, located on the right side of the road.

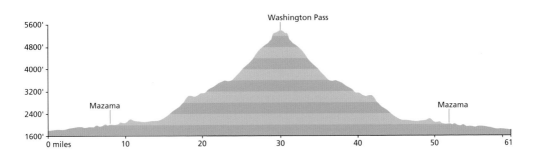

This ride meanders along the sparkling Methow River, with constant hits of stunning Methow scenery—our state's dry version of mountains, valleys, fields, and meadows. The route is pretty straightforward: 30 miles of going up followed by 30 miles of going down.

From Winthrop, head west on State Route 20 for 8 mostly flat, but slightly uphill-trending miles to Goat Creek Road, where you go right.

Enjoy a gentle, rolling riverside cruise through pine forest, dodging pinecones. Admire views of mountains above: Gardner Mountain to the west—almost 9000 feet high—and Goat Peak to the north, where with a decent squint you can spot the fire lookout tower on top. Five miles of this blissful riding might lull you into forgetting what's ahead. But soon enough, upon reaching the tiny "town" of

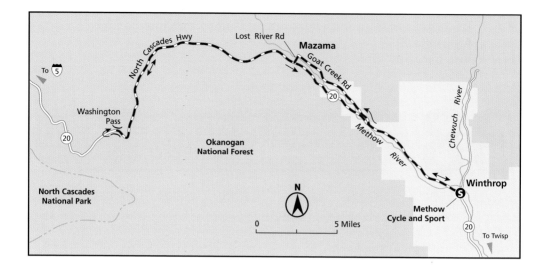

Mazama—population: next to nothing, but home of a terrific general store and café—turn left and head toward State Route 20, where you turn right and get cracking on the climb to Washington Pass.

And what of that climb? Here are the particulars: once on State Route 20, it's roughly 17 miles long and climbs 3300 feet. Which sounds like a lot (because it is), but that's still about 2000 feet less than what Hurricane Ridge climbs over the same distance. (Feel better? I didn't think so.) Unfortunately, headwinds can make this climb even more challenging. The only good thing is that those headwinds will become your tailwinds on what is sure to be one of the best descents of your life.

Basically, the climb goes like this: about 2 miles after you enter State Route 20, the road pitches steeply upward for about 3 miles. It then mellows out for about 5 miles before kicking upward for the steepest part: the final 7 miles just before Cutthroat Lake and through the hairpin turn, and then the last

stretch to the Washington Pass Overlook. But on this last stretch, the shoulder is wide and the awe-inspiring views of Silver Star Mountain, Kangaroo Ridge, and Liberty Bell will surely distract you from any spots of bother. In terms of views, this ride is one of the book's Top 5.

Washington Pass Overlook has restrooms and is a great place to replenish body and soul before heading back down. The descent is a gas, made more so by an ample road shoulder for much of the way. You can follow State Route 20 all the way back to Winthrop (as the map shows), or return the way you came through Mazama.

Note: If possible, take this ride before Memorial Day or after Labor Day, when there is less traffic on the North Cascades Highway (State Route 20). Perhaps the best time is in March or April, when State Route 20 has been plowed from the east side to Washington Pass, but the road is not yet open on the west side.

The hairpin turn just below Washington Pass, where Eastern Washington meets Western Washington >

0.0   From Methow Cycle and Sport in Winthrop, head west on SR 20.
7.9   Right onto Goat Creek Rd.
13.1   Left onto Lost River Rd.
13.5   Right onto SR 20.
30.7   Turn around at Washington Pass to go east on SR 20.
61.0   Return to starting point in Winthrop.

39 WINTHROP TO FALLS CREEK

Difficulty	Strenuous
Time	2½ to 4 hours
Distance	44.5 miles
Elevation Gain	3920 feet

ROAD CONDITIONS: Rural roadway including low-traffic mountain road with chip-seal surface; depending on maintenance and winter's effects, can be rough in spots. Watch for potholes and rough spots. For road conditions, check with Okanogan National Forest.

GETTING THERE: From Burlington, head east on SR 20 (North Cascades Hwy.) for about 130 miles. Just before entering Winthrop, park at Methow Cycle and Sport, located on the right side of the road.

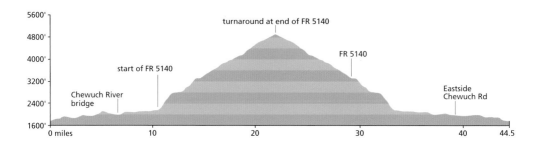

Want to get high (in the mountains) far away from any car-SUV-truck-bus-RV free-for-all? Head for Falls Creek Road, a sexy strip of low- to no-traffic pavement that climbs through the Okanogan National Forest to reach almost 5000 feet at the base of the pristine Pasayten Wilderness. (And yes, a strip of pavement can be sexy.)

From your parking spot just outside of Winthrop, head north on Westside Chewuch Road. The hill-climbing on this first mile will definitely warm up those quads and hamstrings. Continuing north, roll through a mélange of the Methow's trademark ranches, fields, and dry pine forests, climbing ever so gradually along the way. At about 7 miles, take note of the Chewuch River bridge, which you pass on the right; you'll cross that bridge on the return ride.

Just ahead, enter Okanogan National Forest. The road you are pedaling becomes Forest Road 51 and, depending on winter's effects and road maintenance schedules, it can be quite a bit rougher. But you're here to pedal a remote mountain road with stunning vistas, I assume—and you won't be disappointed.

At about 11 miles, turn left onto Forest Road 5140 (Falls Creek Road; the sign just says 5140), and head up. And up. This is the steepest part of the climb, gaining 600 feet in 1.5 miles, for a pitch of 15 percent in spots. As the road climbs deeper and deeper into dry pine forest, it gains about 2800 feet over 11.5 miles.

It's a good, sustained climb, and while its overall grade is steeper than the climb to Washington Pass from Winthrop, it's not nearly as long nor as heavily traveled. You can ride the whole thing without seeing a single vehicle. (However, don't be surprised if you

Heading north out of Winthrop, riders take advantage of smooth, low-traffic roads.

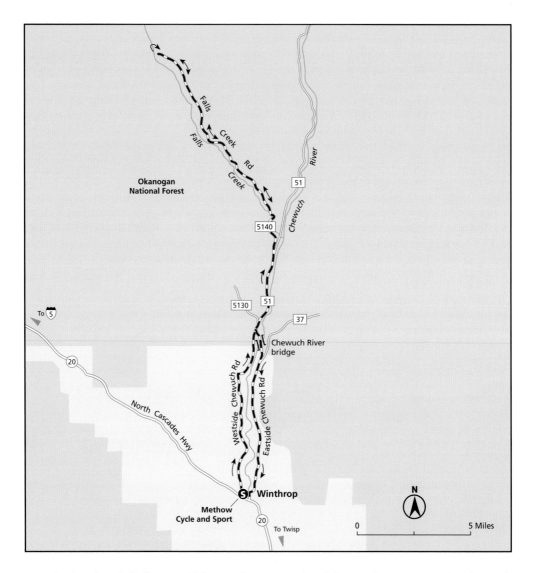

round a bend and find yourself face-to-face with a herd of cattle.) Views are terrific, with myriad peaks along Isabella Ridge rising above the road. (Consider a fall ride, when the needles on the larch trees have gone gold. Stunning.)

Return the way you came, being sure to watch for potholes and even cow pies on your 30-plus miles per hour descent. When you reach the Chewuch River bridge, cross it and just ahead, bear right onto Eastside Chewuch River Road. The road follows the east side of the Chewuch River for about 7 miles back to Winthrop, where you started.

Variation: Not quite enough climbing for you? Add nearby forest roads 5130 (which climbs 750 feet in 5 miles) and 37 (1500 feet in 7 miles) to this route for a 69-mile route that climbs 6330 feet. This longer route is known to locals as the Triple Bypass or Master Blaster.

0.0   From Methow Cycle and Sport in Winthrop, cross SR 20 onto Westside Chewuch Rd.
6.8   Pass Chewuch River bridge.
7.3   Road becomes FR 51.
10.7 Left onto FR 5140.
22.3 Turn around at end of paved road; return the same way.
33.7 Right onto FR 51.
37.5 Left onto Eastside Chewuch Rd; cross bridge.
43.7 Enter Winthrop; road becomes Bluff St.
44.2 Right onto SR 20 W.
44.5 Left to return to starting point.

40 TOUR DE OKANOGAN

Difficulty	Very Strenuous
Time	5 to 9 hours
Distance	103.8 miles
Elevation Gain	6060 feet

ROAD CONDITIONS: Mix of chip-seal surfaces, state highway with narrow shoulder, and rural, lightly traveled roads.

GETTING THERE: From Burlington, head east on SR 20 (North Cascades Hwy.) for about 130 miles. Just before entering Winthrop, park at Methow Cycle and Sport, located on the right side of the road.

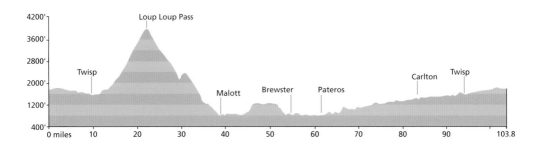

Old Highway 97 cuts across the tabletop of Brewster Flat, not far from the Okanogan and Columbia rivers.

A lot of folks head to the Methow Valley from Puget Sound but never wander much beyond Winthrop. Poor souls—they're missing a lot of great road riding. This epic tour wanders far beyond Winthrop, taking you east and up to Loup Loup Pass, down the other side into Okanogan country, then south to the Columbia River before pointing your way back home along the Methow River.

From Winthrop, head east on Eastside Winthrop–Twisp Road—a terrific, rural alternative to State Route 20 that will take you 10 miles to sleepy Twisp. The tiny burg is your last civilization for 30 miles, before the town of Malott, so make sure you're amply supplied with food and drink as well as spare tubes and the like. (Twisp has no bike shop, but Winthrop does. Malott has no bike shop, but Okanogan does.) From Twisp, head east on State Route 20 and begin making your way toward the day's big climb, Loup Loup

Pass, home to a small, family ski area and campground.

The steady 8-mile climb, mostly through pine forest, gains 2100 feet. That's nothing too painful, but the road's narrow shoulder requires focused concentration.

Once up and over the pass, begin the long (17-mile) descent into Malott, interrupted at Loup Loup Creek by a steep, pesky 1-mile pitch that climbs a couple hundred feet. (You won't like this.) Near the bottom of the descent, turn right onto lightly traveled B and O Road, and head past apple orchards, pastures, and the rocky crags of Fox Mountain. You're still trending slightly downhill here, though winds powering up the Okanogan River valley may challenge you. Or maybe it'll be a tailwind—you never know.

In Malott, pick up Old Highway 97 and continue heading south toward Brewster on a road much like the B and O and with similar scenery—orchards, dry hills, and farmland. Eventually, you have a 1-mile ascent to the Brewster Flat, which affords terrific views south toward the Okanogan River and the dry eastern hills above.

A little past the halfway point of the ride (the 53-mile mark), begin a 2-mile descent into Brewster, hugging the shores of Lake Pateros (also known as the Columbia River).

The biggest town on the route (population about 2000), Brewster has several places to replenish your eats and drinks. Pick up US Highway 97 here and head south along the Columbia River for 7 miles to Pateros. While this stretch of highway can be busy, the road's wide shoulder and smoother pavement offer some comfort. And you'll enjoy the views of the mighty Columbia.

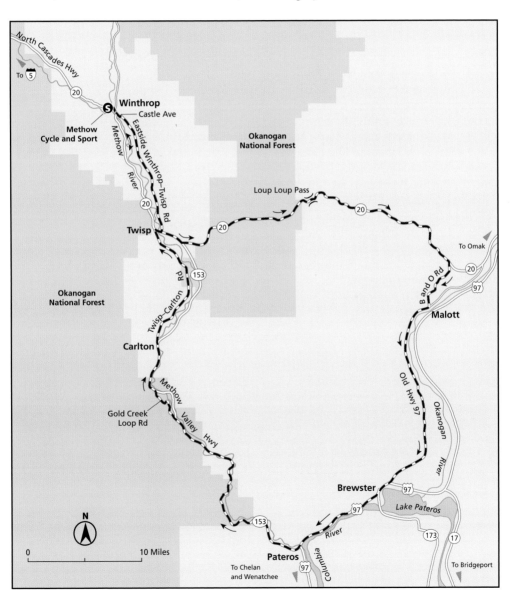

In Pateros begins perhaps the most scenic part of this already scenic ride—the 30-mile return to the Methow Valley via State Route 153. Most of it is along one side or the other of the meandering Methow River. It's potentially the most challenging section as well. It trends slightly uphill the entire way, and in the late afternoons, you can be hammered by headwinds. But the views are terrific, becoming more and more forested the farther you go and the more you climb.

While State Route 153 isn't terribly busy, it doesn't have the widest shoulders in the world. But in tiny Carlton (too small to even have its own Wikipedia page), the route picks up Twisp–Carlton Road, offering a bucolic homestretch into Twisp. From Twisp, return to Winthrop the same way you came.

MILEAGE LOG

0.0	From Methow Cycle and Sport in Winthrop, head east on SR 20.
0.2	Continue straight where SR 20 turns right.
0.3	Right onto Castle Ave. (Becomes Eastside Winthrop–Twisp Rd.)
9.9	Left onto SR 20.
11.8	Left to stay on SR 20.
34.9	Right onto B and O Access Rd. (Becomes B and O Rd.)
38.9	Malott. Right onto Old Hwy 97.
53.4	Brewster. Right onto US Hwy 97.
60.9	Pateros. Right onto SR 153 (Methow Valley Hwy.).
77.7	Left onto Gold Creek Loop Rd.
80.1	Left onto SR 153 (Methow Valley Hwy.).
83.3	Left onto Twisp–Carlton Rd.
93.7	Twisp. Right onto SR 20.
94.1	Left onto Eastside Winthrop–Twisp Rd. (Becomes Castle Ave.)
103.5	Left onto Bridge St.
103.8	Return to starting spot.

CENTRAL CASCADES

Along with routes that scale mountain heights are flatter, mellower ones that follow the banks of meandering, sparkling rivers. Routes through dry pine forests are featured too, as well as ones crisscrossing the fruitful Wenatchee Valley orchard land that's made the area world famous.

41 SKYKOMISH TO LEAVENWORTH (ONE-WAY)

Difficulty	Strenuous
Time	2½ to 5 hours (one-way)
Distance	51 miles
Elevation Gain	4215 feet

ROAD CONDITIONS: Smooth highway with varying shoulder widths; wider near Stevens Pass; narrower near Skykomish and Leavenworth. Much high-speed traffic, especially on weekends.

GETTING THERE: From Monroe, head east on US Hwy 2 for 34 miles to Skykomish. Turn right on 5th St. and park in the mini-grocery parking lot here or on the street in town, just a couple hundred yards across the Skykomish River bridge. To make this a one-way shuttle ride, leave a second car in Leavenworth.

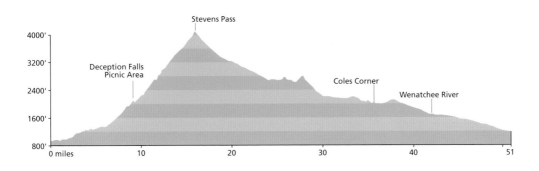

Fantastic mountain scenery, one killer 10-mile climb, and a way-fun descent are all yours on this west-to-east route that busts up and over the Cascade Crest at Stevens Pass. As for the climb, it's a 10-mile thigh-buster that gains about 2700 feet. Not the toughest climb in the book, but nothing to take for granted either. Rewards are huge. Along with stunning alpine scenery—heathery meadows, jagged peaks, and skyline ridges to infinity—you win a screaming-fast descent that seems to go on forever.

Because US Highway 2 is so busy in summers and doesn't offer a super bike-friendly shoulder until about Skykomish, we'll start this route there. From Skykomish, turn right onto US Highway 2 and loosen up on the early miles by pedaling the slightly uphill road for about 6 miles, crossing back and forth across the Skykomish River. Though on

Once over Stevens Pass, it's 35 mostly downhill miles to Leavenworth.

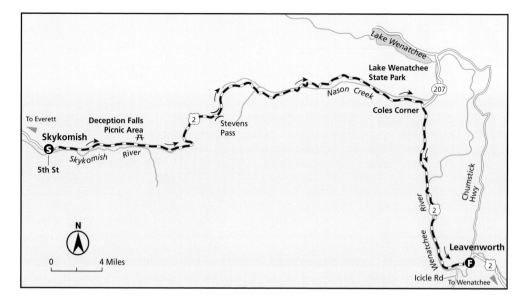

some stretches the shoulder is a bit narrow, the farther you go, passing lanes and pull-over spots for vehicle chain-up offer more breathing room.

Just past the 6-mile mark, remove the "slightly" descriptor from above and just climb uphill, generally gaining about 250 to 300 feet per mile. It's an extremely steady climb, so once you find your rhythm and lock it in, you should be good to go. Thankfully, the road offers a wide, mostly smooth shoulder, so if you need to concentrate or lament your time in the pain cave, you've got room to yourself. As with most mountain pass climbs, be on the lookout for falling rocks. Signs generally point out the most susceptible spots.

Once at the top—wow, have fun! Take a few breaths of that Eastern Washington air and point your bike downward. Except for a mini-bump here and there, the next 35 miles are downhill and fast. And even when you get to Coles Corner at mile 36, and it appears that the road has finally flattened out (it actually doesn't), you usually benefit from the west winds coming down from the mountains.

Another great feature of this ride: on the last 9 miles, you're riding alongside the sparkling, splashing, crystal-clear waters of the Wentachee River as it churns its way through Tumwater Canyon at the foot of Icicle Ridge—it's really quite spectacular.

Count your way down using the highway's mile markers: you enter Leavenworth just past marker 99.

Variations: Return to Skykomish for a century, or stay in one of L-town's numerous Bavarian-themed accommodations and enjoy some of the area's other rides.

MILEAGE LOG

0.0   From Skykomish River bridge, head east on US Hwy 2.
6.1   Climb begins.
15.9   Stevens Pass.
36.0   Coles Corner.
51.0   Arrive in Leavenworth.

42 CHELAN–MCNEIL CANYON

Difficulty	Strenuous
Time	3 to 5 hours
Distance	40.4 miles
Elevation Gain	4100 feet

ROAD CONDITIONS: Rural roads with chip-seal surface, short stretch of US highway with wide shoulder.

GETTING THERE: From Wenatchee, head north on US Hwy 97 Alt. for 35 miles to Chelan. (In Chelan, the highway becomes Woodin Ave.) Turn left onto E. Woodin Ave. (SR 150) and follow for 0.6 mile to Don Morse Park.

Like to climb? Consider yourself a mountain goat? Want to challenge yourself and perhaps even live to tell about it? Then put McNeil Canyon on your tick list.

Simply put, this steep road climbs 2200 feet in 5 miles. Plenty of this book's big climbs gain more elevation, but none climbs so steeply in such a short space. The sign at the bottom of the hill leaves nothing to the imagination: "12 percent grade, 5 miles."

But it's actually a little tougher than that. Near the summit of McNeil Pass, the road angles upward at more than a 15 percent grade. Of course, what goes up must come down. Make sure your brakes are in good shape.

Warm up with a 20-mile loop north from Chelan, first along US Highway 97 Alt., which can be busy, then inland on lightly traveled Apple Acres Road. This is quintessential Eastern Washington—dry, craggy hills, an occasional dead rattlesnake, rough chip-seal roads, wind, and tumbleweeds. About 9 miles in, begin a long descent to the Columbia River and US Highway 97, where you turn right. (Quite possibly directly into a headwind too, but that's likely the least of today's challenges.)

Now heading south, check out the daunting hill ahead of you on the east side of the river—your mission, should you choose to accept it, is to pedal your way to the top of that. At

Among this route's charms: spectacular Lake Chelan, the mighty Columbia River, and the 5-mile beast that is the McNeil Canyon climb

20 miles, cross the Columbia via the Beebe Bridge and just ahead, turn left onto McNeil Canyon Road. Say a prayer, burn an inner tube as an offering to the hill-climbing gods, reach down and strap on your best pair of climbing legs—whatever it takes—but get crackin'. You're given about a mile on McNeil Canyon Road before the 5-mile climb starts, but when it does, expect steep, followed by steeper, culminating in steepest. Seriously, there's no letup.

Also, there's no tree cover, so wind and the hot Eastern Washington sun can make this quite unpleasant. (Don't attempt this climb in the July and August midday sun.) Once at the top—you'll know it by the McNeil Pass summit sign—take a few moments to enjoy the view, let your heart rate drop below 180, then head down. Be careful. Not surpris-

ingly, this is a crazy-fast descent and gravity will entice your bike to hit 50-plus miles per hour in a second. If you're confident in your descending skills, go for it. If not, say a prayer to the descending gods.

Follow McNeil Canyon Road back to the Beebe Bridge, recross the Columbia River, and turn left on Chelan Falls Road (State Route 150). After what you've just been through, the 2-mile hill out of the Columbia River might seem cruel, but perhaps a tailwind will push you along. Soon enough the road levels out. Turn left onto US Highway 97 Alt. and retrace your pedal strokes back to Don Morse Park.

Note: Sections of this ride show up from time to time on the Chelan Century Challenge and Wenatchee Rotary Apple Century organized rides.

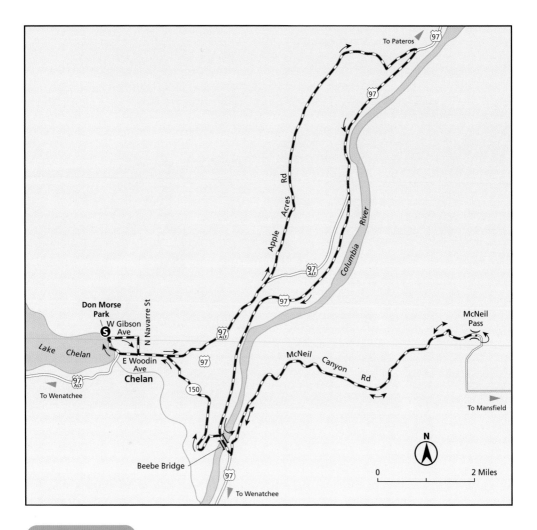

0.0   From Don Morse Park, turn left onto SR 150.
0.1   Right onto W. Gibson Ave. (Becomes N. Navarre St.)
1.1   Left onto E. Woodin Ave. (US Hwy 97 Alt. N.).
1.7   Continue straight to stay on US Hwy 97 Alt. N.
4.5   Left onto Apple Acres Rd.
11.2   Right onto US Hwy 97 S.
21.0   Left onto McNeil Canyon Rd.
23.0   Start of climb.
28.2   Turn around at McNeil Pass summit.
35.4   Right onto US Hwy 97 N.
35.9   Left onto US Hwy 150. (Becomes SR 150.)
38.9   Left onto E. Woodin Ave. (US Hwy 97 Alt S.).
40.4   Return to your starting point at Don Morse Park.

43 LEAVENWORTH–PLAIN LOOP

Difficult	Moderate
Time	2 to 3½ hours
Distance	38.4 miles
Elevation Gain	1490 feet

ROAD CONDITIONS: Some state highway with narrow shoulder (especially busy on summer weekends); rural, low-traveled roads with chip-seal surfaces.

GETTING THERE: Take US Hwy 2 to Leavenworth and park in the middle of downtown at Lions Club Park or wherever street parking is available.

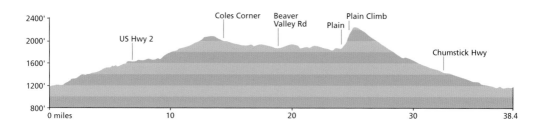

This is a fun, potentially fast, and mostly flat loop that heads out toward Lake Wenatchee and then boomerangs right back to Leavenworth. There is basically just one hill—a steep, switchbacking 1-mile bump that's actually quite fun (if you find that sort of thing fun).

From Lions Club Park (or wherever you park in Bavariaburg), head west out of town on US Highway 2, Leavenworth's main drag. Be aware of four things: the first 9 miles of Highway 2's shoulder is narrow; there can be mucho traffic, especially on summer weekends; the first 13 miles are deceptively uphill (just in case you're wondering why you're not going faster); and there's the potential for rock fall from the cliffs of Tumwater Mountain on your right. (Extra incentive to wear your hel-

met, that.) On the upside, those first 9 miles follow the wildly scenic Wenatchee River, spectacular as it squeezes its way through rocky Tumwater Canyon.

At Coles Corner—notable for the 59 Diner as well as being the turnoff for State Route 207 and Lake Wenatchee—turn right. As if by magic, the route's ambience takes an instant turn for the mellow. Fewer cars, wider shoulders, and a mostly pool-table flat surface (even slightly downhill in spots) make this a pleasant, chip-seal foray through the dry pine forests of Eastern Washington.

Continue in this mode for about 12 miles, turning right on Beaver Valley Road (about 4 miles past Coles Corner) to begin pedaling east toward tiny Plain. Legend has it that the town was originally named Beaver Valley

The fun, not-too-long switchbacking climb just outside Plain

until the postal service deemed it too long a name for so small a town. Residents then asked for a plain, simple name—and they got it. Despite its tininess (population: a handful or two), the town has a nice little general store.

Once through Plain, begin the ride's one true climb: a stiff 1.1-miler that gains 400 feet via several switchbacks. But there is a prize at the end: as soon as you hit the top, you begin an 11-mile descent on what is now the Chumstick Highway, which takes you almost back to Leavenworth. Turn right at the US Highway 2 intersection; Lions Club Park is about a half mile ahead on your right.

MILEAGE LOG

0.0	West on US Hwy 2 from Lions Club Park in Leavenworth.
14.9	Right onto SR 207 at Coles Corner.
18.7	Right onto Beaver Valley Rd. (Becomes Chumstick Hwy.)
23.7	Continue on Chumstick Hwy. where it turns right.
24.2	Plain.
37.7	Right onto US Hwy 2.
38.4	Return to starting point at Lions Club Park.

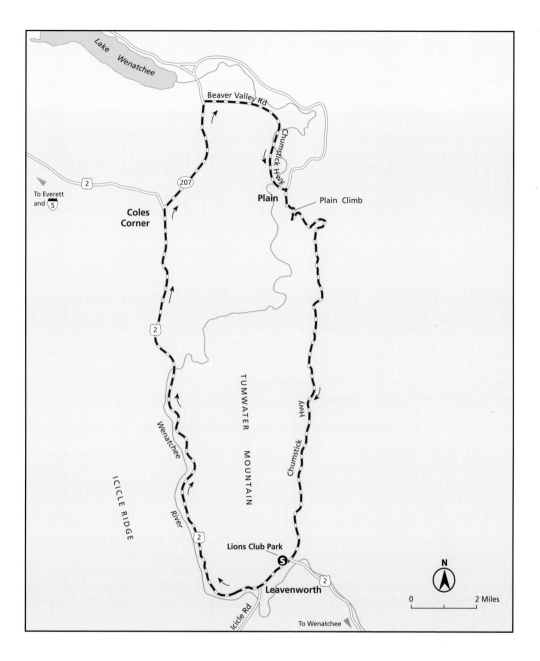

Lake Wenatchee

Beaver Valley Rd

Chumstick Hwy

To Everett
and 5

207

Coles
Corner

Plain

Plain Climb

2

TUMWATER MOUNTAIN

Wenatchee

River

Chumstick Hwy

ICICLE RIDGE

2

Lions Club Park

S

Leavenworth

Icicle Rd

2

To Wenatchee

N

0   2 Miles

44 ICICLE ROAD

Difficulty	Easy
Time	1½ to 3 hours
Distance	28 miles
Elevation Gain	1945 feet

ROAD CONDITIONS: Combo of somewhat rough, chip-seal mountain road and smooth residential and downtown roads. *Note:* Some years, Icicle Road is closed by floods, mudslides, fires, or natural disasters.

GETTING THERE: Take US Hwy 2 to Leavenworth and park smack in the middle of downtown at Lions Club Park or wherever street parking is available.

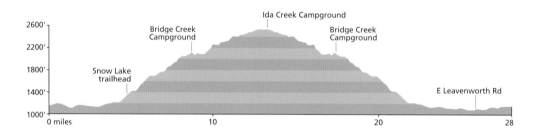

Admittedly, this is a short route, but the Icicle Canyon views are so stupendous, this gateway to the Enchantments deserves serious consideration. From Lions Club Park in Leavenworth, head east on US Highway 2 for about a half mile and turn left onto Icicle Road. That's basically it—one main road for about 15 miles deep into the heart of some of the Alpine Lakes Wilderness's most stunning scenery—an area beloved by rock climbers, hikers, campers, and backpackers. (Consider taking this ride in autumn, when the larch trees on the surrounding mountainsides turn a fiery gold.) The road's a tad rough—chip

seal that only gets rougher the farther you go—but the shoulder is wide and where it isn't, the road's remoteness translates into sparse traffic.

At 4 miles, after passing through a somewhat residential area, the road joins Icicle Creek. It will climb steadily, but not too steeply, the rest of the way. Along with views of the rushing, gushing creek, jagged, sky-reaching peaks are everywhere you turn, some of them appearing to rise right from the roadside. Many are adorned with what look like giant toothpicks—snags from a 1994 forest fire that burned thousands of canyon acres.

Follow this route along Icicle Ridge into the spectacular Alpine Lakes Wilderness. >

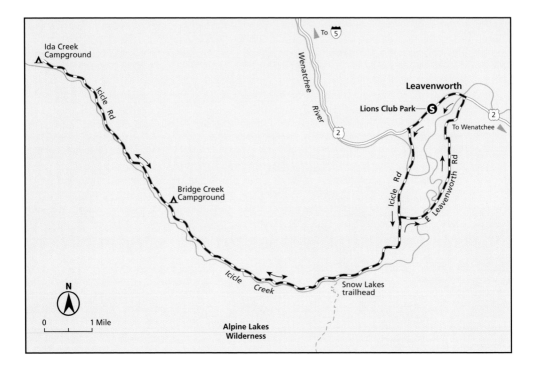

At about 13 miles, the pavement ends by the Ida Creek Campground, making a good turn-around spot. Return the way you came, but for variety, and a sort of behind-the-lederhosen view of Leavenworth, at about 24 miles turn right onto Leavenworth Road, cross Icicle Creek, and follow the road for about 3 miles back to US Highway 2, now on the east side of the Wenatchee River. Turn left; Lions Club Park is less than a mile ahead on the right.

Variation: If the above route isn't long enough, combine it with the Leavenworth–Plain Loop (Tour 43), for a 65-miler that climbs about 3500 feet.

MILEAGE LOG

0.0	From Lions Club Park in Leavenworth, head west on US Hwy 2.
0.6	Left onto Icicle Rd.
3.1	Bear right to stay on Icicle Rd.
4.8	Snow Lakes trailhead.
9.1	Bridge Creek Campground.
13.2	Turnaround by Ida Creek Campground.
23.8	Right onto E. Leavenworth Rd.
26.1	Bear left to stay on E. Leavenworth Rd.
27.2	Left at US Hwy 2 W.
28.0	Return to starting point at Lions Club Park.

45

WENATCHEE–LEAVENWORTH 'N' BACK

Difficulty	Moderate
Time	2½ to 4 hours
Distance	46.3 miles
Elevation Gain	3000 feet

ROAD CONDITIONS: Rural farm roads with narrow to no shoulders; some rough chip-seal surfaces; short stretches of busy highway.

GETTING THERE: Head east on US Hwy 2 and then on US Hwy 2/97 toward Wenatchee. Just before crossing the Columbia River, exit at Euclid Ave. Head south for 0.5 mile and turn left onto Olds Station Rd. Follow for 0.5 mile and turn left into Wenatchee Confluence State Park.

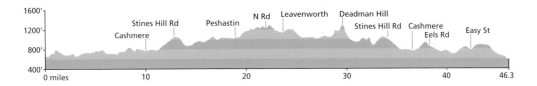

There's more than one road that connects Wenatchee and Leavenworth and this route explores many of them, as well as fields of fruit trees, pointy rock pinnacles, a handful of fruit-packing towns, one sparkling river, and of course, Aplets & Cotlets. While not completely avoiding US Highway 2/97, this route does its darndest.

Head west out of Wenatchee Confluence State Park and after about a mile of various twists and turns, find yourself on Lower Sunnyslope Road, a twisting farm road that follows the Wenatchee River, winds through orchards, vineyards, and farms, and does its best to avoid the hustle and bustle of US Highway 2/97. In spots the roads are so narrow you feel as though you could ride down the middle and pluck an apple from the trees on either side without altering your course. You'll visit fruit-packing towns such as Cash-

mere (of Aplets & Cotlets and Anjou Bakery fame), Dryden, and Peshastin.

Approaching Leavenworth, you'll be struck by the steadily increasing presence of pine forests and jagged peaks and ridges—an alpine environment very different from the round, dry hills of Wenatchee and the Columbia River. It makes sense: Leavenworth is about 400 feet higher than Wenatchee and more than 20 miles closer to the crest of the Cascade Mountains. At 24 miles, reach Leavenworth, the land of lederhosen and all things Bavarian, with plentiful opportunities for food, drink, espresso, and even a bike shop.

The return to Wenatchee starts with 5 miles on US Highway 2. Its wide shoulder and bike signs hopefully will alert vehicle drivers to your presence. Soon, the route continues on the same farm and frontage roads you traveled before. A new one—Deadman Hill—features the steepest climb of the day. It's only about a mile, but with pitches to 10 percent and with an even steeper descent.

Return to Wenatchee proper via Easy Street on the north side of the highway, enjoying expansive views of the Columbia River and surrounding ridges as you enter town.

Variation: This route can be ridden with either Wenatchee or Leavenworth (or any point in between) as the starting point. Keep in mind that Leavenworth is about 400 feet higher than Wenatchee, and that the prevailing wind is from the west.

MILEAGE LOG

0.0   From your parking spot in Wenatchee Confluence Park, head west out onto Olds Station Rd.

0.3   Left onto Olds Station Rd.

0.5   Right onto Chester Kimm Rd.

0.8   Left onto E. Penny Rd.

1.0   Right to stay on Penny Rd.

1.3   Right onto Lower Sunnyslope Rd.

Pedaling below the dry, rounded hills near Cashmere

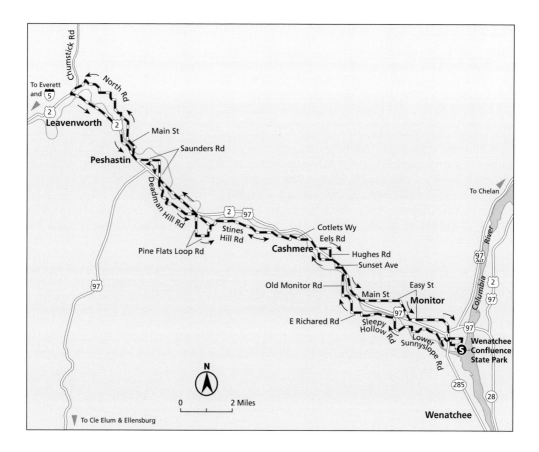

2.9   Left onto Sleepy Hollow Rd.
5.4   Left onto E. Richared Rd.
5.8   Right onto Richared Dr.
6.0   Right onto Fairview Canyon Rd.
6.3   Left onto Old Monitor Rd. Monitor.
6.8   Right to stay on Old Monitor Rd.
7.5   Cross bridge over Wenatchee River.
9.3   Left onto US Hwy 2 W./97 S.
9.9   Left onto Cotlets Wy. (Becomes Cottage Ave. in Cashmere.)
10.7   Left onto N. Division St.
10.8   Right onto Sunset Ave. (Flowery Divide Rd.)
12.2   Bear right onto Stines Hill Rd.
14.5   Bear right to stay on Stines Hill Rd.
15.6   Right onto Johnson Rd.; immediate left onto US Hwy 2 W./97 S.
16.9   Right onto Foster Rd.
17.0   Left onto Saunders Rd.
18.6   Right onto US Hwy 2 W.
18.9   Right onto Main St. in Peshastin.
19.3   Left to stay on Main St. (Becomes North Rd.)

20.8	Left to stay on North Rd.
22.2	Right to stay on North Rd.
23.4	Left onto Chumstick Rd.
23.8	Enter Leavenworth. Left onto US Hwy 2 E.
28.7	Right onto Deadman Hill Rd.
29.9	Left to stay on Deadman Hill Rd. (Becomes Pine Flats Loop Rd.)
31.9	Left to stay on Pine Flats Loop Rd. (Hall Rd.).
32.9	Right onto Stines Hill Rd.
34.8	Bear left stay on Stines Hill Rd. (Flowery Divide Rd.).
36.3	Cashmere. Left onto S. Division St.
36.4	Right onto Cottage Ave. (Becomes Cotlets Wy.)
37.1	Cross US Hwy 2/97.
37.2	Right onto Eels Rd.
37.6	Bear left to stay on Eels Rd.
38.2	Right onto Hughes Rd.
38.7	Bear left to stay on Hughes Rd. (Becomes Sunset Wy.)
39.5	Right onto Red Apple Rd. Immediate left onto US Hwy 2 E./97 N.
40.7	Left onto Easy St. (E. Main St.). Monitor.
42.8	Bear left to stay on Easy St.
45.2	Left onto E. Penny Rd.
45.6	Right onto Euclid Ave.
46.1	Left into Wenatchee Confluence State Park.
46.3	Return to starting point.

46 WENATCHEE–CHELAN–WENATCHEE

Difficulty	Very strenuous
Time	5 to 9 hours
Distance	101.4 miles
Elevation Gain	4440 feet

ROAD CONDITIONS: Mix of paved bike path, busy (and not so busy) highway with wide shoulder, rural chip-seal road, and some town riding on bike lanes.

GETTING THERE: From US Hwy 2/97 in Wenatchee, follow N. Wenatchee Ave. for 1.3 miles to Hawley St. E. and turn left. In 0.5 mile (the road having become N. Miller St.), turn left onto Walla Walla Ave. and just ahead, left into Walla Walla Point Park.

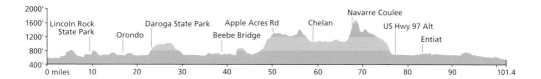

Take one mighty river, add one mighty lake, sprinkle in an awesome coulee climb, and that's this ride in a nutshell. This slightly more-than-a-century ride was once the route of the Wenatchee Rotary Club's Apple Century Ride (and perhaps will be again). It isn't particularly hilly, but wind can be an issue, especially in the afternoons. But so what? The endless orchards, countless bald hills, craggy peaks and canyons, and of course, those sparkling mega-bodies of water make this a must-ride.

From Walla Walla Point Park, hop on the paved Apple Capital Recreation Loop Trail and head north, loosening up for a couple miles as you pedal along the Columbia River through Wenatchee Confluence State Park and Walla Walla Point Park. Just

north of Confluence, follow the trail to the Olds Bridge, which crosses the Columbia River, and hop on the wide shoulder of US Highway 2/97. At the T intersection at the top of the hill, stay on US Highway 2/97 by turning left. Follow it for the next 43-plus miles along—and at one point across—the Columbia River.

Closer to Wenatchee, this road can be busy, but its shoulder is wide and the traffic lessens the farther north you go. In fact, once you're past Orondo, about 15 miles north of the Olds Bridge, traffic can be downright sparse. Mostly, however, this ride is about the Columbia River, which is always in view and always a stunner. On several stretches, the road seems to overhang the riverbanks, and

You're never far from the Columbia River (pictured) or Lake Chelan on this route.

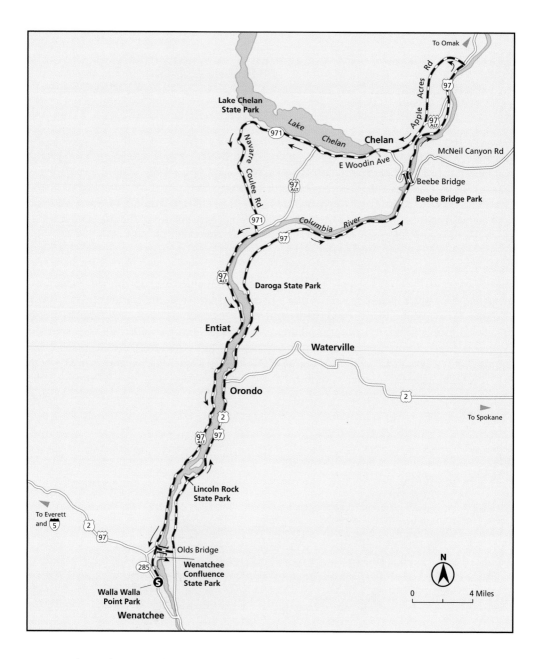

you can almost hear Woody Guthrie singing, "Roll on, Columbia, roll on!"

This area is known as the apple capital of the world, and this ride is lined with orchards and fruit stands, as well as parks such as Lincoln Rock State Park (check out Abe's profile, visible from the road), Daroga, and Beebe

Bridge—all of which offer restrooms. Roadside mini-marts, however, are infrequent.

Cross Beebe Bridge—taking care because there's no real shoulder—and follow US Highway 97 N for about 10 miles to Apple Acres Road. Begin the day's first steep climb. Only a couple miles long, the road gains about 450 feet, mostly at a 5 and 6 percent grade, taking you away from the river in a hurry while offering spectacular views.

The surface is rougher here and the shoulder more narrow, but the road is lightly traveled. It levels out as it squeezes its way through a rocky canyon, providing a backdoor approach to the town of Chelan. After a right turn onto US Highway Alt. 97, enter Chelan at mile 58. You'll find plenty here, as well as a bike lane. Follow Woodin Avenue and then Lakeshore Road along the shores of Lake Chelan—a stunning natural wonder that is 55 miles long, a mile wide, and, at 1400 feet deep, the third deepest lake in the United States, after Crater and Tahoe lakes.

Continue along the lake for about 8 miles, almost until Lake Chelan State Park, and then turn left to commence the second and biggest climb of the route, Navarre Coulee. It's a steep 2-miler into peaceful pine forest with one stretch that climbs 300 feet in less than three-quarters of a mile. But the shoulder is wide and the payoff grand, with terrific lake, mountain, and valley views. From the top, it drops quickly and the following 8 miles are a steep winding descent through horse farms and ranches and pine forest strewn with softball-size pinecones. Eventually, the woods open up, exposing you to strong crosswinds, and you return to the west bank of the Columbia River.

At the bottom of the hill, turn right onto US Highway Alt. 97 and follow it for about 25 miles back into Wenatchee, hoping that the headwind isn't too strong. The road is similar to 97, with decent shoulder, orchards, and views galore, but with fewer parks (and thus restrooms). At mile 84, however, the small town of Entiat has various food and drink establishments.

Back in Wenatchee, cross under US Highway 2/97, and just ahead, regain the Apple Capital Trail and follow it back to Walla Walla Point Park where you started.

Variation: Itching for more hills? Just before crossing Beebe Bridge, go right on McNeil Canyon Road and head up. (And up and up—2200 feet in 5 miles. Of course, once you turn around at McNeil Pass, it become 2200 feet of downs. See the description in Tour 42, Chelan–McNeil Canyon.)

MILEAGE LOG

0.0	From Walla Walla Point Park in Wenatchee, head north on Apple Capital Recreation Loop Trail.
2.6	Right onto US Hwy 2 E./97 N.; cross Columbia River via Olds Bridge.
3.6	Left to stay on US Hwy 2/97.
8.6	Lincoln Rock State Park.
16.1	Orondo. (Road becomes US Hwy 97 N.)
22.1	Daroga State Park.
37.6	Beebe Bridge Park.
37.8	Cross Columbia River via Beebe Bridge.
47.4	Left onto Apple Acres Rd.
54.0	Right onto US Hwy 97 Alt. S.
56.8	Enter Chelan. Road becomes E. Woodin Ave.
61.4	Bear right onto SR 971 S. (S. Lakeshore Rd.)
66.2	Bear left to stay on SR 971 (Ridgeview Dr.). Lake Chelan State Park.
67.0	Left to stay on SR 971 (Barrett Grade/Navarre Coulee Rd.). Big climb.
75.5	Right onto US Hwy 97 Alt. S.
83.1	Entiat.

99.0   Continue straight on Euclid Ave.
99.4   Left to stay on Euclid Ave.
99.5   Right onto Isenhart Ave.
99.7   Right onto Olds Station Rd.
99.8   Left into Wenatchee Confluence State Park.
99.9   Right onto Apple Capital Recreation Loop Trail.
101.4   Return to starting point at Walla Walla Point Park.

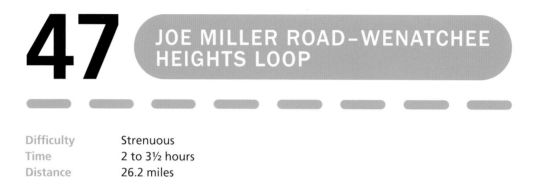

47 JOE MILLER ROAD–WENATCHEE HEIGHTS LOOP

Difficulty	Strenuous
Time	2 to 3½ hours
Distance	26.2 miles
Elevation Gain	2960 feet

ROAD CONDITIONS: Some city riding with bike lanes; state highway with decent shoulder; narrow, rural farm road with little to no shoulder.

GETTING THERE: From US Hwy 2/97 in Wenatchee, follow N. Wenatchee Ave. for 2 miles to N. Miller St. Turn right and, just ahead, left onto Chelan Ave. (SR 285). Continue for 2.2 miles (staying on SR 285 when Chelan Ave. goes straight) to Stevens St. Continue straight on Mission St. Park at Lincoln Park 0.4 mile ahead.

Though relatively short (only 26 miles), this ride includes the Joe Miller–Stemilt Loop climb, a stiff 6.5-miler that rises 1900 feet up from the banks of the Columbia River. If you're the type who seeks out an area's signature climb, this route will taste like nectar of the gods. If you prefer a less strenuous route, something like Wenatchee–Leavenworth 'n' Back (Tour 45) may be more to your liking. If you're on the fence, consider that the last 9 miles of this route are downhill, and that even the climbs are softened by the occasional downhill or flat reprieve. It's not quite as bad as it looks, so give it a try.

From Lincoln Park at Wenatchee's south end, head south out of town for about 4 miles

via the mighty Columbia River–hugging and ample-shouldered Malaga–Alcoa Highway. Eye the high, dry, somewhat daunting Jumpoff Ridge to the south, rising some 3000 feet above you—that's where you're headed. At W. Malaga Road, turn right and head up. The chip-seal road shoulder is narrow, but the "Bikes on Road" sign should alert traffic to your presence.

After a short reprieve, you reach the 6-mile mark, where you turn right onto Joe Miller Road and the climb starts in earnest, zigging and zagging upward through orchard and farmland. If your bike computer has a grade percentage function, you won't want to watch the numbers: 8 percent, 9 percent, 11 percent,

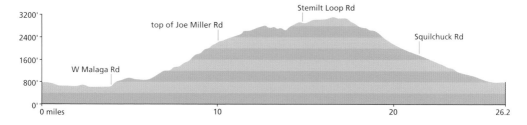

7 percent, 12 percent, 14(!) percent, and on and on for 6.6 miles. But your efforts will be rewarded with views of the rich orchard and ranchland of the Wenatchee Valley, the mighty Columbia River cutting through dusty plateaus and ridges, and seemingly all of Eastern Washington spread out before you. Higher up, on Stemilt Loop Road (which you reach 4 miles into the climb), the route enters dense pine forest.

After you complete your main climb and begin the descent on Stemilt Loop Road, remember that it is a paved mountain road, rough in sections. Employ your best bike-handling skills to navigate the often pothole- and giant pinecone–strewn road.

Racers get their climb on in the annual Wenatchee Omnium bike race. (Charles Naismith)

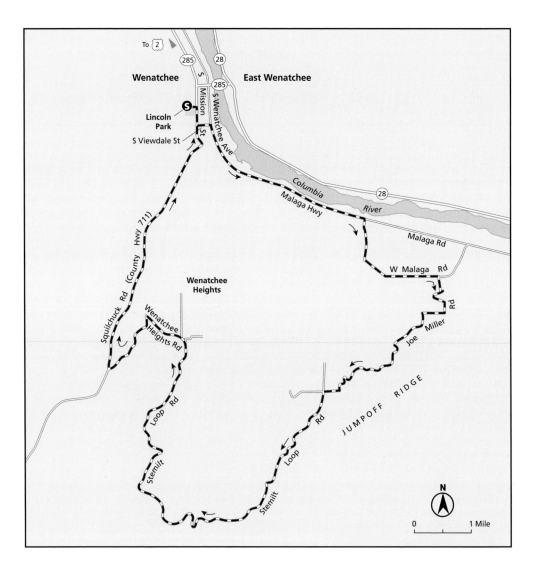

At about 17 miles, after 3 miles of rollers, the road exits the forest, becomes quite smooth, and begins a sweeping descent past Wenatchee Heights and down toward Squilchuck Creek and Squilchuck Road. Turn right, and after 5 more miles of descending, return to the south end of Wenatchee and Lincoln Park.

MILEAGE LOG

0.0   From Lincoln Park in Wenatchee, head east on Crawford Ave.
0.0   Right onto S. Mission St.
0.4   Left onto S. Viewdale St.
0.6   Right onto S. Wenatchee Ave. (Becomes Malaga Hwy.)
4.0   Right onto W. Malaga Rd.

6.1	Right onto Joe Miller Rd. Big climb begins.
7.0	Right to stay on Joe Miller Rd.
8.2	Bear right to stay on Joe Miller Rd.
9.1	Bear left to stay on Joe Miller Rd.
9.9	Right to stay on Joe Miller Rd.
10.2	Left onto Stemilt Loop Rd.
13.9	Left to stay on Stemilt Loop Rd.
16.5	Left to stay on Stemilt Loop Rd.
19.1	Road becomes Wenatchee Heights Rd.
21.1	Right onto Squilchuck Rd. (County Hwy 711; becomes S. Mission St. in town.)
26.1	Turn left onto Crawford Ave.
26.2	Return to Lincoln Park and starting point.

48 BADGER MOUNTAIN– WATERVILLE LOOP

Difficulty	Strenuous
Time	3 to 5½ hours
Distance	50 miles
Elevation Gain	4700 feet

ROAD CONDITIONS: Combination of lightly traveled rural roads (usually with wide shoulders); stretches of roughish chip-seal pavement; hard-packed dirt roads; and some residential streets with bike lanes.

GETTING THERE: Heading east on US Hwy 2/97, cross the Columbia River via US Hwy 2/97 (Hwy 2 and 97 join up near Peshastin and stay that way until Orondo). Turn right onto SR 28 E. (Sunset Hwy.). Follow for 2.3 miles to 19th St. NW in East Wenatchee and turn right, following signs for signs for the Apple Capital Recreation Loop Trail parking lot, just ahead on the left.

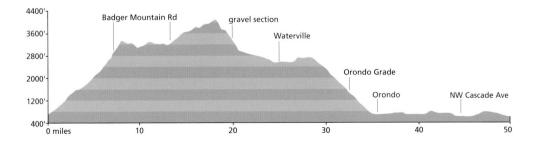

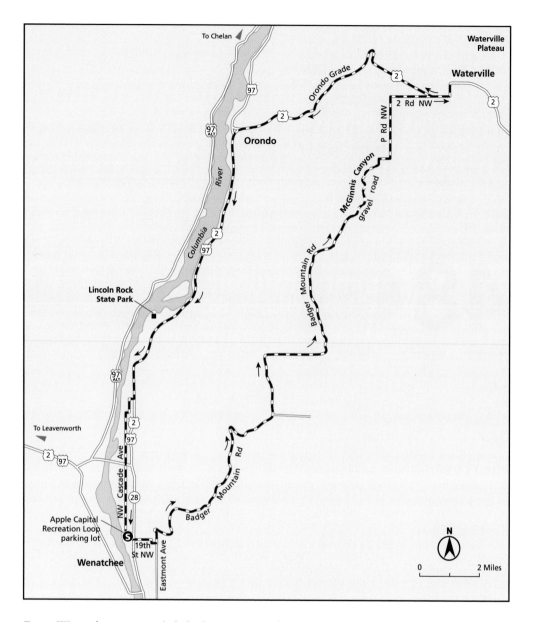

From Wenatchee, you can't help but notice (and perhaps, fear?) the 4000-plus-foot table-top ridge that rises high above the eastern banks of the Columbia River. Maybe you've always wondered how to get up there on a bike. (If not, turn the page; this ride might not be for you.) This route gets you to the top, but that's not all. Should you accept the full-meal deal (including a 2-mile descent down hard-packed gravel road), you'll be treated to an incredible loop across the Waterville Plateau and a long, fast descent down the Orondo Grade to the Columbia River.

Before heading out from the 19th Street entrance of the Apple Capital Recreation Loop Trail parking lot, give the elevation profile one last look. Then, hop on your bike, find a suitably appropriate climbing

High above the east bank of the Columbia River, the Waterville Plateau boasts treeless, straight-arrow roads that seem to go on forever.

gear, and plan to stay in it for a while. This one climbs steadily right from the get-go, even over the first couple miles, as you pedal through the residential/school zone of the old East Wenatchee Bench (bike lane provided through much of this). Soon enough, most signs of civilization are behind you and it's just you, your thoughts, and the ribbon of pavement ahead of you. Climbing consistently at about 7 percent—with short stretches to 12 or so—Badger Mountain Road offers a decent shoulder and is reasonably smooth.

Not an easy climb by any stretch—the toughest section is a 2750-foot climb in 8.3 miles. Badger Mountain Road is unshaded (*waaaay* unshaded) and can be hot as heck.

Windy too. But wow, what incredible views! Take a break at any of the pullout areas along the way to see the whole Wenatchee Valley spread out before you, as well as countless hills, ridges, and ranges: Sage Hills, Jumpoff Ridge, Mission Ridge, Tronsen Ridge, the Wenatchee Range—seemingly *all* of the Central Cascades.

A little more than 8 miles in, the grade levels out and the road rolls slightly up and down through sagebrush hills on the Waterville Plateau. The chip seal is a bit rougher here, the road shoulder narrower, but chances are it'll feel as though you have the entire plateau to yourself. Pass the occasional farm or ranch, as well as the big white balls of Orbcomm (a satellite-tracking company), and soon you'll enter pine forest. Here the road starts climbing again, though not as relentlessly as before. Just past the 18-mile mark, the climb tops out at just over 4100 feet. At this point you can turn around and head back the way you came, or you can brave 2 miles of steep descent through forested McGinnis Canyon on unpaved, hard-packed dirt road. The surface is firm and not too washboardy, but it *is* steep, dropping about 1000 feet in a little more than 2 miles.

As the forest opens up near the bottom of the hill, you'll probably notice some trees and buildings to the north—that's Waterville. After a couple turns here and there through dry wheat fields, reach Waterville at the 25-mile mark, the first opportunity for food and drink. From here, just about all of your climbing is behind you. After a mile-long jaunt west from Waterville on US Highway 2, encounter the Orondo Grade, 6.5 miles of uninterrupted downhill. (The sign says 6 percent descent for 6 miles.)

The shoulder is narrow and the surface is not exactly smooth. For best results, time your ride so it's neither the heat of the day (melting tires are so yesterday) nor a busy weekend (RVs and semis don't make the best road partners).

Once down by the banks of the Columbia, turn left onto US Highway 2/97 and head south for about 15 miles, crossing your fingers that the headwind is negligible. Though traffic can be of the high-speed variety, the shoulder is generally wide and you get to look for Abe Lincoln's profile when you pass Lincoln Rock State Park on the riverside. If the traffic is too much, turn right on NW Cascade Avenue about 9 miles south of Orondo and follow it for the last 5 miles as it parallels US Highway 2/97 (and then State R 28) back to where you parked.

Variations: Turning around where the pavement ends atop Badger Mountain (mile 18.4) makes for a 36.8-mile out-and-back route that climbs about 4200 feet. No services at any point along the way.

MILEAGE LOG

0.0	From the Apple Capital Recreation Loop Trail parking lot in Wenatchee, turn right onto 19th St. NW.
1.1	Left onto Eastmont Ave. (Becomes Badger Mountain Rd.)
9.1	Bear left to stay on Badger Mountain Rd.
18.4	Bear left to stay on Badger Mountain Rd. Pavement ends.
22.0	Left onto P Rd. NW.
24.5	Right onto 2 Rd. NW. (Becomes US Hwy 2 just ahead in Waterville.)
25.5	From Waterville, head west on US Hwy 2.
27.4	Bear right to stay on US Hwy 2.
28.7	Begin long descent.
35.3	Left to stay on US Hwy 2/97 S.
45.0	Right onto NW Cascade Ave.
49.9	Left onto 19th St. NW.
50.0	Return to parking lot.

49 ELLENSBURG TO LEAVENWORTH (BLEWETT PASS) (ONE-WAY)

Difficulty	Strenuous
Time	3 to 5 hours
Distance	57.6 miles (one-way)
Elevation Gain	3570 feet

ROAD CONDITIONS: Mostly smooth pavement with wide shoulders. Busy weekend traffic.

GETTING THERE: From I-90 at Ellensburg, take exit 105. Follow W. University Wy. toward Ellensburg. Take the first right onto N. Dolarway Rd. (which becomes W. Dolarway, then Railroad Ave.) and follow for 1.4 miles to N. Pacific St. Turn right and in 0.1 mile, turn right again onto W. 5th Ave. Park in West Ellensburg Park, a few hundred yards ahead. To make this a one-way shuttle ride, park a second car in downtown Leavenworth at Lions Club Park or wherever street parking is available.

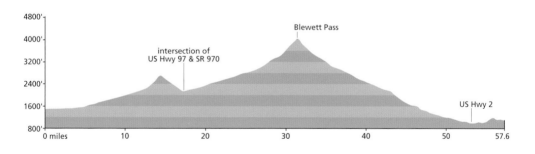

This one-way ride, from the dry, windswept Kittitas Valley up and over Blewett Pass and down into the timbered Wenatchee River valley, features a couple of nice climbs. First, a warm-up hill to get you out of the valley and, after a couple-mile descent, a more sustained—though not overly steep—14-mile climb to Blewett Pass.

From Ellensburg, head northwest out of town first on State Route 10, then US Highway 97. Hopefully, the headwind isn't too bad—valley winds seem to be the strongest in late spring and early summer—and won't dishearten you so much that you can't enjoy the stunning views up ahead of Mount Stuart and her Stuart Range siblings.

After 15 miles, crest the first hill and commence a sweeping descent through a wide-open forest of wind turbines. Stay right at the intersection where State Route 970 merges with US Highway 97 and begin the gradual (at first) 14-mile climb to the pass. Marvel at your surroundings here in the Swauk Creek valley. The dry brown hills of the Kittitas Valley have been replaced by lush green pine forest that gets only lusher (izzat a word?) the higher you climb.

Car and truck traffic usually increases here,

but the road's wide shoulder offers somewhat of a buffer. Your route passes the unincorporated community of Liberty, site of a former gold-mining camp from the 1870s, which today offers a café in case you need some eats or drinks.

While the first 12 miles of the Blewett Pass climb gain a little more than 100 feet per mile—an average grade of about 2 percent—the last 2 miles climb about 600 feet, almost 6 percent. Once up and over the pass, partake in the bugs-in-the-teeth grinning that comes with a 20-mile descent, just about all the way to the intersection with US Highway 2 and the town of Peshastin. Turn left at the intersection and from there, it's a 5-mile straight shot along the Wenatchee River to the renowned Bavarian-themed town of Leavenworth.

Variation: Old Blewett Pass via Forest Road 7320 has many little switchbacks. While certainly less crowded than US Highway 97, the road is much rougher and is not always passable because of snow.

MILEAGE LOG

0.0   Head east out of West Ellensburg Park on W. 5th Ave.
0.3   Left onto N. Wenas St.
0.5   Left onto W. University Wy.

Wind is to the Kittitas Valley as rain and clouds are to Puget Sound.

1.8   Right onto Reecer Creek Rd.
1.9   Left onto Old Highway 10 (Becomes US Hwy 97.)
4.2   Right to stay on US Hwy 97.
17.4   Right to stay on US Hwy 97.
31.8   Blewett Pass.
52.7   Left onto US Hwy 2.
56.8   Leavenworth.
57.6   Lions Club Park.

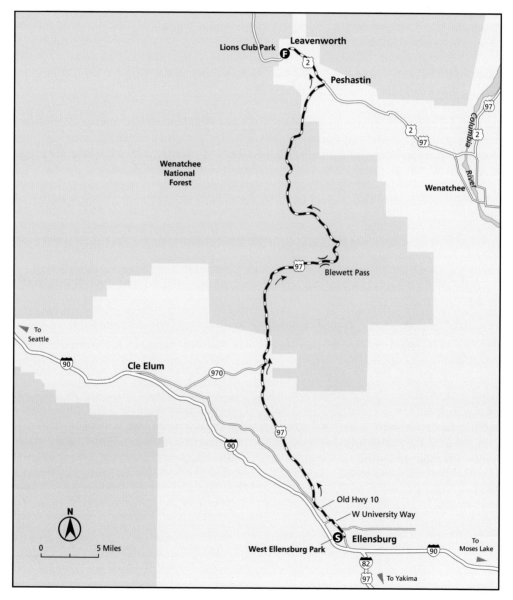

50 MANASTASH METRIC CENTURY

Difficulty	Moderate
Time	3½ to 6 hours
Distance	63.4 miles
Elevation Gain	2225 feet

ROAD CONDITIONS: Rural roads and state highway, much of it with chip-seal surface; and varying shoulder width; potential for much wind.

GETTING THERE: From I-90 in Ellensburg, take exit 105. Follow W. University Wy. toward Ellensburg. Take the first right onto N. Dolarway Rd. (which becomes W. Dolarway, then Railroad Ave.) and follow for 1.4 miles to N. Pacific St. Turn right and in 0.1 mile, turn right again onto W. 5th Ave. West Ellensburg Park is a few hundred yards ahead.

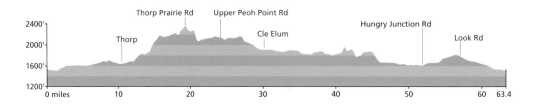

This 60-some-mile-loop heads west from Ellensburg on the south side of the Yakima River to Cle Elum, where it turns around and heads back via the north side. Along with said river, this route shows off impressive Manastash Ridge to the south, as well as the rolling hills, dales, and dry open fields of the Kittitas Valley. You can expect wind too—a prevailing westerly that'll likely be at your back for the home stretch. (Remember this when riding the Ellensburg area: Wind is to the Kittitas Valley as rain is to Seattle.)

This route roughly follows the Manastash Metric Century, an organized ride held each fall as a fundraiser for Ellensburg's "RSVP" (Retired and Senior Volunteer Program).

Head south out of West Ellensburg Park

via Railroad Avenue; after passing through an industrial area, turn right onto Umptanum Road. Just beyond Interstate 90 and the Yakima River—cross under the first and over the second—turn right onto Brown Road and commence heading toward Cle Elum—first on Brown Road, then on S. Thorp Highway, then on a linking series of northwest-trending rural roads. Pass through farm and pastureland at the foot of 5000-foot Manastash Ridge, which accompanies you to the south.

About 10 miles in, after passing through tiny Thorp and crossing to the north side of Interstate 90, begin the route's biggest sustained climb. (Actually, it isn't so much one climb as it is a series of rollers.) Over the next

Ride the tailwind while following the sparkling Yakima River from Cle Elum to Ellensburg.

7 miles, you'll gain about 700 feet, much like climbing giant rounded steps. Views north to the Stuart Range and the Enchantment peaks open up. Much closer, are views of the giant wind turbines that have begun showing up in recent years throughout the Kittitas Valley. (And you might find yourself fighting one of the giant headwinds that drew those turbines here in the first place.)

After paralleling the freeway for about 6 miles, cross back to the south side of Interstate 90 on Upper Peoh Point Road to the base of Cle Elum Ridge. Begin a forested descent through the foothills into south Cle Elum and, after crossing to the north side of the Yakima River and Interstate 90, into Cle Elum proper. Plenty of places here to stock up on food and drink as well as a bike shop should you need one.

From here the ride begins the return trip to Ellensburg, first through town (Cle Elum, that is) and then east via State Route 10, a fun road that rolls up and down (mostly down) alongside the Yakima River for about 20 miles. There are plenty of places to pull over and ogle the sparkling river, the nesting ospreys, and the stunning Yakima River canyon. With luck, you'll be aided and abetted much of the way by a killer tailwind.

Approaching Ellensburg, the route detours north and then east for a 10-mile rural road exploration near the Ellensburg airport. Back in town, the route skirts the busy downtown to reenter West Ellensburg Park via 5th Avenue.

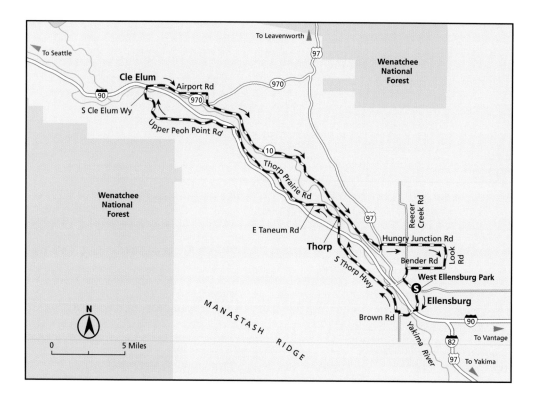

MILEAGE LOG

0.0	From Ellensburg, head south out of West Ellensburg Park onto W. 5th Ave.
0.2	Right onto N. Railroad Ave.
1.3	Right onto Umptanum Rd.
2.0	Right onto Brown Rd.
2.7	Left to stay on Brown Rd.
2.9	Right onto Brown Rd. (Rte. 6).
4.7	Right onto Hanson Rd., immediate left onto S. Thorp Hwy.
12.1	Left onto Bruton Rd./E. Taneum Rd.
14.7	Right onto Thorp Prairie Rd.
22.2	Bear left onto Upper Peoh Point Rd.
28.9	Left onto Lower Peoh Point Rd. (Becomes S. Cle Elum Wy., then Railroad Ave.)
30.4	Right onto W. 2nd St.
31.7	Right onto N. Short Ave.
31.8	Left onto E. 1st St.
32.2	Left onto Airport Rd.
35.6	Left onto SR 970 E.
35.8	Right onto SR 10 E.
50.1	Left onto McManamy Rd./Poor Farm Rd.
51.9	Left onto US Hwy 97 N.
52.3	Right onto Hungry Junction Rd.

56.5	Right onto Look Rd.
58.4	Right onto Sanders Rd. (Becomes Bender Rd.)
60.9	Left onto Reecer Creek Rd.
61.6	Left onto W. University Wy.
62.8	Right onto N. Wenas St.
63.1	Right onto W. 5th Ave.
63.4	Return to West Ellensburg Park.

51 LION ROCK CLIMB

Difficulty	Strenuous
Time	3 to 4½ hours
Distance	44.8 miles
Elevation Gain	4350 feet

ROAD CONDITIONS: Rural, low-traffic road with chip-seal surface. Nine-mile stretch of winding, one-lane paved forest road. Potential for strong cross-winds.

GETTING THERE: From I-90 at Ellensburg, take exit 105. Follow W. University Wy. toward Ellensburg. Take the first right onto N. Dolarway Rd. (which becomes W. Dolarway, then Railroad Ave.) and follow for 1.4 miles to N. Pacific St. Turn right and in 0.1 mile, turn right again onto W. 5th Ave. Park in West Ellensburg Park, a few hundred yards ahead.

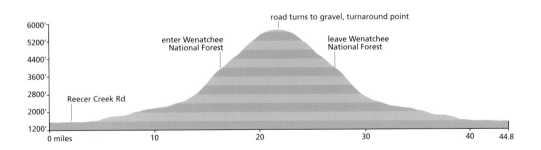

Here's a ride that's sure to put a sting in your legs. (And lungs. And heart.) Though not as long as climbs to Paradise on Mount Rainier or Hurricane Ridge outside Port Angeles, this route's featured ascent is significantly steeper. In just 6 miles, it gains more than 2600 feet elevation. By comparison, the west approach to Paradise takes about 11 miles to gain as

Up, up and away: the Lion Rock route climbs 2,600 feet in 6 miles!

much elevation. Clearly, this is not a climb for the faint of heart. (Or lung. Or quad.) But like most climbs, it pays off with superlative views, these overlooking the Kittitas Valley.

Another challenge of the Lion Rock Climb is that much of it follows a winding, one-lane paved national forest road. Traffic is low, but with just one lane, extra care is required, especially on the potentially fast descent.

From West Ellensburg Park, head west out of town via University Way. Turn north onto Reecer Creek Road and follow it across the wind-swept valley to the forested ridgeline of Table Mountain. Note the dozens of giant wind turbines taking advantage of the notorious Ellensburg wind. (Certainly a four-letter

word if you have to ride straight into it.)

When you're about 15 miles outside of Ellensburg, Reecer Creek Road curves to the right, becomes the one-lane Forest Road 35, and starts climbing in earnest, switching back and forth—up, up, and more up—about a dozen times. The higher you go, the deeper the road enters the lovely pine stands of Wenatchee National Forest. The road's remoteness makes you feel as though you are hiking or mountain biking through the woods.

The entire climb is actually 9 miles, but it's just the first 6 miles that are unusually steep. Once you hit the intersection with Forest Road 3517 (you continue straight ahead on FR 35), the toughest part is behind you. On the last part—a 2-percent grade versus the steady 8 to 10 percent grade—you'll feel as though you're going downhill.

The end of the pavement is the turnaround point for this route. Return the way you came, being careful of oncoming cars during your fast descent on the one-lane road.

Variation: This being a road bike book, the route ends where the pavement ends. However, as the sign at the end of the pavement states, a gravel road continues for a number of miles to Haney Meadow. It's up to you whether you want to put your bike through that, especially with a rough gravel descent.

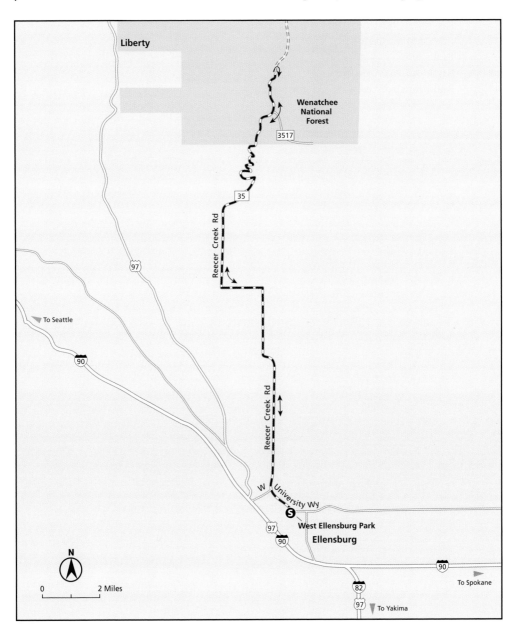

0.0	From Ellensburg, head north out of West Ellensburg Park onto W. 5th Ave.
0.4	Left onto N. Wenas St.
0.6	Left onto W. University Wy.
1.8	Right onto Reecer Creek Rd.
9.4	Continue on Reecer Creek Rd. where it turns left.
13.4	Reecer Creek Rd. becomes one-lane FR 35.
22.4	Pavement ends; turnaround point. Return the same way.
43.0	Left onto W. University Wy.
44.2	Right onto N. Wenas St.
44.4	Right onto W. 5th Ave.
44.8	End route back at West Elllensburg Park.

OLYMPIC AND KITSAP PENINSULAS

Appealing port towns and waterfront communities, dense ancient forests, and hilly island-esque riding are among the features of this region's routes. Oh yeah, the state's biggest climb too—Hurricane Ridge where the views, as well as the 17 uphill miles to get there, will absolutely take your breath away.

52 PORT ANGELES–LAKE CRESCENT–JOYCE LOOP

Difficulty	Moderate
Time	2 to 3½ hours
Distance	42.3 miles
Elevation Gain	3555 feet

ROAD CONDITIONS: Rural, chip-seal roads (many with "Bikes on Road" signs); narrow mountain and lakeside roads; a couple stretches of busy US Hwy 101.

GETTING THERE: From US Hwy 101 in Port Angeles, turn right onto S. Bean Rd. and follow for 0.5 mile to S. Lauridsen Blvd. Turn left and park in Lincoln Park just ahead on the right.

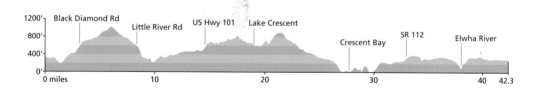

This visually rewarding route boasts a bevy of what the Olympic Peninsula is known for—breathtaking mountains, deep dark forests, a really deep lake (Lake Crescent is the second deepest lake in the state), and a shoreline jaunt along the mighty Strait of Juan de Fuca.

The beginning is a little tricky, since you have to maneuver across busy US Highway 101. But it's better to do that at the beginning of the ride than at the end, right?

From Lincoln Park, pedal east toward Port Angeles via Lauridsen and after turning right onto Tumwater Truck Road, meet US Highway 101. Carefully go left (grateful for the wide, wide shoulder) and in a half mile, turn left onto Pine Street. Climb steeply and follow it to the left over 101, where it becomes Black Diamond Road.

Heading up toward the Olympic Mountains, Black Diamond climbs up and up for about 4 miles, past forests and farms—and even a winery—until it intersects with and becomes Little River Road. This narrow mountain road starts at a thousand feet above sea level, and flying down it is serious fun. (Traffic should be light, but the road is narrow, so be alert for vehicles traveling in the opposite direction.)

Just past the bottom of the hill, at the 10-mile mark, the route goes left onto US Highway 101, which it follows for about 7.5 miles to Lake Crescent. With its high-speed traffic, 101 is not ideal for a cycling excursion, but its surface is smooth, its shoulder wide, and from time to time, it affords stunning mountain views (as well as Mad Max-esque scenes of whole hillsides logged to devastation). You'll also find the occasional general store or mini-mart should you need to replenish.

Upon reaching Lake Crescent, go right onto E. Beach Road and after a short stiff climb, drop down lakeside for a scenically spectacular 2-mile stretch. The road is narrow, rough in spots, and affords poor visibility. But it's a stunner. On one side is the 600-foot-deep lake, with its mesmerizing blue-green hue. (The lake's low nitrogen content makes it difficult for algae to grow, so the water is exceptionally clear.) Across the lake is a 4000-foot wall of trees—Sourdough Mountain and Aurora Peak. On the opposite side of the road, a nearly tropical scene of cascading falls, lush ferns, thick moss, and drooping trees announce that you are riding through the Olympic rain forest. Several pullouts offer spots to stop and admire your remarkable surroundings.

Leaving the shoreline, the primitive road climbs steeply for about a mile before beginning a 5-mile descent to Crescent Bay on the Strait of Juan de Fuca. Along the way, at about the 25-mile mark, you pass through tiny Joyce, which has a general store you can use for resupplying. Crescent Beach Road offers terrific views of the massive Strait of Juan de Fuca—a 15-mile-wide trough of roiling

Follow the shoreline of crystal-clear Lake Crescent, the state's second deepest lake.

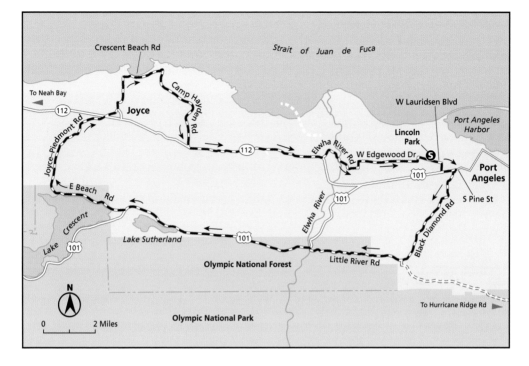

water surging in from the Pacific Ocean and separating you from Vancouver Island. Winds are likely strong and from the west here, which means (*whoohoo!*) a tailwind back to Port Angeles.

Continue east and make your way up and away from the sea by climbing a couple short steep pitches on Camp Hayden Road. Eventually you will intersect with State Route 112, where you turn left. This 5-mile stretch of highway can be busy, but like the earlier stretch along US Highway 101, it offers a decent shoulder and scenic views—valley farmland below the snowy peaks of the Olympics.

Leave State Route 112 by turning left onto Elwha River Road, taking a sec to peer down into the deep gorge. Follow a series of mostly residential roads back to W. Lauridsen Boulevard and Lincoln Park. Should you need post-ride refreshment, a mini-mart is located just outside the park.

Variation: An interesting option should you have a cyclocross bike, beefy tires, and/or quads of steel is to follow Little River Road east. It is gravel for about 4 miles to where it meets up with Hurricane Ridge Road. From there, it's a 12-mile, 3500-foot climb to the ridge.

MILEAGE LOG

0.0   From Lincoln Park head east on W. Lauridsen Blvd.
0.7   Right onto Tumwater Truck Rd.
0.9   Left onto US Hwy 101.
1.5   Left onto S. Pine St.
1.7   Left to continue on S. Pine St. (Becomes Black Diamond Rd.)
6.2   Bear right as road becomes Little River Rd.
9.6   Right onto Olympic Hot Springs Rd.

9.8	Left onto US Hwy 101.
17.4	Right onto E. Beach Rd.
20.6	Bear right as road becomes Joyce–Piedmont Rd.
24.9	Right onto SR 112. (May be unsigned.)
24.9	Left onto Crescent Beach Rd.
25.3	Left to stay on Crescent Beach Rd.
27.1	Right to stay on Crescent Beach Rd. (Becomes Camp Hayden Rd.)
28.7	Bear left to stay on Camp Hayden Rd.
31.9	Left onto SR 112.
37.2	Left onto Elwha River Rd.
39.1	Left onto Laird Rd.
39.3	Follow to right as road becomes W. Edgewood Dr. (Becomes W. Lauridsen Blvd.)
42.3	Return to starting point in Lincoln Park.

53 HURRICANE RIDGE

Difficulty	Very strenuous
Time	2½ to 4 hours
Distance	37.6 miles
Elevation Gain	5100 feet

ROAD CONDITIONS: Chip-seal surface road with ample shoulders; smoother pavement once past the park entry station. Many pullouts to let cars pass.

GETTING THERE: Take US Hwy 101 west to Port Angeles. Once in town, turn left onto Race St. and continue for two blocks to E. Second St. Park in the Civic Field parking lot just ahead on the right.

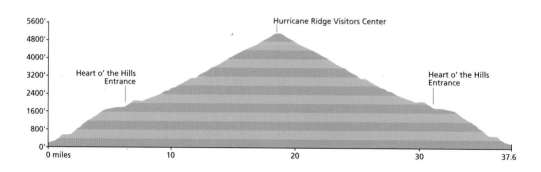

This is the big one—the longest, most relentless, sustained, elevation-gobbling ride in this book, rising from sea level to a mile high in 19 miles. There's no beating about the bush either; this one starts climbing from the first pedal stroke; in fact, the steepest section is the first 4.5 miles.

But it's not without mega-rewards. Views from the top of Hurricane Ridge—a sea of peaks and and valleys stretching in all directions as far the eye can—are mesmerizing. It's easy to understand why Teddy Roosevelt got the ball rolling on turning this into a national park more than 100 years ago.

Views aren't bad on the way up either. Several pullouts offer airplane-wing look-sees of the northern Olympic Peninsula edging into the Strait of Juan de Fuca, with Vancouver Island beyond. In high summers, the wildflowers are glorious, as are the heathers in early fall.

From the Civic Field parking lot in Port Angeles, head south (up) Race Street for about a mile to the Olympic National Park Visitors Center. Just past the park entrance, bear right onto Heart o' the Hills Road and fasten your seatbelts for 17 more miles of whole-grained uphill goodness. These early

The road to Hurricane Ridge is the longest, sustained climb in the state. (Which means it's also the longest, sustained descent too!)

miles are densely forested with a consistent 8 to 9 percent grade. About a mile before the park pay station (a nominal five-dollar fee at press time), the grade lessens to 4 and 5 percent. After all that climbing, you will feel as if you're riding downhill.

Resume climbing, then climb some more. It's fairly relentless the rest of the way, though not quite as steep as the initial miles. Three short dark tunnels keep you on your toes. Take your sunglasses off and be sure that the drivers of cars sharing your tunnel time can see you. Then climb, climb, and climb some more. As with all alpine rides, however, the views improve the higher you go, which certainly tempers one's fatigue and loss of energy.

Once at the top, take in the "Hills-Are-Alive-with-the-Sound-of-Music" vista. Enjoy a short hike (if you don't mind doing it in your socks). Take plenty of pics. The Hurricane Ridge Visitors Center offers a snack bar, restrooms, water, and protection from the elements should you need it. The weather comes in quickly here and often quite harshly—there's a reason it's called Hurricane Ridge.

When you're ready, head down that hill you spent so much effort climbing, secure in the knowledge that you won't have to pedal the cranks a single stroke unless you want to (which you might, to prevent your legs from cramping). It's downhill all the way, a screaming fast descent you'll never forget.

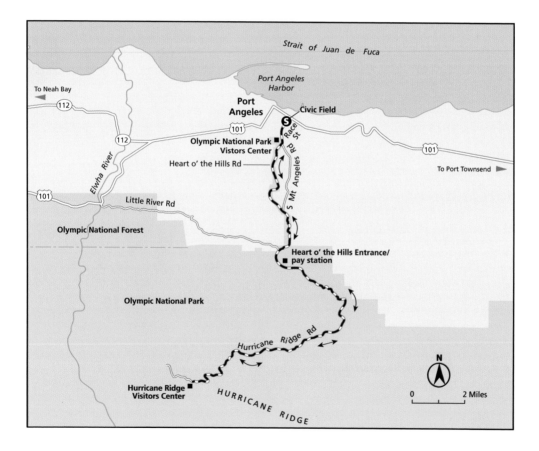

0.0   From the Civic Field parking lot in Port Angeles, go left onto E. Second St. then left onto Race Street.

1.0   Bear right onto Heart o' the Hills Rd. (Becomes Hurricane Ridge Rd.)

6.2   Heart o' the Hills entrance and pay station.

18.8   Hurricane Ridge Visitors Center.

36.7   Left onto Mount Angeles Rd. (Becomes Race St.)

37.6   Right onto E. Second St. and your starting point in the Civic Field parking lot.

54   SEQUIM–SPIT LOOP

Difficulty	Easy
Time	1½ to 3 hours
Distance	33.3 miles
Elevation Gain	1425 feet

ROAD CONDITIONS: Mellow country and residential roads, some with chip-seal surface; short stretch of busy US Hwy 101; city riding with bike lane.

GETTING THERE: From US Hwy 101 just east of Sequim, turn right on E. Washington St. and follow for 1.2 miles to S. Blake Ave. Turn right and follow for 0.3 mile to Carrie Blake Park on the right.

Noted for its location in the rain shadow of the Olympic Mountains (it receives less than half the annual precipitation of Seattle), Sequim offers sundry cycling opportunities including scenic bonuses such as the Olympic Mountains, the Strait of Juan de Fuca, lavender fields, and lovely, open countryside. Bike racers might recognize sections of this route that show up on the annual Tour de Dung, so named because of its proximity to Dungeness Spit.

Begin by heading west across Sequim, first through residential streets and finally exiting the town proper via Old Olympic Highway, which is highway in name only. With US Highway 101 a mile or so away, all the fast

This route features several of the state's more, um, intriguingly named roads.

traffic is over there; this road is just a pleasant low-speed, wide-shouldered country road past farms and fields and with mega-views of the snowy, oft fog-shrouded Olympic Mountains. The road heads due west, so headwinds can be an issue on this part of the ride. (Of course, on the return, they can become tailwinds. And I prefer to be a glass half-full guy.)

About 7 miles in, turn right on Kitchen-Dick Road (first interesting name) and begin heading down toward the Strait of Juan de Fuca and Dungeness Spit. Shortly after passing Woodcock Road (ahem), the route passes Dungeness Recreation Area (restrooms available) before heading down to Marine Drive and following the shoreline proper. Cline Spit, a mini-spit within Dungeness, offers a short

steep ride down to the water for close-up views of the spit, the strait, and even far-off views of Mount Baker, which on sunny days looms large though it's some 80 miles away.

Leaving the water, pedal up E. Anderson Road, which becomes Sequim–Dungeness Way—part of the Tour de Dung route—and follows a series of country roads through farmland, fields, and forest until eventually reaching Schmuck Road. (I'm not making this up.) A few rollers later land you by Sequim Bay and John Wayne Marina, so-named because it was built on land donated by the movie great. Turn right onto Whitefeather Way (sometimes unsigned, but just past the marina), and begin several stairlike pitches that constitute the route's one big climb.

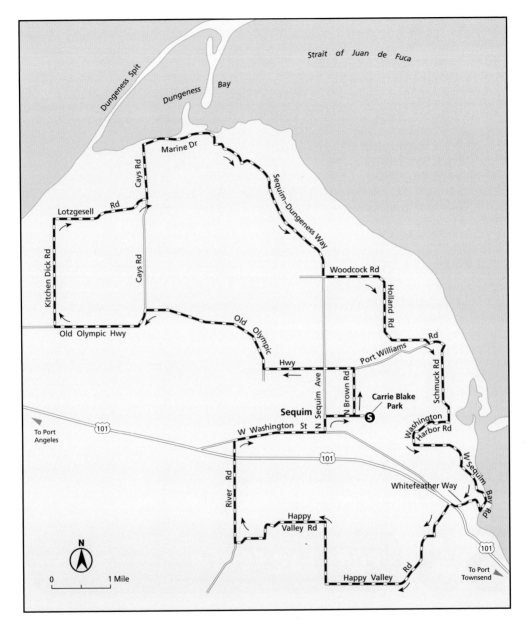

After crossing the Discovery Trail, White-feather intersects with busy US Highway 101. Go right and very carefully pick your way across to Happy Valley Road, a few hundred yards ahead on your left. Resume climbing through forest, farmland, and peaceful valley on chip-sealy country road.

At about 30 miles, go right on River Road and follow back into Sequim. Cross over US Highway 101 via a bridge and at the round-about, go right on W. Washington Street (bike lane provided). Follow that east across town to Sequim Avenue and turn left. You'll find Fir Street and then Carrie Blake Park just ahead on your right.

0.0	From parking in Sequim's Carrie Blake Park, head west on Fir St.
0.2	Right onto N. Brown Rd.
1.0	Left onto Port Williams Rd. (Becomes Old Olympic Hwy.)
2.5	Bear right to stay on Old Olympic Hwy.
5.0	Left to stay on Old Olympic Hwy.
6.7	Right onto Kitchen Dick Rd.
8.4	Right onto Lotzgesell Rd.
10.1	Left onto Cays Rd.
11.0	Bear right as Cays Rd. becomes Marine Dr.
12.3	Left onto Twin View Dr.
12.9	Left onto E. Anderson Rd. (Becomes Sequim–Dungeness Wy.)
15.4	Left onto Woodcock Rd. (Becomes Holland Rd.)
18.1	Right onto Graysmarsh Ln.
18.2	Left onto Port Williams Rd.
18.4	Right onto Schmuck Rd.
19.7	Right onto Washington Harbor Rd.
20.6	Left onto W. Sequim Bay Rd.
22.7	Right onto Whitefeather Wy. (Might be unsigned.)
23.2	Right onto US Hwy 101.
23.4	Left onto Happy Valley Rd.
26.3	Right to stay on Happy Valley Rd.
28.6	Right to stay on Happy Valley Rd.
29.1	Right onto River Rd.
30.8	At roundabout, right onto W. Washington St.
32.3	Left onto N. Sequim Ave.
32.6	Right onto E. Fir St.
33.3	Return to starting point in Carrie Blake Park.

55 PORT T TO FORT F

Difficulty	Moderate
Time	2½ to 4 hours
Distance	47 miles
Elevation Gain	2600 feet

ROAD CONDITIONS: Urban streets with bike lanes, short stretch of gravel bike path, rural road with chip-seal surface, state highway with wide shoulder.

GETTING THERE: On the Kitsap Peninsula, take SR 16/3 north. Cross the Hood Canal Bridge and turn right on SR 19 N. to Port Townsend. Follow it and then SR 20 E. to the ferry terminal. Or take the Coupeville–Port Townsend ferry from Whidbey Island. Find street parking near the ferry terminal.

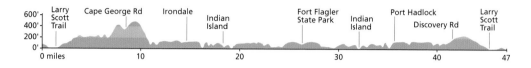

This Olympic Peninsula route offers seaside vistas by the ton—an island exploration, an historic fort, and of course, Port Townsend, famous and beloved for its rhodys and Victorian homes. Fort Flagler too, at the tip of Marrowstone Island, built in the late nineteenth century as a way to safeguard Puget Sound from enemy attack.

From your parking place near the Port Townsend ferry terminal, go left on Water Street and make your way to the Larry Scott Trail. Though unpaved, this short stretch offers stunning water and far-off mountain views as well as an alternative to hassling with all the cars, trucks, and RVs recently disembarked from the ferry and now making their ways

Along with its terrific riding, Port Townsend is beloved for its bounteous rhododendrons and historic Victorian homes.

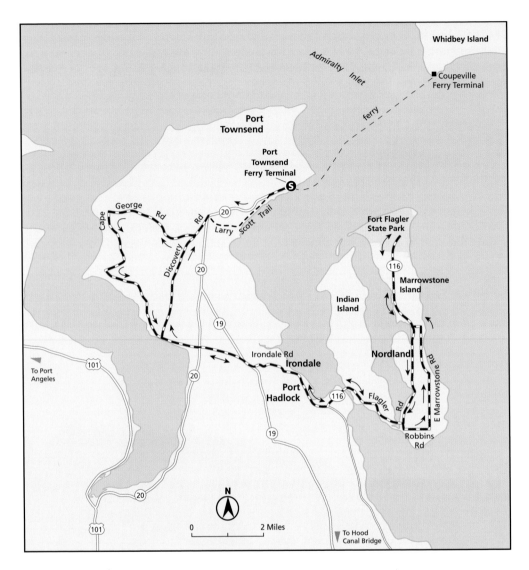

to all points peninsular. If you don't want to pedal the gravel, follow Water Street as it becomes E. Sims Way and then W. Sims Way (always State Route 20) for 3 miles to Discovery Road; you will have a dedicated bike lane most of the way. Port Townsend, of course, should be explored and enjoyed before you leave, if only to sample its Victorian architecture, wander some art galleries, eat, drink, and stock up on supplies.

Head south on Discovery Road and then turn right onto Cape George Road—and

take a deep sigh. You are on rural country road here, wooded rolling hills broken up by the occasional farm or field, with peek-a-boo views of the Olympic Mountains. Follow the road as it trends south, eventually finding yourself high above the sparkling waters of Discovery Bay. After a sweeping descent, go right and make your way east across Quimper Peninsula toward Irondale and Port Hadlock. The roads are busier here, but smoother and with ample shoulders.

In Port Hadlock, at a major intersection

(which oddly is unsigned for the east–west crossroad) go left, following State Route 116 (Oak Bay Road, then Flagler Road) and head for the islands: Indian and Marrowstone. Its smooth road offers a wide shoulder and, along the south shore of Indian Island, terrific views through the madrona trees of Oak Bay, and if you're lucky, Mount Rainier as well as the Olympic Mountains.

Continue east, crossing a bridge onto Marrowstone Island, and commence a terrifically mellow 12-mile upside-down lollipop loop. It's rural island riding at its finest—small farms, peaceful forests, water views. State Route 116 at the north end of the island is a little busier, but certainly not a freeway. After exploring Fort Flagler State Park, with its nineteenth-century gun batteries, return south, this time following State Route 116 all the way back to Port Hadlock. Along the way, while still on Marrowstone Island, pass through scenic Nordland. The town sign reads "Slow down, Oysters at Play," and the town itself boasts a nice general store.

From Port Hadlock, retrace your pedal strokes to Discovery Road. (Coming from this direction, be sure to sneak-sprint the Irondale city limits.) Go right and follow the rural road north for about 3.5 miles to Port Townsend and the Larry Scott Trail.

MILEAGE LOG

0.0	From street parking near the Port Townsend ferry terminal, go left onto Water St. /SR 20. (Becomes E. Sims Wy./SR 20.)
0.7	Left onto Jefferson St.
0.9	Right onto Washington St.
1.0	Left onto Larry Scott Trail.
2.9	Right onto Mill Rd.
3.0	Left onto Discovery Rd.
3.7	Right onto Cape George Rd.
5.7	Bear left to stay on Cape George Rd.
8.6	Bear left to stay on Cape George Rd.
11.3	Right onto Discovery Rd.
12.5	Cross SR 20; road becomes 4 Corners Rd.
13.8	Right onto SR 19 (Rhody Dr.).
14.0	Left onto Irondale Rd.
14.6	Enter Irondale.
15.8	Enter Port Hadlock.
16.0	Left onto SR 116 (Oak Bay Rd.); might be unsigned.
16.8	Left to continue on SR 116 (Flagler Rd.).
17.7	Bear right to stay on SR 116 (Flagler Rd.).
19.6	Right onto Robbins Rd.
19.8	Left to stay on Robbins Rd.
20.5	Left onto E. Marrowstone Rd.
23.4	Left onto E. Beach Rd.
23.6	Right onto SR 116 (Flagler Rd.).
26.5	Turn around at Fort Flagler State Park.
29.5	Nordland.
32.0	Right to stay on SR 116 (Flagler Rd.).

33.9	Left to stay on SR 116 (Flagler Rd.).
34.9	Right to stay on SR 116 (now Oak Bay Rd.).
35.7	Right onto Irondale Rd.
37.7	Right onto SR 19 (Rhody Dr.).
37.9	Left onto 4 Corners Rd.
39.4	Cross SR 20; road becomes Discovery Rd.
40.8	Bear right to stay on Discovery Rd.
44.0	Right onto Mill Rd.
44.2	Left onto Larry Scott Trail.
46.0	Right onto Washington St.
46.2	Left onto Jefferson St.
46.4	Right onto E. Sims Wy. (SR 20). Becomes Water St.
47.0	Return to parking and/or starting point near ferry terminal.

56 SILVERDALE–PORT GAMBLE–EAST BREMERTON

Difficulty	Moderate
Time	2½ to 4 hours
Distance	51 miles
Elevation Gain	3270 feet

ROAD CONDITIONS: County and rural roads, urban riding with bike lanes, and stretches of busy state highway.

GETTING THERE: From SR 3 near Silverdale, take exit 45. Head south on SR 303 (NW Waaga Wy.), which becomes Kitsap Mall Blvd. NW. In 0.6 mile, turn right onto Silverdale Wy. NW and follow for 0.3 mile to NW Bucklin Hill Rd. Turn left and park at Silverdale Old Mill Park, 0.3 mile ahead on the right.

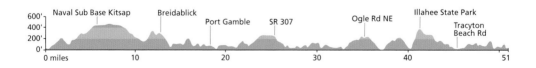

This 50-plus miler explores a couple northerly lobes of Kitsap Peninsula. Along the way it includes some rollers to keep you on your toes, but nothing to make you curse the author. Parts of this route often show up on the Tour de Kitsap, an annual summer ride

This route features some fine waterfront riding along Port Washington Narrows.

put on by the West Sound Cycling Club, a Silverdale-based group. (Silverdale boasts a terrific bike shop as well.)

From Old Mill Park on Bucklin Hill Road, maneuver through Silverdale's busting-at-the-seams commercial core and head north out of town via Clear Creek Road. Expect a fair share of rollers, mini-bumps, and longish gradual hills, as well as a shoulder that disappears from time to time. Happily, most of the high-speed traffic is on State Route 3, which parallels your route. Naval Submarine Base Kitsap is on your left, while a mix of forest, farms, and fields occupy your right. Eventually, however, at the 13-mile mark and a spot on the map called Breidablick, Clear Creek intersects with State Route 3, which you travel for 4 miles to the Hood Canal Bridge.

After you pass the bridge, the traffic thins out (most of it crossed the bridge), the road becomes State Route 104, and you enter the historic mill town of Port Gamble. Located

right on a mini-peninsula that bears its name, much of this charming New England–style village is a National Historic Landmark. Pedal around town a bit to enjoy the turn-of-the-century architecture and perhaps to refuel.

Back on the route, continue south on State Route 104 and then west across the peninsula on Bond Road, through forest and field and on mostly smooth roads with wide comfortable shoulders. At 28 miles, reach historic—and very Scandinavian—Poulsbo, where you'll find some great places to eat and drink. Leaving Poulsbo, also known as "Little Norway," begin making your way south toward East Bremerton, about 15 miles away. You'll be riding a mix of busy urban roads (though most with bike lanes and/or wide shoulders as well as "Bikes on Road" signs) and residential streets, many along Liberty Bay and Port Orchard Passage. Pass Illahee State Park, which offers restrooms.

In East Bremerton, after cutting west across

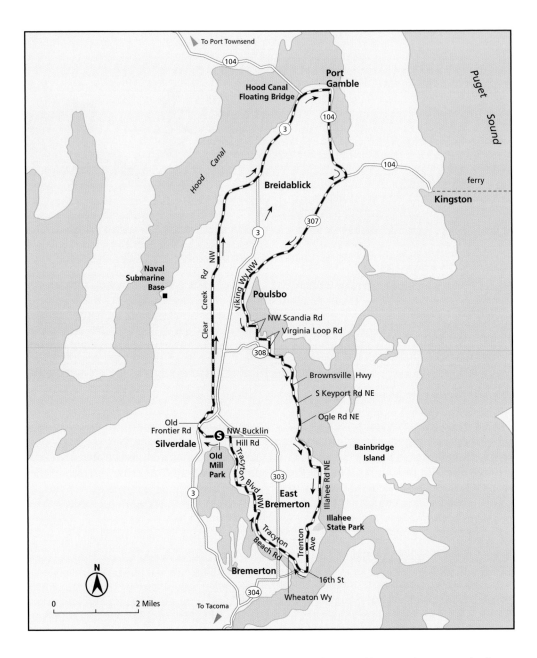

town via Wheaton Way, go right on Tracyton Beach Road for 2 miles of really fine waterfront riding. Eventually, the Tracyton Beach Road heads north away from the water and becomes Tracyton Boulevard, which is more residential and has stretches of nice bike lane.

(Watch for speed bumps, however, which can jolt your hands off the handlebars in a hurry.) About 6 miles north of East Bremerton, reach Bucklin Hill Road and the outer reaches of Silverdale. Turn left. Old Mill Park is a half mile ahead on the left.

0.0   From Old Mill Park in Silverdale, go left onto NW Bucklin Hill Rd.
0.3   Left onto Silverdale Wy. NW.
0.6   Right onto NW Anderson Hill Rd.
1.3   Right onto Old Frontier Rd.
1.9   Continue straight where Old Frontier Rd. goes left.
2.3   Left onto Clear Creek Rd. NW.
13.0 Left onto SR 3.
17.0 Pass Hood Canal Floating Bridge. (Becomes SR 104.)
18.0 Port Gamble.
22.0 Right onto SR 307 (Bond Rd.).
27.7 Right onto Lindvig Wy. Skirt the northern reaches of Poulsbo.
27.9 Left onto Viking Wy. NW.
30.2 Left onto NW Scandia Rd.
31.0 Left onto Virginia Loop Rd.
31.5 Right to stay on Virginia Loop Rd.
32.1 Left onto SR 308.
32.9 Right onto Brownsville Hwy.
33.6 Left onto S. Keyport Rd. NE.
35.2 Left onto Ogle Rd. NE.
36.7 Left onto Brownsville Hwy.; quick left onto Illahee Rd NE. (Becomes Trenton Ave.)
41.4 Pass Illahee State Park. Enter East Bremerton.
42.9 Right onto 16th St.
43.3 Right onto Winfield Ave.
43.5 Left onto 18th St. (Becomes Wheaton Wy.)
44.2 Left onto Lebo Blvd. (Becomes Tracyton Beach Rd.)
46.8 Left onto NW Riddell Rd.
46.9 Bear right onto May St. NW. (Becomes Tracyton Blvd. NW.)
47.5 Bear left to stay on Tracyton Blvd. NW.
47.7 Bear left to stay on Tracyton Blvd. NW.
50.5 Left onto NW Bucklin Hill Rd.
51.0 Left into Old Mill Park where route started.

57 BELFAIR STATE PARK–TAHUYA–SEABECK LOOP

Difficulty	Strenuous
Time	3½ to 6 hours
Distance	64.7 miles
Elevation Gain	3620 feet

ROAD CONDITIONS: Rural chip-seal roads with low traffic and "Bikes on Road" signs; some smooth county roadways with wide shoulders.

GETTING THERE: From SR 3 near Port Orchard, head south on SR 3 for about 8 miles to Belfair. Exit onto SR 300 W. and follow for 3.2 miles to Belfair State Park on the left.

Here's a route that's off the beaten path and that offers hours of remote forest riding as well as some seaside jaunts along Hood Canal. Probably best to ride this route with a buddy—there's a 35-mile chunk in the beginning with no services.

From Belfair State Park, head west, first on the last couple miles of State Route 300 (which becomes North Shore Road), a scenic stretch along the fjord with views across Hood Canal to forested hillsides that call to mind a ride along the Inside Passage. For about 11 miles, the road winds along this shoreline, never more than 10 or 20 feet above sea level. The road is narrow, so be alert, but it's mostly lightly traveled and has numerous "Bikes on Road" signs.

About 11 miles in, leave the shoreline, turn right onto Belfair–Tahuya Road, and com-

mence a bit of a cruel climbing—about 400 feet over the next mile, with stretches at 14 percent. But it gets you up high and deep into the woods, the working forests of Tahuya State Forest and Mason County where, for the next 20-plus miles, you meander up and down and back and forth as the road snakes this way and that. The road surface can be a bit rough, and there's no real shoulder, but traffic is fairly sparse. Do watch for logging vehicles and ORV enthusiasts, however, as this area is a hotbed for both.

At about 31 miles, after reaching the elevation high point of the ride and just before passing the shores of Tahuya Lake, begin a long, mostly gradual, 8-mile descent that lands you in Seabeck, along the northerly arm of Hood Canal. (Along the way, shortly after turning left onto NW Holly Road, a

After starting out gently along Hood Canal, this route cuts through the heart of the vast Tahuya State Forest—twice. >

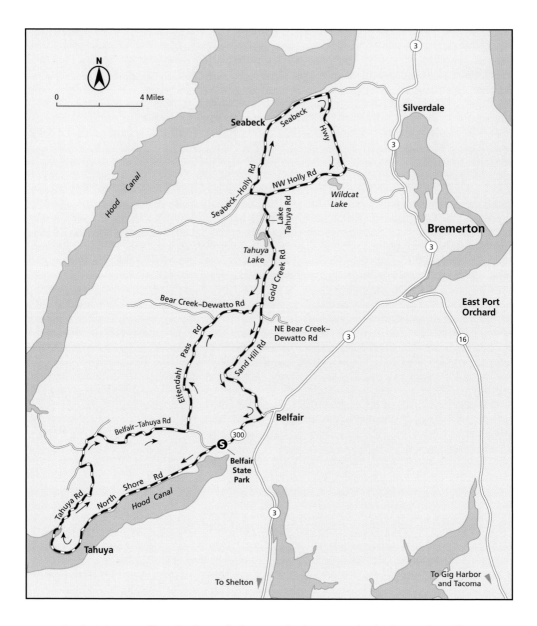

gas station/mini-mart offers the first refueling stop of the trip. It's at about the 35-mile mark, but you may want to wait until Seabeck.)

With water views and the Olympic Mountains looming large across the canal, Seabeck is a stunner. It offers a cute general store and café and some terrific shoreline riding along Seabeck Highway (which unfortunately doesn't last very long). Seabeck Highway—not really

a highway in the high-speed traffic sense—heads inland and commences the second long climb of the day—a stiff 2-miler that gains about 500 feet. A fun, rolling-hill loop on smooth, wide-shouldered road out to Wildcat Lake follows before a return—and climb back up—to the chip-seal roads and working woods of Tahuya State Forest.

After turning left onto Bear Creek–Dewatto

Road, begin the snaking, deep-woods descent back to your starting point at Belfair State Park. (Do your best to obey the Mission Creek Correction Center for Women signs that advise you not to pick up hitchhikers.)

Be careful on the final 2-mile stretch on State Route 300 before the park; the road is narrow, the speed limit 45, and you can encounter many eager RVers headed for the park.

MILEAGE LOG

0.0	From Belfair State Park, head west on SR 300, which becomes North Shore Rd.
11.0	Right onto Belfair–Tahuya Rd.
21.9	Left onto Elfendahl Rd.
27.9	Right at Bear Creek–Dewatto Rd. (T intersection might be unsigned.)
30.0	Left onto Gold Creek Rd. (Becomes Lake Tahuya Rd.)
35.4	Left onto at NW Holly Rd.
36.3	Right onto Seabeck–Holly Rd.
39.8	Seabeck. (Road becomes Seabeck Hwy.)
42.7	Follow as Seabeck Hwy. goes right.
46.4	Right onto NW Holly Rd.
50.6	Left onto Lake Tahuya Rd. (Becomes Gold Creek Rd.)
56.0	Left onto NE Bear Creek–Dewatto Rd.
56.8	Right onto Sand Hill Rd.
62.6	Right onto SR 300.
64.7	Return to starting point at Belfair State Park.

58 BURLY BURLEY–KEY PENINSULA ROUTE

Difficulty	Moderate
Time	2½ to 4 hours
Distance	48.8 miles
Elevation Gain	3185 feet

ROAD CONDITIONS: Low-traffic rural roads with shoulders of varying widths; some with chip-seal surface; some with "Bikes on Road" signs. Stretch of highway with smooth wide shoulder.

GETTING THERE: From I-5 in Tacoma, take exit 132. Head west on SR 16 for 13.4 miles, across the Tacoma Narrows Bridge to the SR 302 W. (Purdy Key Center) exit. Merge onto Purdy Dr. NW and head north for 1.7 miles to 154th St. NW. Turn left and follow as the road bears right and becomes 66th Ave. NW. Reach Burley in 1 mile; park in the grocery store parking lot. (*Note:* Eastbound traffic must pay a toll to cross the Tacoma Narrows Bridge.)

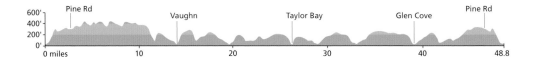

This foray over low-traffic roads explores the rural reaches of Key Peninsula, the island-like finger of land that extends south from Kitsap Peninsula. It winds through a mix of dense forest, open farmland, and small communities such as Burley, Vaughn, Home, Lake Bay, and Key Center. This is one of the more remote rides in this book, so expect to find just yourself, your bike, and the open road ahead. Keep in mind that you won't find many places to resupply with food and drink, so take advantage of the few gas station mini-marts you pass along the way.

This route features a lot of ups and downs—blame it on the mile-thick ice age sheet that 20,000 years ago gouged out countless ridges on the peninsula as it receded. The first part of the elevation profile resembles Bart Simpson's head—12 miles of ups and downs on a mix of smooth roads with wide shoulders (and "Bikes on Road" signs) as well as narrower country roads through pastoral farmland.

Begin in Burley (which started out in the late nineteenth century as a socialist community). At the 20-mile mark, about a mile after

Minter Bay's history includes a time when local Native Americans met here with members of Vancouver's Expedition in 1792.

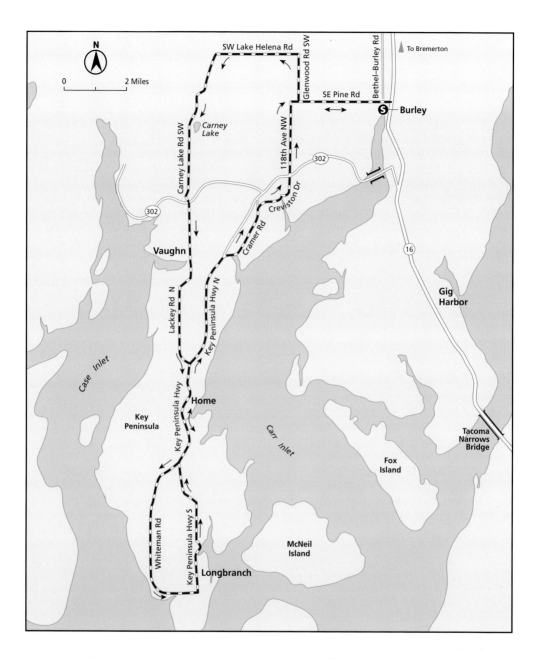

you turn right onto Key Peninsula Highway, pass through tiny Home, a former anarchists' enclave. There's a mini-mart here, but you will pass through this town on your return trip, at the 34-mile mark.

Turn right onto Whiteman Road. It lacks shoulder but also traffic, making it a win-win. Pedal through moss-hung forest, rolling fields, and the occasional farm hidden in the trees. Follow the chip-sealed road's ups and downs, including a quick ride-by of Taylor Bay, before climbing back up and turning left onto smooth, wide-shouldered Key Peninsula Highway, from whence you head back north.

Pass through Home (who says you can never go home again?), and turn right onto 92nd Street/Cramer Road, where a small grocery store offers the chance for some supplies. A fun little stretch on winding narrow country roads—down by Glen Cove and undulating along Minter Creek—follows, eventually delivering you onto 118th Avenue NW and the last climb of the day. It's a gradual 2-miler that, when you turn right onto Pine Road, you'll recognize as part of the Bart Simpson–head climb that began this ride. Pedaling in the opposite direction affords you a nice descent. The last mile back to Burley drops almost 300 feet.

Enjoy.

MILEAGE LOG

0.0	From the grocery store parking lot in Burley, head north on Bethel–Burley Rd. SE.
0.4	Left onto SE Pine Rd.
3.2	Right onto Glenwood Rd. SW.
4.7	Left onto SW Lake Helena Rd.
7.2	Left onto J. M. Dickenson Rd. SW. (Becomes Carney Lake Rd. SW, then Wright–Bliss Rd.)
14.2	Pass through Vaughn.
14.5	Bear left onto Lackey Rd. N.
17.8	Right onto Key Peninsula Hwy.
19.3	Pass through Home.
21.1	Right onto Whiteman Rd.
27.2	Left onto Key Peninsula Hwy. S.
28.2	Pass through Longbranch.
31.6	Stay straight on Key Peninsula Hwy.
33.7	Pass through Home.
38.6	Right onto 92nd St. Kp. N.
38.6	Left onto Cramer Rd. Kp. N.
41.2	Right onto Creviston Dr. Kp. N.
42.4	Left onto 118th Ave. NW. (Becomes Glenwood Rd. SW, then SW Pine Rd.)
48.4	Right onto Bethel–Burley Rd. SE.
48.8	Return to start.

EASTERN WASHINGTON

These routes feature a whole lot of everything: epic climbs, long stretches beside the winding Columbia River, fragrant pine forests, bounteous orchards and vineyards, the wheat fields of Palouse, and more. (Such as wind.) The only thing lacking in abundance is traffic—many of these rides are on low-traveled roads that surprise and delight with their remoteness.

59 TONASKET–OROVILLE–PALMER LAKE LOOP

Difficulty	Very Strenuous
Time	4½ to 8 hours
Distance	79.5 miles
Elevation Gain	5925 feet

ROAD CONDITIONS: Rural roads with varying degrees of chip-seal chunkiness and shoulder widths; multiple cattle guards on Loomis–Oroville Rd.

GETTING THERE: Head north on US Hwy 97/SR 20 to Tonasket, about 24 miles north of Omak. In town, the highway becomes Whitcomb Ave., Tonasket's main street. Look for street parking.

This 80 (or so)-miler is like two separate rides in one route. The first half climbs into the high dry forest and open farmland of the Okanogan highlands, passing tiny Sitzmark Ski Area before heading down (almost 20 miles' worth) to Oroville. Upon crossing the

Okanogan River, just 4 miles south of the US-Canada border, the route heads west toward the Cascades, chasing the Similkameen River through gorge and canyon before offering a serene ride along Palmer Lake. The route finishes off with miles and miles of Okanogan

Riders follow the glistening Similkameen River for almost 17 miles from Oroville to Palmer Lake.

orchard riding, just above the winding river of the same name.

Climbing commences from the get-go on this route, as heading out of Tonasket you begin pedaling upward past dry open fields and into hillsides fringed with pines. The road is narrow, with a chip-seal surface and occasional shoulder, but traffic is very light to nonexistent. The consistent climb—which continues for almost 20 miles—has some steep bits (up to 9 percent) but is not brutal. Besides, the sweeping views into the north Okanogan Valley are worth any sting to the legs. Plus, riding through the Okanogan highlands makes you feel as though you are riding through the sets of an old Western movie—dodging the occasional tumbleweed; passing endless hay fields and wheat fields broken up only by pasture, ranchland, and bands of pine forest; checking out barns and farmhouses where it looks as though the lifestyle hasn't changed in decades; and visiting tiny spots on the map such as Havillah (no services; seemingly no people).

Just past 19 miles, reach Sitzmark Ski Area (one chair lift, one rope tow), having climbed about 3600 feet to get there. And thus begins a potentially fast 17-mile descent into Oroville, down basically the same field-farm-forest landscape you spent the past few hours climbing up. (The descent is like watching a video of the climb on fast-reverse.) Though traffic is still light on this stretch (Chesaw Road into Oroville), do be aware that it's steeper and that the narrow farm road surface can be rough. The shoulder is somewhat vague too (and at times gravelly), so concentration is key.

Dropping back into the orchard-rich Okanogan Valley, enter Oroville at mile 36, the first

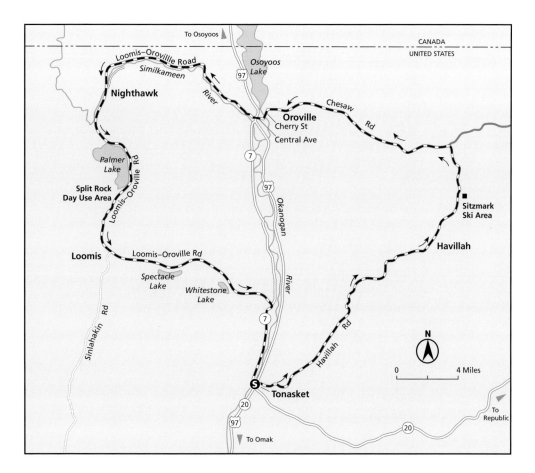

opportunity for food and drinks. (The last one, too, for about 25 miles, until the route passes through the small town of Loomis.) At Oroville, located on the southern shore of 14-mile-long Osoyoos Lake, which straddles the US-Canada border, cross the Okanogan River and begin the 42-mile western lobe of this route on Loomis–Oroville Road.

Never letting the Similkameen out of its sight, the snaking road follows the snaking river up and down a series of rollers through a breathtaking rocky gorge, eventually emerging above a verdant valley near tiny Nighthawk (no services). The chip-seal surface is chunky and given that much of this is rangeland, be on the lookout for cattle, cattle guards, and cattle exhaust, as it were.

Reach Palmer Lake just 4 miles south of Nighthawk at about mile 54, and enjoy a pleasant lakeside jaunt, bounded on the left by ranches, orchards, and towering forested hillside. The lake itself is a stunner, situated against a backdrop of 4000-foot peaks that appear to be peering around smaller Grandview Mountain in the foreground. Split Rock Day Use Area, at the south end of the 4.5-long, kidney bean–shaped lake, offers restrooms.

Reach the tiny town of Loomis at mile 62, which offers a mini-grocery for food and drinks. From there, head east past orchard and farmland, as well as a couple smaller lakes, finally dropping fairly steeply to just above the Okanogan River, where the road becomes State Route 7 (there's no sign). A 5-mile, mostly flat homestretch lands you just across the river from Tonasket; cross the bridge and you're back where you started.

Variations: For shorter routes, do either route lobe—the Palmer Lake segment on the west side of the Okanogan River (mostly flat), or the Havillah-Sitzmark Ski Area section (east of the river and featuring a 3000-plus-foot climb)—and once you hit Oroville, head south back to Tonasket via State Route 7 on the west side of the Okanogan River. US Highway 97, on the east side works too, but is busier than State Route 7. The shortened Havillah-Sitzmark loop is about 55 miles with 4300 feet elevation gain whereas the shortened Palmer Lake route is about 61 miles with 2700 feet of climbing.

MILEAGE LOG

0.0	From Tonasket, head north on Whitcomb Ave./US Hwy 97.
0.3	Right onto Jonathan St. E. (Becomes Havillah Rd.)
0.6	Continue onto Havillah Rd.
19.5	Sitzmark Ski Area.
23.7	Turn left onto Chesaw Rd.
36.0	Left to stay on Chesaw Rd. (Becomes Cherry St.) Enter Oroville.
36.6	Right onto Central Ave. (Becomes Loomis–Oroville Rd.)
49.9	Nighthawk.
53.9	Palmer Lake.
58.2	Split Rock Day Use Area.
62.5	Loomis.
74.0	Right onto SR 7. (No sign.)
79.3	Left onto 4th St. Bridge into Tonasket.
79.5	Return to where you parked.

60 OMAK LAKE–NESPELEM LOOP

Difficulty	Very Strenuous
Time	4½ to 8 hours
Distance	79.2 miles
Elevation Gain	5275 feet

ROAD CONDITIONS: Low-traffic rural road and state highway. Frequent chip-seal surfaces, though Columbia River Rd. does have a nice 15-mile stretch of smooth pavement. Watch for cattle guards (signed). **Note:** Largely without shade, this route is the very definition of a multi-bottle ride. With almost no towns along the route, the only chance to refuel is in Nespelem, which isn't reached until the 44-mile mark.

GETTING THERE: Drive US Hwy 97/SR 20 north to Omak and take the exit signed for SR 155 S./Grand Coulee Dam. Turn left onto Dayton St., left again onto 5th Ave. E., and then right onto Columbia St. Follow for 0.3 mile into Eastside Park.

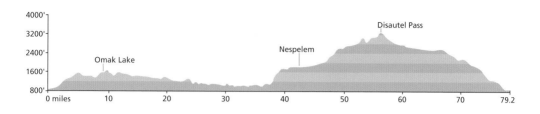

Similar to Tour 59, this is another 80-miler that presents itself as two completely different 40-milers. The first half, from Omak to the Columbia River, follows mostly deserted road (much of it smooth asphalt too!) along a sce-nic lake through an unshaded mix of scrubby rollers and verdant valleys, finishing with a 13-mile stretch along the Columbia River.

Part two, from Nespelem back to Omak, climbs gradually through dry pine forest,

Pedaling beside the Columbia River before climbing up out of the basin to Nespelum and Disautel Pass beyond (Andy Kindig)

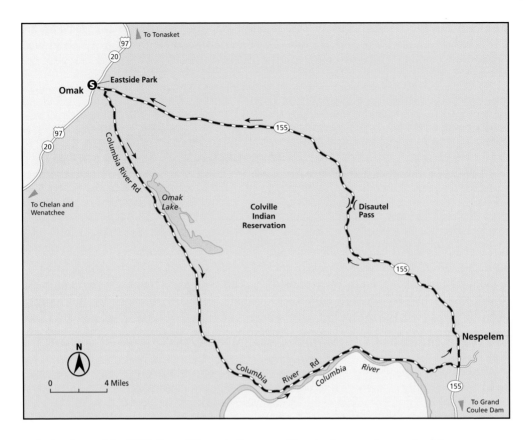

culminating with 3252-foot Disautel Pass before serving up a gradual 20-plus-mile descent into the Okanogan Valley.

From Eastside Park in Omak, work your way east out of town, following the sign for Disautel Pass but turning right onto Columbia River Road just outside of town. (You'll crest that pass on the second half of the ride.) Passing scrubby forest and open farmland, the rural road ascends for the first 5 miles or so, gaining 600 feet as it climbs up above Omak Lake, the first views of which you're treated to at about 7 miles. Turquoise in color, it might remind you of Diablo Lake, off the North Cascades Highway. It's Washington's largest saline lake, with no creek outlet for drainage and creates a stunning contrast against the arid landscape of scrubby hills, dry forest, and volcanic rock.

Continuing south past the lake on unusually smooth (for Eastern Washington) pavement, pass through a rolling shadeless landscape of open meadows, brushy fields, and not only zero traffic but pretty much no signs of human life. There's no cell service and things can feel pretty deserted out here in the vast Colville Indian Reservation. At Saddle Horse Flat, after a short steep descent, the road heads east, rolling up and down for about 13 miles alongside the Columbia River, tamed here by the Chief Joseph Dam in Bridgeport. Down beside the river, it's cooler and there's more greenery, though the road has returned to more typical narrow-shouldered chip seal.

At about mile 38, flip the record over and begin the second half of the route, which starts with a consistently steep 2-mile climb up out of the valley (with some pitches at 9 percent).

Turn left onto State Route 155 and in about 2 miles—much of it on a dedicated bike lane!—reach Nespelem, which offers a gas station mini-mart and thus a chance to resupply.

Back in the saddle, continue climbing but not quite as steeply as before. Though it's a state highway with a 60 miles per hour speed limit, State Route 155 is by no means one of the busy ones and the riding—a consistent 10-mile uphill tick that climbs ever higher into wonderfully dry Eastern Washington pine forest—is quite enjoyable.

At the 57-mile mark, reach 3252-foot Disautel Pass, about 2200 feet higher than your earlier cruise beside the Columbia River. Heading down, the descent is not super-screaming fast though one needs to be aware of the potential for falling rocks from roadside cliffs. Eventually, you break out of the forest and it feels as if the entire Okanogan Valley has opened up just for you, made even more stunning by the Cascade Range backdrop.

Continue down, down, down, eventually returning to Eastside Park in Omak.

MILEAGE LOG

0.0	From Eastside Park in Omak, go left onto Omak Ave./SR 155 N.
1.2	Right onto Columbia River Rd.
1.9	Take the first right to stay on Columbia River Rd. (Omak Lake Rd.)
9.0	Omak Lake.
38.2	Start of 2-mile climb.
41.5	Left onto SR 155 N.
43.7	Nespelem.
56.7	Disautel Pass.
79.2	Return to your starting point at Eastside Park.

61 CHELAN–BRIDGEPORT–MANSFIELD

Difficulty	Very strenuous
Time	5½ to 9 hours
Distance	93.4 miles
Elevation Gain	4220 feet

ROAD CONDITIONS: US highway with wide shoulders; low-traffic rural roads, most with chip-seal surface.

GETTING THERE: From Wenatchee, head north on US Hwy 2 E./US Hwy 97 N. for 39 miles toward Chelan. (Road becomes just US Hwy 97 N. past Orondo.) Beebe Bridge Park is on the left just south of Beebe Bridge. Park there.

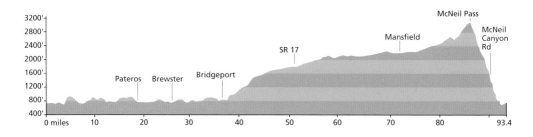

Follow the Columbia River north to Brewster and the wide expanse of Lake Pateros, where you begin the gradual climb up and across the wide, dry, treeless flatlands of the Columbia Plateau. Finish it off with a 6-mile drop down McNeil Canyon that just might be your fastest descent ever. Views are plentiful but thankfully, cars and trucks aren't. Neither is shade, however, so ride smart—take multiple bottles and don't ride the bulk of this route during the heat of a July or August afternoon.

From Beebe Bridge Park, carefully cross the bridge and head north on US Highway 97 along the Columbia River. Though at times busy, the chip-seal road offers a wide shoulder and terrific riding below the gorge's dry craggy cliffs and boulder fields, and along neat rows of fruit trees. Pass Wells Dam at about mile 12 (restrooms available), the main hydropower producer for Douglas County and the barrier that temporarily transforms the Columbia River into Lake Pateros.

Continue north through the small town of Pateros—plenty of places for eats and

Built in 1950, the Columbia River Bridge at Bridgeport is listed on the National Register of Historic Places.

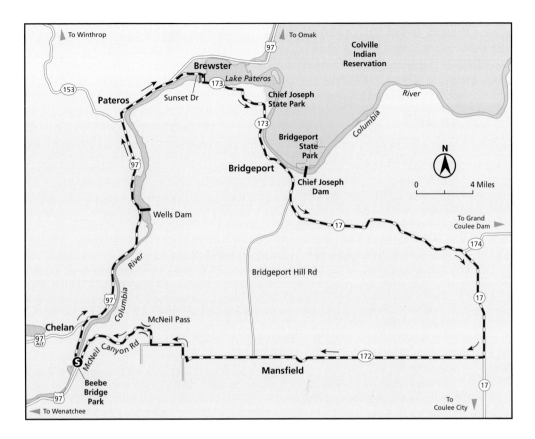

drinks here, as well as at Brewster, 6 miles up the road—and note that when the road swings east, the high rocky canyon walls almost disappear and the surrounding dusty hills become more soft and rounded. Cross the river/lake at Brewster, and with the now-expansive lake on your left, follow the rural, narrow-shouldered road past orchards, farm fields, and, in season, hillsides decked out in wildflowers. Eventually find yourself in yet another small town, Bridgeport. Check your bottles and your nutrition level, for this is the last chance to resupply for 37 miles.

Just beyond Bridgeport, now on State Route 17, pass the Chief Joseph Dam and begin the climbing portion of the route, which—and I'm only telling you this because I love you and know that you can handle it— continues for about the next 50 miles. For the most part, as you work your way out of the river gorge and onto the plateau, it's a gradual climb, maybe a 4 percent grade at the steepest but mostly 2 and under; if you're blessed with a tailwind, much of it can seem negligible.

Head east, then south, then west across the plateau, much of the scenery along the ride completely the same—dry, scrubby, treeless, and for the most part, traffic-less. Shoulder width and road smoothness vary but with so little traffic, it doesn't much matter. Do be aware of the giant farm trucks that ply these roads—they're big, they drive fast, and they can scare the heck out of you when they come up behind you.

Now heading due west, with a lineup of Cascades in the distance, reach the small town of Mansfield at about mile 74. Pound down some food and drink should you need it and finish off the last 20 miles of this route, which require only 14 miles of pedaling (albeit with about a thousand feet of climbing); the final 6 miles, on smooth, wide-shouldered road from McNeil Pass down to Beebe Bridge Park, drops 2300 feet. Whoa!

Variation: This loop can be shortened to about 68 miles by turning right onto Bridgeport Hill Road just east of Bridgeport.

MILEAGE LOG

0.0	From Beebe Bridge Park in Chelan, go left onto US Hwy 97 N. toward Beebe Bridge and then follow it north.
19.1	Pateros.
24.5	Right onto Brewster Grange Rd.
24.7	Left onto Sunset Dr.
25.7	Right onto S. 7th St. Enter Brewster.
26.0	Left onto W. Bruce Ave.
26.6	Right onto SR 173/Bridge St. Cross Lake Pateros/Columbia River.
35.6	Enter Bridgeport. Bear left onto 10th St.
35.8	Right onto Columbia Ave.
36.3	Right onto 17th St.
36.4	Left onto Foster Creek Ave.
37.1	Right onto SR 17 S.
53.1	Bear right to stay on SR 17 S.
60.7	Right onto SR 172 W.
73.7	Right onto Main St., Mansfield. Continue on SR 172 W.
82.0	Right onto McNeil Canyon Rd.
86.3	McNeil Pass summit.
93.4	Cross US 97 N.; return to starting point in Beebe Bridge Park.

62 YAKIMA CANYON

Difficulty	Moderate
Time	2 to 3½ hours
Distance	45.5 miles
Elevation Gain	2110 feet

ROAD CONDITIONS: Scenic road with chip-seal surface and mostly decent shoulder.

GETTING THERE: From I-82/US Hwy 97 near Ellensburg, take exit 3 and head west toward SR 821 (Canyon Rd.) on Thrall Rd. In 0.5 mile, turn left on Canyon Rd. and park just ahead at Helen McCabe State Park on the left.

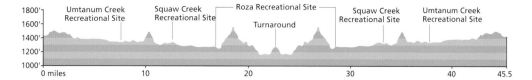

Take a breathtaking ride through a geologic wonder, Yakima Canyon, where the wily Yakima River snakes its way through a thousand-foot-deep gorge, boring through desert hills and basalt cliffs. Look for bighorn sheep ambling up and down the hillsides, golden eagles and osprey riding the thermals out of the canyon, and, should you stop, watch your step, pardner, for this be rattlesnake country.

This route can be ridden from either direction, but we'll start at the north (Ellensburg) end. From the parking lot at Helen McCabe State Park, hop on State Route 821 and head south. The road offers a narrow shoulder but "Bikes on Road" signs and a low(ish) speed limit (45 mph) add some degree of comfort. Another comforting thought is that anybody who wants to make time between Ellensburg and Yakima will take the freeway, not a winding two-lane road with a couple of dozen squiggly hairpin turns to it.

At about 2 miles, the road butts right up against the river and pretty much stays there for the next 20 miles. From time to time, it rises a few hundred feet or so above the Yakima River, offering terrific bird's-eye views into the canyon while also keeping your climbing legs busy. Numerous pullouts

The 1,500-foot-high basalt cliffs of Yakima Canyon

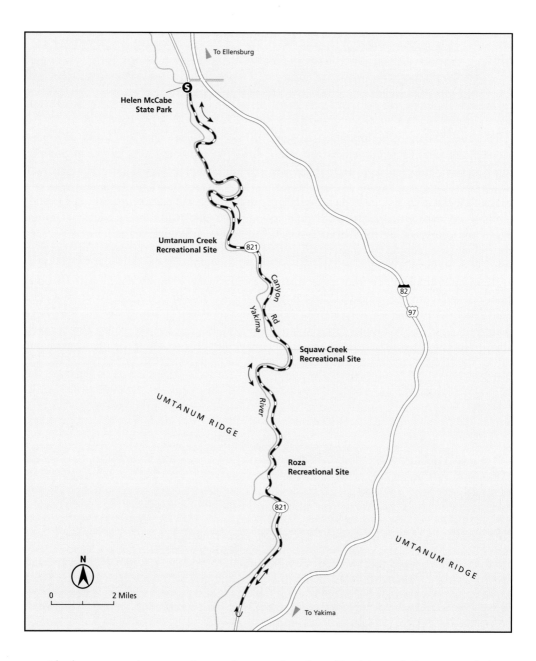

provide the opportunity to gaze in wonder at the rounded hills and rocky cliffs surrounding you.

There are no food or drink establishments along the canyon road, though three recreational sites (Umtanum Creek at mile 8.5, Squaw Creek at 12.7, and Roza at 17.3) have pit toilets. The biggest hills are a mile-long climb just past the Roza Recreational Site (mostly 5 percent) and another one just after the turnaround, as the road climbs about 400 feet over 2.5 miles. Wind is also a factor and seems to blow from any direction.

At about 22 miles from the start, the

canyon opens up, revealing Selah and the outskirts of Yakima. Should you need replenishment, ride to Selah, 5 miles south of the canyon entrance. Otherwise, turn around and do it all again, heading back to the Ellensburg end of the canyon.

Note: On the return route, you'll be riding in the hillside lane. Be aware that several spots are prone to falling rocks from the cliffs above. Keep your eyes peeled and your head covered.

Variation: If you'd like the opportunity to ride the canyon sans car, truck, and RV traffic, each May Crimestoppers of Yakima holds the Your Canyon for a Day Bike Tour, a 35-mile fundraising ride during which the road is open to bikes only.

MILEAGE LOG

0.0	From Helen McCabe State Park, head south on SR 821 S./Canyon Rd.
8.5	Umtanum Creek Recreational Site.
12.7	Squaw Creek Recreational Site.
17.3	Roza Recreational Site.
22.7	Canyon opens up. Turn around and return the same way.
45.5	Return to starting point at Helen McCabe State Park.

63 NACHES HEIGHTS–WENAS LAKE

Difficulty	Moderate
Time	2½ to 4 hours
Distance	46.5 miles
Elevation Gain	2490 feet

ROAD CONDITIONS: Low-traffic rural farm roads with chip-seal surface; some residential and urban roads.

GETTING THERE: From US Hwy 12 in Yakima, take the N. 40th Ave./Fruitvale Blvd. exit. Head south on N. 40th Ave. for 0.2 mile to the shopping center on the right.

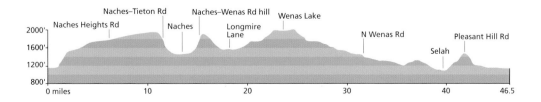

A fake elk guards this roadside ranch.

Here's a near-50-miler that scales the orchard-'n'-vineyard-rich heights above the Naches Valley before dropping down, crossing the Naches River, and heading north for the wide-open roads (and possible winds) of the Wenas Valley. The word "heights" implies climbing, no surprise that you'll have to pedal up a steep mile to get up there. The word "valley" should not imply climbing, but to get to Wenas Valley requires surmounting another mile-long spot-of-bother that's even steeper: the Naches–Wenas grade, which has pitches to 12 percent. Yikes! But this route also features a 10-plus-mile gradual descent that, aided as you'll likely be by a tailwind, should have you feeling fast and strong and 20 years younger.

From the shopping center parking lot, head west on Powerhouse Road and in just over a mile, turn left onto aptly named Naches Heights Road, which heads up in a hurry, climbing at a 7 to 9 percent grade for a mile before mellowing out at the ridge's spine. While the grade lessens, this low-traffic stretch continues climbing gradually along that spine for the next 8 miles or so, the road zigging and zagging through orchard, vineyard, and farmland. Though the road is narrow, with a come-and-go shoulder and occasionally rough chip-seal surface, the surrounding views are spectacular—soft, rounded hills and ridges extending in all directions, with mounts Adams and Rainier peeking over from afar.

Just past the 11-mile mark, now on Naches–Tieton Road, bear right and follow as the road drops like a stone into the Naches Valley, losing 500 feet of elevation in 2 miles. It's a crazy-fast descent—the shoulder narrow and guard-railed, and the vibe a bit claustro—be careful. Turn left at the bottom of the hill and, just after crossing the sparkling

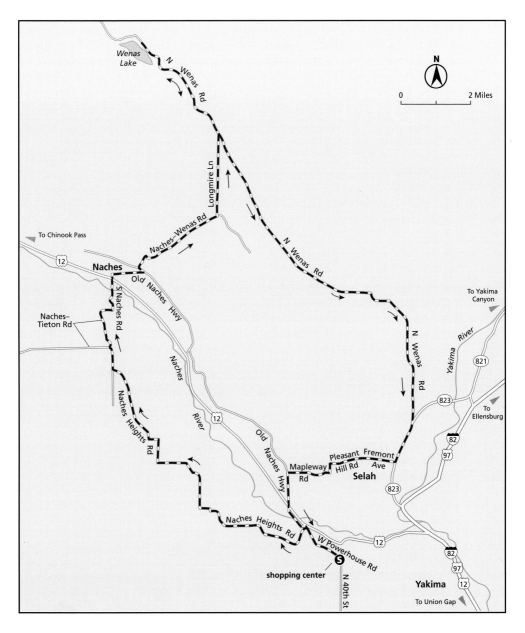

Naches River and busy US Highway 12, find yourself in the small town of Naches, which offers food and drink.

Head east out of town and at about mile 15, begin the Naches–Wenas climb—take 'er slow and easy, and you'll be fine. The truly steep part is less than a mile, and once you're on top, you'll be rewarded with a sweeping descent across a windswept, rolling, sagebrush valley. Continue north and at mile 20, turn left onto N. Wenas Road for an 8-mile out-and-back foray to Wenas Lake (where you will find a small store).

On the way out you'll likely be bucking a headwind. But the way back features a killer, 10-mile, slightly downhill stretch with a probable tailwind. How cool is that? Also cool is the Wenas Creek Mammoth, which likely lumbered across this valley some 16,000 years ago; in 2005 remnants from one of the species' bones was found in this valley and paleontological digs have been going on ever since in the hope of being able to piece more of the big critter together.

At mile 40, return to civilization (as it were), entering Selah. The last 6 miles or so follow mostly residential streets and outlying roads—with one more big hill (on ironically named Pleasant Hill Road, which climbs 370 feet in 2 miles). Just after crossing US Highway 12, you're back on W. Powerhouse Road. Follow it for 2 miles back to where you started.

MILEAGE LOG

0.0	From the shopping center parking lot in Yakima, turn right onto W. Powerhouse Rd.
1.2	Left onto Naches Heights Rd. Steep climb.
4.8	Left to stay on Naches Heights Rd.
5.0	Right to stay on Naches Heights Rd.
7.3	Right to stay on Naches Heights Rd.
8.1	Left to stay on Naches Heights Rd.
10.7	Bear right onto Naches–Tieton Rd.
11.3	Bear right to stay on Naches–Tieton Rd.
11.6	Right to stay on Naches–Tieton Rd.
12.8	Left onto S. Naches Rd.
13.7	Cross US Hwy 12. Enter Naches. Road becomes Naches Ave.
13.8	Right to stay on Naches Ave.
13.9	Right onto 2nd St.
14.1	Bear left onto Old Naches Hwy.
14.9	Left onto Naches–Wenas Rd.
15.1	Right to stay on Naches–Wenas Rd. Begin steep climb.
17.9	Left onto Longmire Ln.
20.4	Left onto N. Wenas Rd.
24.0	Turn around at Wenas Lake. Return via N. Wenas Rd.
35.9	Right to stay on N. Wenas Rd.
40.0	Right onto E. Fremont Ave.
41.1	Left onto Pleasant Hill Rd.
41.2	Left to stay on Pleasant Hill Rd.
42.0	Left onto Selah Heights Rd.
42.2	Right onto Mapleway Rd.
43.5	Left onto Old Naches Hwy.
44.4	Cross US Hwy 12; Old Naches Hwy. becomes W. Powerhouse Rd.
46.5	Return to starting point in shopping center parking lot.

64 YAKIMA–WHISTLIN' JACK

Difficulty	Strenuous
Time	3½ to 5½ hours
Distance	72.8 miles
Elevation Gain	2650 feet

ROAD CONDITIONS: Narrow farm road and state highway. Because it is an east–west corridor, SR 410 can be busy; a good time to ride this route is in the spring before the mountain passes have been cleared of snow and Chinook Pass is open all the way.

GETTING THERE: From US Hwy 12 in Yakima, take the N. 40th Ave./Fruitvale Blvd. exit. Head south on N. 40th Ave. for 0.2 mile to the shopping center on the right.

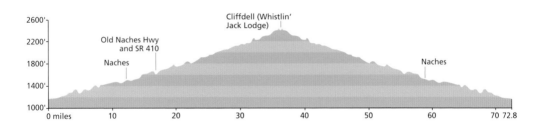

After a scenic 17-mile ramble through the agriculturally rich orchard and farmland of the Naches Valley, this route hops onto State Route 410 and heads toward Chinook Pass and the Cascade Crest. It's up to you—and seasonal snows—to decide how far you want to ride. For our purposes, we'll turn around in Cliffdell, home of Whistlin' Jack, a beloved lodge, tavern, mini-grocery, and gas station that is a veritable town unto itself.

From the shopping center, head west on W. Powerhouse Road and in little more than a mile, turn left onto S. Naches Road. The narrow, low-traffic route winds past orchards and ranchland, offering terrific views not just of the Naches River below, but to the dry hills and ridges beyond. The pavement is a bit

chippy and sections still feel as though they were only recently dug out of the hillside. Also, be careful not to get conked on the head by falling rock. But it's a terrific ride and just 4 miles from the franchise hustle and bustle, you'll feel as though you're in the middle of nowhere, more likely to come across a tractor moseying down the road than a speeding car.

Continue though this mix of farms, orchards, and fields for the next 13 miles; it's interrupted only when you cross the river and pass through the small town of Naches. The farms and fields on the north side are even more expansive. At about 17 miles, the Old Naches Highway, which you've been riding since the town of Naches, comes to an end at the intersection of US Highway 12 and State

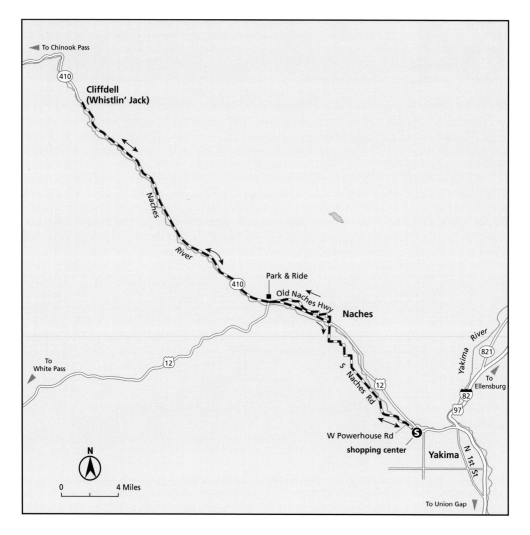

Route 410. Turn right onto 410 and with the river still by your side, head west.

The next 20 miles climb gradually to Whistlin' Jack. Also called the Chinook Scenic Byway, the road offers spectacular views up to Cleman Mountain and Bethel Ridge, and you'll enjoy that lovely, dry Eastern Washington pine smell as you enter Wenatchee National Forest. The road offers a decent shoulder, and its surface is fairly smooth, though it becomes rougher the higher it goes.

Reach Cliffdell, home to Whistlin' Jack, at mile 37. Food and drink are available here, as well as opportunities to gaze at the Naches

River while enjoying your refreshments. The return route is the same with one alteration. Assuming there's a tailwind and it's not during weekend hours when it's mobbed with traffic, continue straight onto US Highway 12 at the US Highway 12–State Route 410 intersection. Follow US Highway 12 for a little more than 4 miles to Naches. From there, turn right onto S. Naches Road and return to your starting point the way you left.

Variations: Ride all the way to Chinook Pass and back for a big day of about 130 miles with 7600 feet of elevation gain. For a shorter ride to Chinook Pass and back, start at the

Park & Ride by the intersection of US Highway 12 and State Route 410 and head to the pass from there; it's 95 miles round trip with 5800 feet elevation gain.

MILEAGE LOG

0.0	From the shopping center parking lot in Yakima, go right onto W. Powerhouse Rd.
1.5	Slight left onto S. Naches Rd.
11.9	Enter Naches. Right onto Naches Ave.
12.0	Left onto 3rd St.
12.2	Right onto Old Naches Hwy.
12.4	Left to stay on Old Naches Hwy.
13.3	Bear left to stay on Old Naches Hwy.
17.0	Right onto SR 410 W.
36.8	Turn around in Cliffdell at Whistlin' Jack. Return via SR 410 E.
56.6	Road becomes US Hwy 12.
61.0	Right onto S. Naches Rd.
70.2	Right onto W. Powerhouse Rd.
72.8	Return to starting point in shopping center parking lot.

A chilly spring ride on Old Naches Highway

65   KONNOWAC PASS LOOP

Difficulty	Easy
Time	1½ to 3 hours
Distance	28.5 miles
Elevation Gain	885 feet

ROAD CONDITIONS: Rural farm road with chip-seal surface; county highway.

GETTING THERE: From I-82/US Hwy 97/12 in Yakima, take exit 33B and head east on E. Yakima Ave., which becomes Terrace Heights Wy. Turn right on N. Keys Rd. and follow for 1 mile to Yakima Sportsman State Park, located on the right.

This mostly flat, pleasant ramble offers a taste of something that has made the Yakima Valley world famous: its vineyards and orchards. The route also passes through Union Gap, which geology geeks will recognize is the narrow canyon where the Yakima River squeezes between Ahtanum Ridge and the Rattlesnake Hills.

From Yakima Sportsman State Park, make your way south past orchards and vineyards—a horse ranch or two as well—on pancake-flat road. The surface is chip seal, but the traffic and speed limit are low. Tractors will seem as common as cars.

At about 7 miles, the road hooks up with the Yakima River (as well as with Interstate 82/US Highway 12, but those high-speed roads are safely beyond the barriers). The road pushes through Union Gap, where massive 800-foot-high ridges covered with sagebrush rise above you on both sides.

After passing under the freeway, the road becomes the Yakima Valley Highway, which

offers a decent shoulder and not too much traffic. At 14 miles, turn left onto Konnowac Pass Road and begin the route's one and only climb. Past vineyards, orchards, and other agricultural concerns—including the Yakima Agricultural Research Laboratory—the road rises gradually, not steeply. (It's as if it's afraid of offending someone.)

The surrounding hills and ridges are beautiful, but also treeless the higher you go, so this ride can be hot during the dry Eastern Washington summers. Once at the top, let 'er rip—it's a gradual descent, the road becoming smoother the lower you go, eventually ending up on the outskirts of the small town of Moxee City. From there, it's 7 more miles of flat orchard-vineyard riding across the valley floor back to Yakima Sportsman State Park.

Variations: Options are many, including continuing on Yakima Valley Highway to Zillah for about a 45-mile ride, or on to Sunnyside for about a 75-miler.

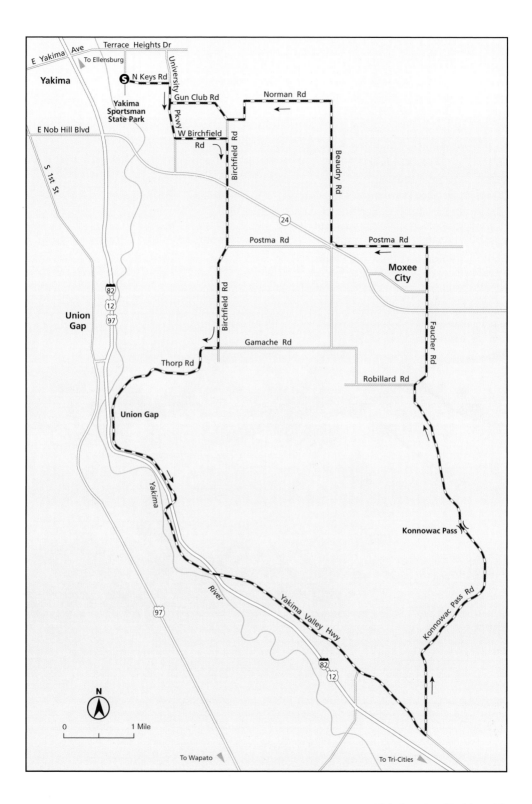

Yakima

E Yakima Ave

Terrace Heights Dr

To Ellensburg

S N Keys Rd

University

Gun Club Rd

Yakima
Sportsman
State Park

Norman Rd

E Nob Hill Blvd

S 1st St

Pkwy

W Birchfield
Rd

Birchfield Rd

Beaudry Rd

24

Postma Rd

Postma Rd

Moxee
City

82
12
97

Union
Gap

Birchfield Rd

Gamache Rd

Faucher Rd

Thorp Rd

Robillard Rd

Union Gap

Yakima

Konnowac Pass

River

97

Yakima Valley Hwy

82
12

Konnowac Pass Rd

N

0   1 Mile

To Wapato

To Tri-Cities

0.0	From Yakima Sportsman State Park, turn right onto N. Keys Rd.
0.6	Right onto University Pkwy.
1.4	Left onto W. Birchfield Rd.
2.2	Right onto Birchfield Rd.
5.1	Right onto Thorp Rd. (Becomes Yakima Valley Hwy.)
14.1	Left onto Konnowac Pass Rd.
19.8	Becomes Faucher Rd.
21.6	Left onto Postma Rd.
23.0	Right onto Beaudry Rd. (Becomes Norman Rd.)
26.4	Right to stay on Norman Rd.
26.6	Turn right onto Birchfield Rd. (Gun Club Rd.)
27.7	Right onto University Pkwy.
27.9	Left onto N. Keys Rd.
28.5	Return to starting point at Yakima Sportsman State Park.

Spring blossoms along the Yakima Valley Highway

66 KENNEWICK–CLODFELTER ROAD LOOP

Difficulty	Moderate
Time	2½ to 4 hours
Distance	45.9 miles
Elevation Gain	2375 feet

ROAD CONDITIONS: Rural farm roads with chip-seal surface; some urban riding with and without bike lanes. Several new(ish) roundabouts, with more likely to come.

GETTING THERE: Take I-82 and I-182 east toward Tri-Cities. In Richland, take I-182 exit 5A and head south on SR 240 E./George Washington Wy. for 1.5 miles. Turn left onto Columbia Park Trail and head east for 1.4 miles. Park in the Wye Park gravel parking lot to the north (Columbia River side), near the N. Columbia Center Blvd. intersection.

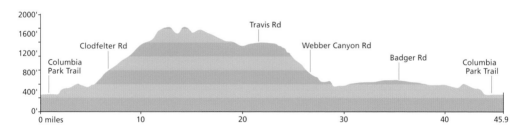

From deep in the heart of the bustling Tri-Cities, this 45-miler heads up into the Horse Heaven Hills south of town, where the traffic is just about nil and the treeless views across endless fields of grain are grand. Be aware that she's a windy one up here, as evidenced by the ever-increasing presence of giant wind turbines slowly spinning away along the nearby ridge. Near the end of this route, enjoy a pleasant 12-mile cruise through a mix of orchard-vineyard-ranch farmland, where, if you are lucky, you'll be given a push by a tailwind.

Begin by leaving Wye Park on the banks of the Columbia River and making your way west on a busy suburban roadway, passing through a roundabout or two along the

way. (The road does offer a bike lane as well as "Bikes on Road" signs.) After some careful maneuvering, turn left onto Leslie Road and begin climbing up out of the river valley. Over the next 4 miles or so, you pass through residential and gradually decreasing numbers of gas-station-fast-food-big-box sprawl—maneuvering through a couple more roundabouts—until you find yourself on Clodfelter Road, where the fun begins.

Heading up into the wide-open hills, Clodfelter leaves the Tri-Cities in its wake, climbing higher through wheat field upon wheat field. It's a low-traffic road so the minimal shoulder isn't a big deal. The climb is a fairly consistent 3 to 4 percent grade, though a couple pitches do get a bit uppity at 8 percent.

From on high, the sweeping views down to the Columbia River and her environs are tremendous. The wind? Hmm, maybe not so much. But if it's in your face now, soon enough it'll be at your back.

At about 16 miles, after a few rollers along the ridge top, head due west on straight-arrow Sellards Road before turning right and, tailwind at your back (fingers crossed), begin heading north. (Mostly shadeless; be aware that this route can be hot and the middle 35 miles offer no places to stop for liquid or other refreshment.)

At 24 miles, begin a 5-mile descent back into the valley toward Benton City through Webber Canyon, passing huge hills along the way and being treated to valley floor views of orchards and vineyards. Thankfully, the road here is smooth and the shoulder wide, so the fast drop feels safe. At the bottom, turn right on Badger Road (Benton City is 2 miles ahead should you go straight), and follow for a truly pleasant 12 miles east across the farm and ranchland valley. At Leslie Road, turn left and follow the route back to the start.

Endless fields of wheat (and wind) in the Horse Heaven Hills

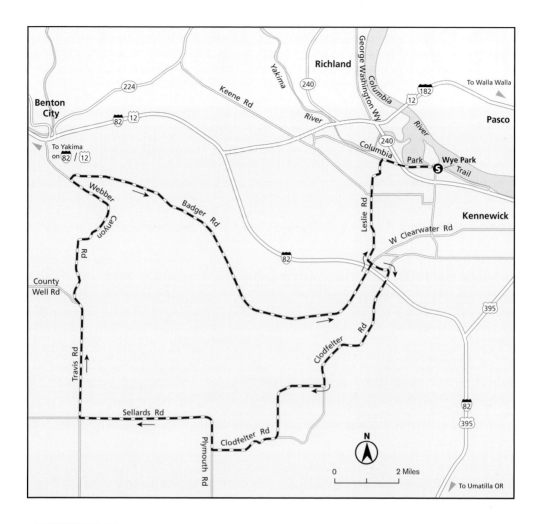

MILEAGE LOG

0.0   From Wye Park, head west on Columbia Park Trail (a paved road).
1.7   Left onto Leslie Rd.
5.8   Right onto Clodfelter Rd.
11.3 Bear left to stay on Clodfelter Rd.
15.3 Right onto Plymouth Rd. (Becomes Sellards Rd.)
20.2 Right onto Travis Rd.
23.8 Continue straight onto Webber Canyon Rd.
28.7 Right onto Badger Rd.
40.8 Left onto Leslie Rd.
44.2 Right onto Columbia Park Trail.
45.9 Return to starting point in Wye Park.

67

SPRINGDALE–HUNTERS–CHEWELAH LOOP

Difficulty	Very Strenuous
Time	4½ to 8 hours
Distance	81.7 miles
Elevation Gain	5235 feet

ROAD CONDITIONS: Rural chip-seal farm roads and some stretches of state and US highway.

GETTING THERE: From US Hwy 2 at Reardan, about 25 miles west of Spokane, head north on SR 231. In 31 miles, reach Springdale, where the highway becomes W. Shaffer Ave., Springdale's main street. Look for street parking.

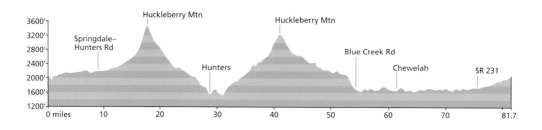

This terrific 80-some mile loop features just about everything you'd want in a ride: a couple challenging climbs; some fast sweeping downhills; a pastoral setting of farms, fields, forests, and wide-open river valleys; and rural, low-traffic roads. As a bonus, the ride swings past the Columbia River, here in its dammed Lake Roosevelt form (named for Franklin D.). A few small towns along the way—Hunters, Cedonia, Chewelah, and the start-finish town of Springdale—add a little spice and charm as well as providing places to refuel.

Heading west from Springdale, warm up with a pleasant 10 miles through Camas Valley, following various threads of Chamokane Creek. The narrow-shouldered, chip-seal sur-face road takes you through a mix of ranch-, pasture-, forest-, and farmland. Red-tailed hawks perch on about every fifth telephone pole and magpies swoop across the road.

Soon the road heads upward through dry Inland Northwest pine forest, beginning your first ascent of Huckleberry Mountain. You'll gain about 1200 feet in 8 miles, with the last 1.5 miles rising to pitches of 10 and 11 percent.

Rolling over the summit, fly down an 11-mile descent into Hunters, a small community with a corner grocery on the main (and only) corner. Located at mile 29, it's the last store you'll see for 32 miles, so to take advantage of it.

Bundle up for a winter road ride. >

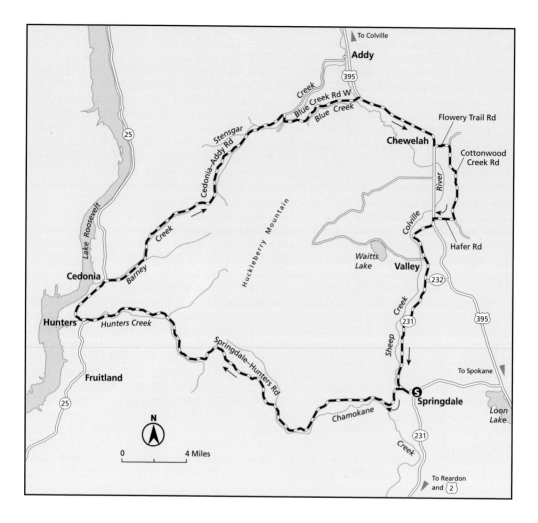

Back on the road, head north along Lake Roosevelt, climbing along a narrow-shouldered stretch of State Route 25 that can be busy with lake enthusiasts hauling their boats to the water. Thankfully, this section is short (about 3 miles) and at tiny Cedonia, you turn right onto Cedonia–Addy Road to begin your second ascent of Huckleberry Mountain, this time along its northern shoulder. Because it starts lower, this Huckleberry climb is bigger—1700 feet in 10 miles—though never as steep as the first one. Once you reach the top, you'll drop like a stone, and the freefall doesn't let up for about 13 miles. Along the way, you wind along rural farm roads, through forest, past scenic farms, and across a lovely pastoral creek valley, eventually winding up at US Highway 395.

Turn right and follow the busy, but smooth, wide-shouldered road for 6 miles into Chewelah, which has a grocery store and various other establishments from which to purchase food or drink. The remaining 20 miles south back to Springdale follow mostly flat farm roads and state highway through the Colville Valley, the river of the same name never far from view.

0.0	From Springdale, head west on SR 231.
0.7	Turn left onto Springdale–Hunters Rd.
18.0	Reach top of Huckleberry Mountain.
28.6	Right onto SR 25 N.
29.1	Enter Hunters. Right to stay on SR 25 N.
32.5	Right onto Cedonia–Addy Rd. (Eventually becomes Addy–Gifford Rd.)
41.7	Reach top of Huckleberry Mountain.
49.6	Right onto Blue Creek Rd. W.
50.1	Left to stay on Blue Creek Rd. W.
55.5	Right onto US Hwy 395 S.
61.5	Cheweleh. Left onto E. Main Ave. (Becomes Flowery Trail Rd.)
62.4	Right onto Cottonwood Creek Rd.
64.4	Take the first right onto Cottonwood Creek Rd./Lower Cottonwood Rd.
67.3	Right onto Hafer Rd.
68.6	Left onto US Hwy 395 S.
68.8	Right onto SR 231 S.
81.7	Return to starting point in Springdale.

68 MOUNT SPOKANE

Difficulty	Strenuous
Time	3 to 6 hours
Distance	55.7 miles
Elevation Gain	4740 feet

ROAD CONDITIONS: Everything from rural farm roads to state highway to narrow, winding, chip-seal mountain road. Best to ride during weekdays or early on weekend mornings to beat the crowds. *Note:* Because of heavy snowfall, the last 4 miles of road to the summit are clear of snow most years from sometime in May until sometime in October.

GETTING THERE: From I-90 in Spokane, head north on US Hwy 2/395 for 7 miles to Country Homes (a sprawling and ironically named suburb) to North Division Bicycle Shop. Park here or look for parking a couple blocks west at Whitworth College or at any of the nearby shopping areas.

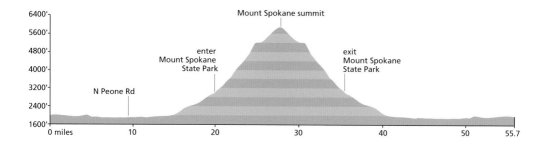

For riders ever on the hunt for roads that point endlessly upward, here's the Lilac City's offering: Mount Spokane, centerpiece for both Mount Spokane Ski and Snowboard Park and Mount Spokane State Park. Depending on how much of the road to the top is open, riders can climb all the way to almost 6000 feet (5883 ft.), a 13-mile, 3800-foot ascent in one shot. Ooh, me likee.

Of course, big mountain climbs mean big vistas and this is no exception: when conditions are right one can see not only the entire Spokane metro area but all the way to Canada and Montana.

From North Division Bicycle Shop near Whitworth University, head east on E. Hawthorne Road through a suburban sprawl of retail and fast-food franchises. Thankfully,

Nearing the summit of Mount Spokane (Mike Sirott)

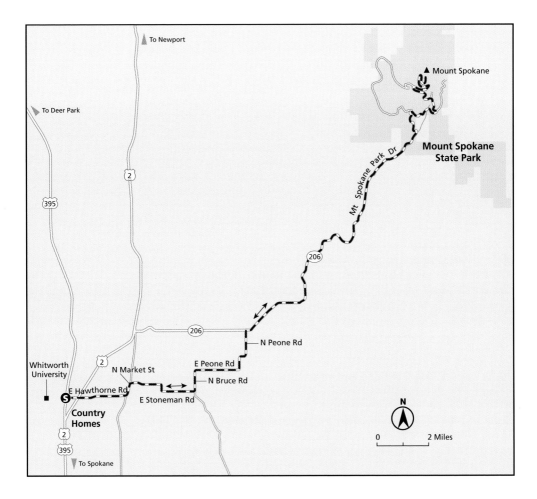

in about 2 miles, the road takes a turn for the rural, and soon enough you are pedaling through the rich agricultural fields northeast of Spokane, a land of tidy farms, ranches, combines, and tractors, with big-ticket farmhouses overlooking all.

At about 10 miles, turn right onto State Route 206 and before you looms daunting Mount Spokane, towering over the surrounding Selkirk Mountains. At about 15 miles, swing to the right and begin the climb, pedaling upward through forest on a chipseal mountain road. With Deadman Creek tumbling down the hill just to the right, the climb's first 6 miles aren't particularly steep. It's not until you enter Mount Spokane State

Park that the climb starts getting serious, entering (and remaining in) the 8 to 11 percent range. Consolations are that the road is smoother and a bit wider once inside the park and that the climb is shaded.

Continue up as far as the snow level and road closure gates allow, turning left onto N. Summit Road at mile 24 (turning right leads to the cross-country ski trails) and following it for 4 more switchbacking, elevation-gobbling miles to the top. (This 4-mile road to the top is often gated because of heavy snowfall.) Enjoy the views, catch your breath, and when you're ready, head back down, taking care on the narrow road's many turns. Return the way you came to your starting point.

0.0	From North Division Bike Shop, go left onto E. Hawthorne Rd.
2.5	Left onto N. Market St./Pend Oreille Hwy. (May be unsigned.)
2.9	Right onto E. Parksmith Dr./E. Stoneman Rd. (May be unsigned.)
5.7	Left onto N. Bruce Rd. (N. Argonne Rd.)
6.4	Right onto E. Peone Rd.
8.0	Bear left to stay on E. Peone Rd. (Becomes N. Peone Rd.)
9.7	Right onto SR 206. (Becomes Mount Spokane Park Dr.)
15.0	Climb begins.
20.8	Enter Mount Spokane State Park.
23.9	Left onto N. Summit Rd.
24.2	Bear left to stay on N. Summit Rd.
25.0	Bear left to stay on N. Summit Rd.
25.6	Sharp right to stay on N. Summit Rd.
27.9	Reach the summit! Turn around to head back down.
30.1	Sharp left to stay on N. Summit Rd.
30.7	Bear right to stay on N. Summit Rd.
31.5	Bear right to stay on N. Summit Rd.
31.8	Right onto N. Mount Spokane Park Dr.
46.0	Left onto N. Peone Rd.
46.9	Bear right to stay on N. Peone Rd.
49.3	Left onto N. Bruce Rd.
50.1	Right onto E. Stoneman Rd.
52.8	Turn left onto N. Market St./Pend Oreille Hwy.
53.3	Right onto E. Hawthorne Rd.
55.7	Right onto N. Division St.; return to your starting place.

69   CHENEY–ROCK LAKE LOOP

Difficulty	Strenuous
Time	4 to 6½ hours
Distance	76.1 miles
Elevation Gain	3160 feet

ROUTE CONDITIONS: Low-traffic rural Palouse farm roads with chip-seal surface. One stretch of not-too-busy state highway.

GETTING THERE: From I-90/US Hwy 395 between Cheney and Spokane, take exit 270. Head south on SR 904 (Lt. Col. Michael P. Anderson Memorial Hwy.) for 7 miles into Cheney, where it becomes W. 1stSt. Park in the public lot on the left just past the intersection of K and 1st streets or in the grocery store parking lot across the street.

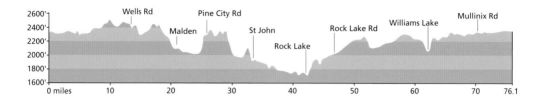

Here's a route that's mind-boggling in its diversity. From the rollout in Cheney, home of Eastern Washington University, it passes through lovely Inland Northwest pine forest and pasture before delving into the Palouse, Washington's wheat- and lentil-growing mecca and landscape of high rounded mounds that follow one after another—in all directions—seemingly forever. Riding twixt and around these dry, treeless hills—some

Riders take turns at the front of the paceline in the annual Cheney–Rock Lake road race. (Kimberly Brittain)

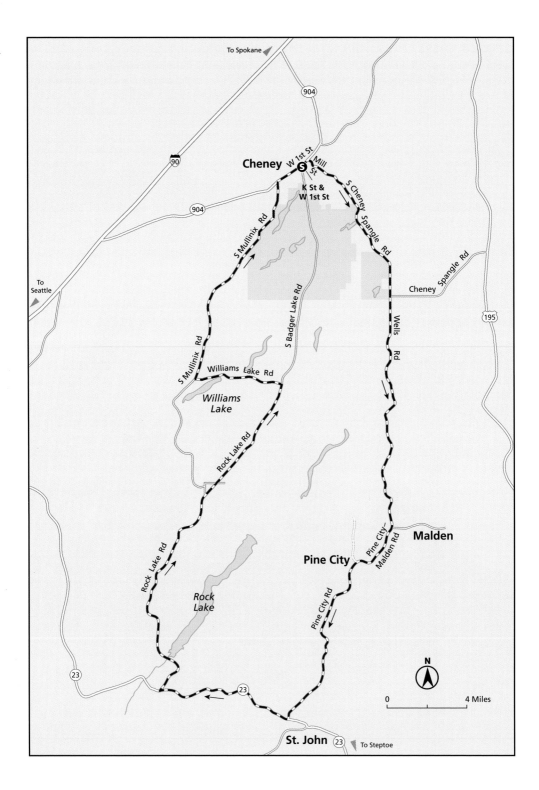

To Spokane

904

To Seattle

I-90

904

Cheney

W 1st St

Mill St

S

K St & W 1st St

S Cheney Spangle Rd

Spangle Rd

S Mullinix Rd

Cheney Spangle Rd

195

S Badger Lake Rd

Wells Rd

S Mullinix Rd

Williams Lake Rd

Williams Lake

Rock Lake Rd

Rock Lake Rd

Rock Lake

Malden

Pine City

Pine City–Malden Rd

Pine City Rd

N

23

23

St. John

23

To Steptoe

0

4 Miles

of them hundreds of feet high—burns one's quads and hammies, that's for sure. But in a good way, a hurts-so-good way. (Thanks for this route to the Spokane Rocket Velo club members, who use it for their annual Cheney–Rock Lake Road Race.)

Head south out of town via S. Cheney Spangle Road through a mix of open forest and farmland, passing a peaceful pond and assuming that this will be your landscape for the next 70 miles. Au contraire, mon frère. At about 8 miles, you emerge from the forest and into the Palouse: humpy hillocks of wheat and grain that extend in all directions. It's shadeless and likely windy, so put your head down and have fun, following one lovely ribbon of road after another as they wind up, down, and around and around these lumps and bumps. These mini-mountains of wheat are multi-hued too, and vary in color throughout the seasons, from spring green to summer gold, to rich, dark tones after the fall harvest.

Much of the rest of the route passes through this hilly landscape. As for places to stop for food and drink, the route doesn't pass through any towns per se, but a couple—Malden, at mile 21, and St. John, at mile 33—are less than a mile off the route (see Mileage Log).

At mile 33, turn right onto State Route 23, a slightly busier roadway that follows Cottonwood Creek, cutting through the hills and even trending downhill for the next 7 miles (although your pace may be slowed by a headwind). At mile 40, turn right onto Rock Lake Road and resume roller-coastering the hills, passing Rock Lake along the way. At about mile 52, reach a stretch of straight-arrow road through open pastureland that just begs to be hammered as hard as you can. So, go for it!

Just ahead, reenter that mix of forest and farmland that began this route. After turning left onto Williams Lake Road—and gritting it out up a short steep pitch—turn right onto S. Mullinix Road and begin the homestretch back to Cheney. Along the way, enjoy a ride-by of Turnbull National Wildlife Refuge, with more than 130 marshes, wetlands, and lakes.

MILEAGE LOG

0.0	In Cheney, head north from the public parking lot on W. 1st St.
0.4	Right onto S. Cheney Spangle Rd.
8.9	Continue straight onto Wells Rd.
21.0	Right onto Pine City–Malden Rd. (Malden is a couple hundred yards to the left.)
23.7	Left onto Pine City Rd.
33.0	Turn right onto SR 23 (St. John is a half mile to the left.)
40.4	Turn right onto Rock Lake Rd.
58.9	Left onto Williams Lake Rd.
63.5	Right onto S. Mullinix Rd.
74.7	Turn right onto W. 1st St./SR 904.
76.1	Return to starting point in Cheney.

Difficulty	Strenuous
Time	3 to 5½ hours
Distance	64.4 miles
Elevation Gain	3275 feet

ROAD CONDITIONS: Low-traffic state highway and rural farm roads with varying shoulder widths; narrow mountain road to the top of Steptoe Butte.

GETTING THERE: From I-90 in Sprague, north of Ritzville, take exit 245. Head east on SR 23 for 43 miles to US Hwy 195. Turn right and head south for 10 miles to Colfax and SR 272. Turn left onto SR 272 and follow for 11 miles to Palouse. In town (and in quick succession), turn right on N. Fir St., left on W. Whitman St., right on N. Mill St., and right onto W. Main St. Park at Hayton Green Park, just ahead on the left.

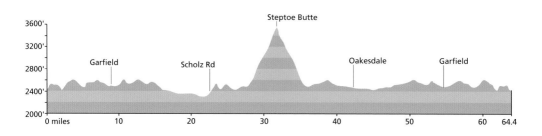

This route's calling card is Steptoe Butte, a quartzite mound that rises more than a thousand feet above the surrounding Palouse Hills. Though steep in parts, the climb is only about 3 miles long and since you reach the summit not by switching back and forth but by spiraling around the mountain, you are treated to 360-degree views all the way up.

Start in the town of Palouse and head north on State Route 27 on chip-seal roads that head north through dry open fields and hills, offering a decent enough shoulder but absolutely no shade. (There's none anywhere on the route.)

Reach Garfield at 9 miles (food and drink opportunities available), and after passing through town, continue 3 more miles to Dry Creek Road, where you turn left. Second verse same as the first—a Palouse landscape of hilly fields of grain broken up by the occasional farmhouse 'n' grain silo compound. At about the 28-mile mark, enter Steptoe Butte State Park and soon find yourself at the foot of Steptoe Butte.

This is not the toughest climb in the book, but its spiraling ascent of the butte makes it a one-of-a-kind. Expect a consistent 6 to 8 percent grade, with the steepest pitches (up to 12 percent) in the first third. From the top, the surrounding humps and bumps resemble ocean swells, albeit green,

From Steptoe Butte, the wheat fields of the Palouse appear to change color at the whim of the clouds.

gold, and brown ones, and when clouds pass over, they reveal even more shades from the hills' multi-hued repertoire.

Because the road is narrow and rough, take great care on the descent and keep an eye open for car and RV traffic. At the bottom, head left out of the park onto Hume Road and in 7 miles, reach Oakesdale, where you'll find places for food and drink. From Oakesdale, it's 20 miles of Palouse riding to Palouse, the repeated rollers keeping you on your toes.

MILEAGE LOG

0.0	From Hayton Green Park in Palouse, turn right onto W. Main St.
0.2	Left onto SR 27 N./Division St.
9.1	Garfield.
12.0	Left onto Dry Creek Rd.
22.5	Right onto US Hwy 195 N.
23.0	Right onto Scholz Rd.
24.1	Bear right onto Hume Rd.
28.1	Left into Steptoe Butte State Park.
32.2	Reach the top! Turn around and head back down.
36.3	Left onto Hume Rd.
43.5	Right onto SR 27 S. (Oakesdale is 0.3 mile ahead to the left.)
54.8	Garfield.
64.1	Right onto W. Main St. in Palouse.
64.4	Return to starting point at Hayton Green Park.

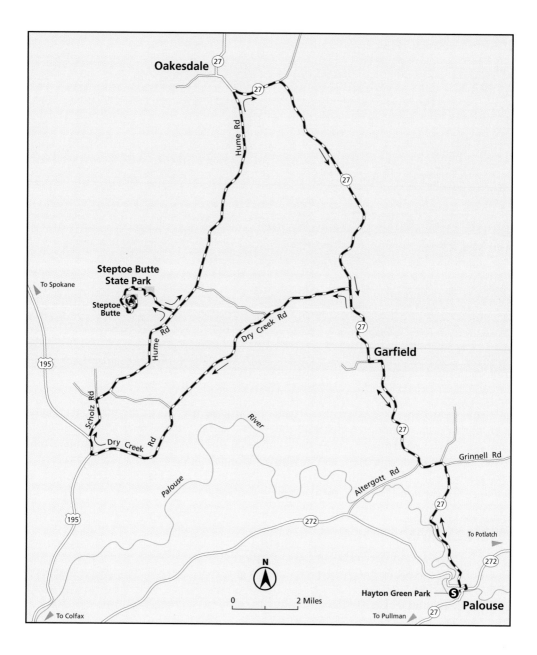

Oakesdale

To Spokane

Steptoe Butte
State Park

Steptoe
Butte

Hume Rd

Dry Creek Rd

Garfield

Scholz Rd

Dry Creek Rd

Palouse

River

Altergott Rd

Grinnell Rd

To Potlatch

272

N

0   2 Miles

Hayton Green Park

Palouse

To Colfax

To Pullman

71 DAYTON–BLUEWOOD SKI AREA

Difficulty	Moderate
Time	2½ to 4 hours
Distance	43.4 miles
Elevation Gain	3320 feet

ROAD CONDITIONS: Low-traffic, rural mountain road with chip-seal surface.

GETTING THERE: From Walla Walla, head northeast on US Hwy 12 for 31 miles to Dayton. In town, the highway becomes Main St.; look for street parking near the E. Main St. intersection with S. 4th St.

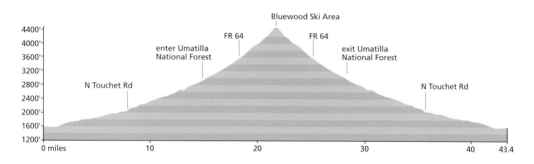

Most roads to ski areas switch back and forth ever more steeply, tightening the screws the higher one goes. Not so N. Touchet Road, which takes you from charming downtown Dayton to the 4300-foot level of southeast Washington's Blue Mountains and Bluewood Ski Area via nary a switchback and at a gentle gradient that's rarely more than 4 percent.

Pedaling the pleasant wide streets of Dayton, head south out of town following signs for the ski area. Soon find yourself on N. Touchet Road, which follows the North Fork of the Touchet River as it begins its gradual ascent of the Blue Mountains. At first you pass through a short stretch of the big rounded hills characteristic of southeast Washington, overlain with open farms and ranches as well as fringes of forest. Gradually, however, those forest fringes become the predominant landscape and by 11 miles, you're riding a narrow mountain road in the woods. In 4 miles, you enter Umatilla National Forest and the road becomes Forest Road 64.

The road surface can be rough in stretches—mountain roads tend to get beaten up by the weather—and the shoulder narrow or nonexistent, but traffic is so minimal that it doesn't matter too much. Reach the ski area just before mile 22. Eat, drink, slap yourself on the back, and then head down. Hopefully, you've packed a jacket as this zippy descent can be nippy.

Variation: Add this to the Walla Walla–Middle Waitsburg Loop (Tour 72) for a killer 95-mile route that climbs about 6500 feet.

0.0   In Dayton, head north on E. Main St. toward S. 4th St.
0.1   Right onto S. 4th St. (Becomes N. Touchet Road)
15.0   Enter Umatilla National Forest; road becomes FR 64.
21.6   Bluewood Ski Area. Turn around; head back down.
42.0   Reenter Dayton, now on S. 4th St.
43.3   Left onto E. Main St.
43.4   Return to your starting point in Dayton.

Built in 1887, Dayton's Columbia County Courthouse is the oldest operating courthouse in the state.

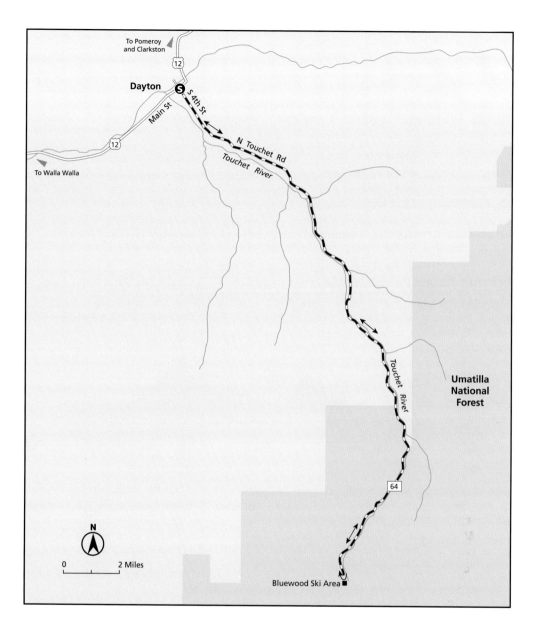

To Pomeroy
and Clarkston

12

Dayton

S 4th St

Main St

12

To Walla Walla

N Touchet Rd

Touchet River

Touchet River

**Umatilla
National
Forest**

64

N

0   2 Miles

Bluewood Ski Area

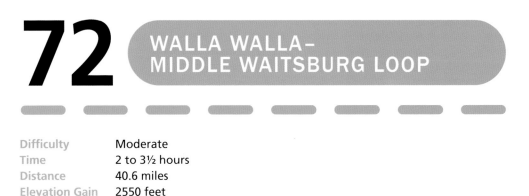

72 WALLA WALLA– MIDDLE WAITSBURG LOOP

Difficulty	Moderate
Time	2 to 3½ hours
Distance	40.6 miles
Elevation Gain	2550 feet

ROAD CONDITIONS: Rural farm roads with chip-seal surface; busy US highway with wide shoulder.

GETTING THERE: From the Tri-Cities area, head east on US Hwy 12 to Walla Walla. Once in town, exit onto E. Rees Ave. and park at Borleske Stadium just ahead on the left.

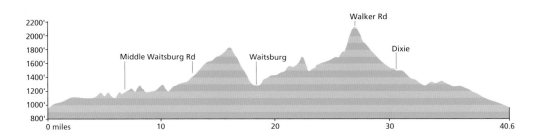

This classic loop heads north, snaking its way up, down, and around the rollercoaster wheat fields 'twixt Walla Walla and the small town of Waitsburg. Mostly following low-traffic farm roads, this route features plenty of hills (and views), but most are not very big and you'll likely find yourself picking bugs out of your teeth from smiling during so many fun descents. (Parts of this route are featured on the Tour of Walla Walla road race and time trial.)

From the Borleske Stadium parking lot, wind your way north out of Walla Walla—taking great care when crossing US Highway 12 (there's no traffic light)—and turn right onto Middle Waitsburg Road. It's your magic carpet for the next 17 miles as you surf the great rounded hills of wheat. The road shoul-

der is narrow, but the traffic level is low and there are "Bikes on Road" signs. (Do be aware that, sadly, in 2011, there was a bicycle fatality on this road when a cyclist was struck by a vehicle.) With no trees on the route, shade is nil (prepare accordingly) and in these hills, winds can seem to come from several directions at once. (In general, Walla Walla winds are from the south.)

Most of the hills are quick ups and downs, but at about mile 11, they begin trending upward and for the next 5 miles, gain about 100 feet of elevation per mile, the payoff being that at mile 16, you commence a fun, fast, smooth descent to Waitsburg.

After a quick left into and right out of Waitsburg (places to refuel here if you need), head out onto even more rural farmland on

Racers roll out of Waitsburg during the annual Tour of Walla Walla.

Wilson Hollow Road. More farms and fields of grain follow as well as some gentle rollers. After about 3.5 miles on this road, pavement ends and you come to an unsigned fork in the road. Panic not. Take the right fork, crest a small hill, and pavement immediately resumes. After a short descent, turn left onto Coppei Road and follow Coppei Creek for more farmland foraying.

Continue for another 3 miles or so of way-off-the-beaten-path rural riding, slightly (just slightly) uphill much of the way, before swinging to the right onto Walker Road and commencing a steep 1-mile climb out of the hollow, with a pitch or two at 10 percent. Once over, find yourself at the 28-mile mark and an intersection with US Highway 12, where you turn left.

The remaining 12 miles back to Walla Walla are downhill and flat, and though Highway 12 is certainly busier than the other roads on this route, it offers a wide shoulder and smooth surface. At mile 30, pass through the small town of Dixie, which has a small market, and then pedal on to your starting point in Walla Walla.

Variations: Add this to the Dayton–Bluewood Ski Area route (Tour 71) for a killer 95-mile route that climbs about 6500 feet. Add it to the Kooskooskie–Cottonwood Ride (Tour 73) for a 72-mile route with about 4100 feet of ups.

MILEAGE LOG

0.0	From Borleske Stadium in Walla Walla, turn left onto E. Rees Ave.
0.2	Left onto E. Sumach St.
0.5	Bear left to stay on E. Sumach St.
0.7	Left onto N. Clinton St.

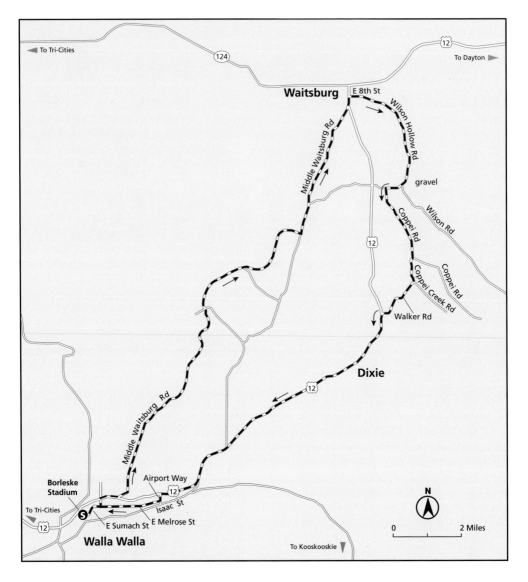

0.8   Carefully cross US Hwy 12.
0.9   Right onto Middle Waitsburg Rd.
10.9   Bear right to stay on Middle Waitsburg Rd.
17.9   Left onto US Hwy 12 E.
18.2   Right onto E. 8th St. (Becomes Wilson Hollow Rd.)
22.2   Short gravel stretch; bear right at fork onto McCown Rd. (May be unsigned.)
22.9   Left onto Coppei Rd.
25.4   Right onto S. Fork Coppei Creek Rd.
26.2   Right onto Walker Rd.
27.8   Left onto US Hwy 12 W.
30.1   Dixie.

37.3	Left onto Airport Wy.
37.8	Right onto E. Melrose St.
40.1	Bear left onto E. Sumach St.
40.4	Right onto E. Rees Ave.
40.6	Right to your starting point at Borleske Stadium.

73 KOOSKOOSKIE–COTTONWOOD RIDE

Difficulty	Moderate
Time	2 to 3 hours
Distance	38.7 miles
Elevation Gain	1780 feet

ROAD CONDITIONS: Rural farm and mountain roads with chip-seal surface; some city streets with and without bike lanes.

GETTING THERE: From the Tri-Cities area, head east on US Hwy 12 to Walla Walla. Once in town, exit onto E. Rees Ave. and park at Borleske Stadium, just ahead on the left.

Face it: Kooskooskie, that tiny unincorporated spot on the map just to the right and a little below Walla Walla, is fun to say. Try it: *Kooskooskie.* It makes for a fun ride too—a 15-mile (one-way) jaunt in which the landscape transforms from open fields of waving grain to a forested canyon in the lower reaches of the Blue Mountains. Turn around where pavement ends (and Oregon begins) and enjoy a killer return ride. The route

finishes with a 12-mile loop past orchards, vineyards, and of course, wheat fields, south of town.

Head east out of town on E. Isaacs Avenue, which, just past Walla Walla Community College, becomes Mill Creek Road. You'll follow this for the next 10 miles all the way to Kooskooskie on the Washington-Oregon border. At about the 5-mile mark, bear left at the fork intersection to stay on Mill Creek

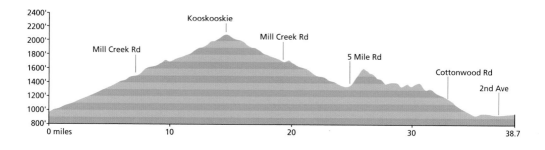

A lone rider has the roads and hills just about all to himself.

Road. (On the way back from Kooskooskie, you'll go left here onto 5 Mile Road.)

What follows is a lazy, slightly uphill meander past orchards, tony wineries, and vineyards, and to the left, amber Walla Walla wheat fields. Rushing Mill Creek chatters through greenery in the hollow to the right. The rural road is somewhat narrow and the shoulder vague, but traffic is light and hopefully, the multiple "Bikes on Road" signs alert drivers to your presence. (These signs are on most roads throughout this route. Creepily, it's not unusual to see one riddled with bullet holes.)

Climbing gradually—1100 feet in 15 miles—the route becomes more and more forested until you find yourself at the end of the pavement. There's no sign for Kooskooskie, it's too small to be a town, but the sign for Camp Kiwanis here pretty much marks the Washington-Oregon border and our turnaround spot.

Heading back, throw it into the big chain ring in front and one of the tiny gears in back and let 'er rip—the 2 and 3 percent descent is the kind that makes you feel stronger than the most doped-up rider on a Five-Hour Energy binge. Just be sure that you're not going so fast that you miss the hard left turn (135-degree) onto 5 Mile Road.

After a steep 1-mile climb, the next 9 miles follow mostly mellow farm roads that wander through the area's rich agricultural bounty on display in wheat fields, orchards, and vineyards. One particularly scenic stretch on 5 Mile sweeps below the rolling foothills of the Blue Mountains with views up toward Kooskooskie.

At 36 miles, reenter Walla Walla from the south and make your way through the pleasant college town via city streets, most with bike lanes.

0.0   From Borleske Stadium in Walla Walla, turn left onto E. Rees Ave.

0.2   Left onto E. Sumach St.

0.5   Bear right onto E. Melrose St.

2.7   Right onto Airport Wy.

2.8   Left onto E. Isaacs Ave.

3.8   Continue straight now on Mill Creek Rd.

5.3   Bear left to stay on Mill Creek Rd.

14.7   Kooskooskie turnaround. Return the same way.

24.3   Sharp left onto 5 Mile Rd. (Becomes Russell Creek Rd.)

27.8   Left onto Foster Rd.

28.7   Bear right to stay on Foster Rd.

30.7   Right onto Cottonwood Rd.

34.7   Bear right to stay on Cottonwood Rd.

36.2   Left onto Spruce St.; immediate right onto S. 2nd Ave.

38.1   Right onto E. Cherry St.

38.3   Left onto N. Palouse St.

38.4   Right onto E. Pine St.

38.6   Right onto E. Rees Ave.

38.7   Left to return to your starting point at Borleske Stadium.

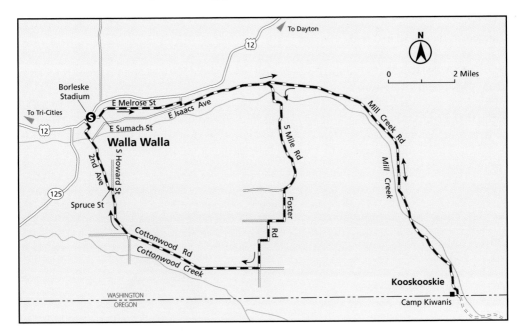

CROSS-STATE ROUTES

Though each of these state-crossing routes is roughly 330 miles long, it's hard to imagine how they could be more dissimilar. The east–west Anacortes-to-Spokane route crosses two big mountain passes—Washington and Loup Loup—while showcasing everything from the state's lush forests to the high, dry desert of Eastern Washington. Conversely, much of the north–south Blaine-to-Vancouver route stays low, hugging shoreline, lakefront, and river-bed while passing through a major metropolitan area and numerous small cities and towns.

74 ANACORTES TO SPOKANE (ONE-WAY)

Difficulty	Very Strenuous
Time	3 to 6 days or more
Distance	331.6 miles
Elevation Gain	18,650 feet

ROAD CONDITIONS: Everything from smooth, wide-shouldered roads to narrow, rural farm roads with chunky chip seal.

GETTING THERE: Take I-5 to exit 230 in Burlington and head west on SR 20 for 12 miles. Continue straight on SR 20 Spur for 3 more miles to Commercial Ave. and bear right, following for 1.3 miles into Anacortes to 15th St. Park in the shopping center on the right or look for on-street parking.

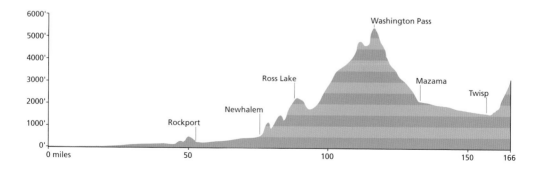

Under the bluest of Eastern Washington skies, riders pedal away the morning's chill.

Just as there are multiple ways to skin a cat, there are multiple routes via which to cross the roughly 330 miles of Washington State. To include the most spectacular route across the Cascades—Rainy and Washington passes—as well as the highest and most challenging one, this ride follows Highway 20 east to the Columbia River, throwing in 4020-foot-high Loup Loup Pass along the way.

The route begins at Anacortes where, after making your way across Fidalgo Bay via the Tommy Thompson Parkway trestle bridge, you traverse the Skagit Flats on State Route 20 and head toward Sedro-Woolley. "Gateway to the North Cascades," reads the town sign, which should let you know what you're in for. But not for many miles yet, for the true climbing won't start until about the 77-mile

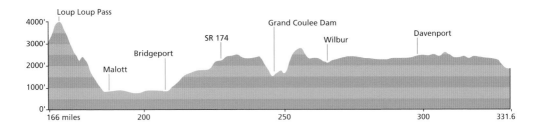

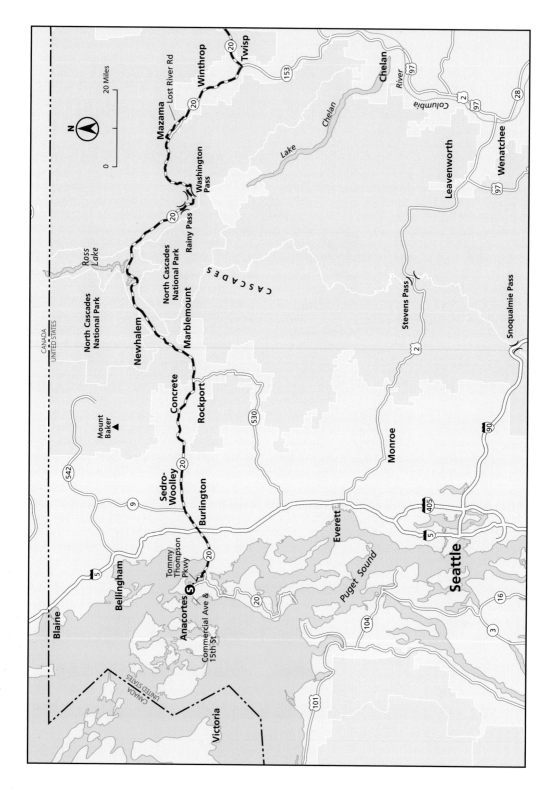

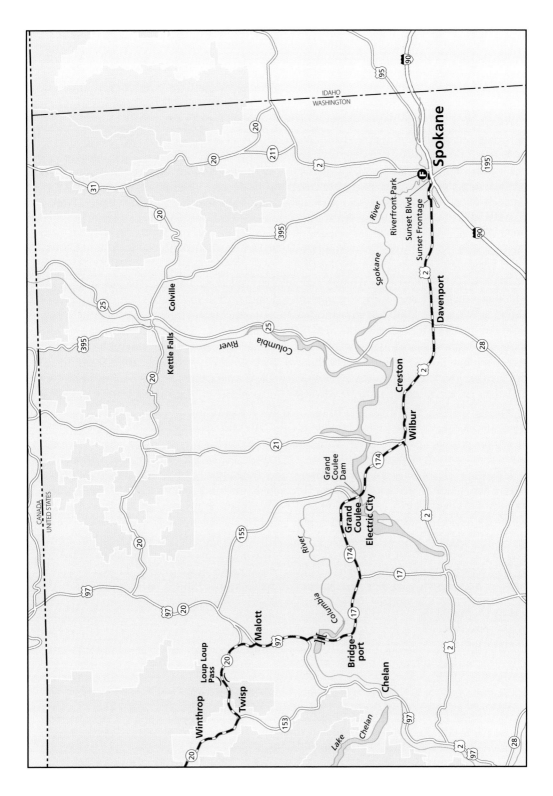

mark at the Seattle City Light company town of Newhalem. Until that point, State Route 20 (also known as the North Cascades Highway) passes through small towns such as Concrete, Rockport, and Marblemount.

(Reached at mile 62, Marblemount is the last chance to credit-card camp—that is, stay in a motel—for about 75 miles until you reach Mazama. There are, however, a number of campgrounds—Newhalem Creek and Goodell Creek in Newhalem, and Colonial Creek at mile 86—along the way. Also bear in mind that cell service is sketchy to nonexistent on most of the Newhalem to Mazama stretch.)

At Newhalem, where a small general store presents your last chance to resupply until Mazama—the road begins angling upward, climbing more than 5000 feet over the next 44 miles, much of it gradually. The final 3.4 miles, however, which culminates with 5477-foot Washington Pass—gain 900 feet. Enjoy the views at the Washington Pass Overlook, and then let 'er rip down into the Methow Valley and Winthrop, reached at mile 149. Many places here to eat and stay, both indoors and under the stars. Pearrygin Lake State Park is just 4 miles north of Winthrop.

Following the course of the Methow River, the gradual descent continues for another 11 miles through Twisp before State Route 20 leaves the river behind and begins the 8-mile, 2100-foot climb to Loup Loup Pass. Mileage-wise, the top of the pass (mile 171) is a hair past the halfway point of this route. Climbing-wise, it's way past halfway, since you've climbed about 13,000 feet so far. The rest of the route climbs *only* about 5600 more feet.

Enjoy another big, fast descent, this one into the Okanogan Valley. Cross the Okanogan River at Malott (food and drink opps here) and head south to the Chief Joseph Bridge (just west of Chief Joseph Dam) where, at the 209-mile mark, you cross the Columbia River at Bridgeport. (Nearby Bridgeport State Park offers camping, and Brewster, about 10 miles west of Bridgeport, offers a motel.)

Now on the south side of the Columbia River, climb up and across the Columbia Plateau—not as steep as the earlier Washington Pass and Loup Loup climbs but at 25 miles long, a grind in its own right—and at mile 246, after a long sweeping descent, reach Grand Coulee Dam. It's one of the world's largest concrete structures as well as the largest hydroelectric producer in the United States. The towns of Grand Coulee and Electric City offer plenty of places to eat, drink, and lodge for the night.

Another steady climb out of the Columbia River/Banks Lake/Roosevelt Lake basin ensues before the route makes a beeline for US Highway 2 and Wilbur at mile 266. From here, the route follows US Highway 2 across the state's channeled scablands and wheat fields, passing through small towns such as Creston, Davenport, and Reardan before entering the Spokane metropolitan area. After some urban maneuvering, the route ends at Spokane's beautiful Riverfront Park.

MILEAGE LOG

0.0   From the shopping center in downtown Anacortes, head south on Commercial Ave.
0.3   Left onto 17th St.
0.4   Right onto Tommy Thompson Pkwy.
3.4   Slight right onto March's Point Rd.
4.3   Left onto S. March Point Rd.
6.7   Right to stay on S. March Point Rd.
7.8   Left onto SR 20.

16.0	Burlington.
21.0	Sedro-Woolley.
33.4	Right onto Hamilton Cemetery Rd.
44.6	Concrete.
62.0	Marblemount.
77.0	Newhalem.
113.3	Rainy Pass.
118.3	Washington Pass.
135.6	Lost River Rd. to Mazama.
148.8	Winthrop.
160.1	Left to stay on SR 20 E.
171.2	Loup Loup Pass.
183.3	Right onto B and O Access Rd.
187.2	Left onto Old Hwy 97.
187.3	Right onto B and O Rd. Malott. Cross Okanogan River.
187.7	Right onto US Hwy 97 S.
199.3	Left toward SR 17 S.
201.0	Left to stay on SR 17 S.
208.8	Cross Columbia River near Bridgeport.
225.0	Slight left onto SR 174 E.
246.0	Grand Coulee and Grand Coulee Dam.
265.8	Left onto US Hwy 2. Wilbur.
275.1	Creston.
295.8	Davenport.
326.4	Left onto W. Sunset Frontage Rd.
327.0	Right onto S. Grove Rd.
327.0	Left onto W. Sunset Hwy.
329.7	Slight left onto W. Sunset Blvd.
329.9	Slight left to stay on W. Sunset Blvd.
330.2	Right onto W. 3rd Ave.
330.6	Left onto N. Howard St.
331.6	Arrive Riverfront Park in Spokane.

75

BLAINE TO VANCOUVER (ONE WAY)

Difficulty	Very Strenuous
Time	3 to 6 days or more
Distance	329.7 miles
Elevation Gain	10,830 feet

ROAD CONDITIONS: Everything from urban streets to paved bike trail to busy smooth-surface state highway to rural farm roads with chunky chip seal.

GETTING THERE: From I-5 exit 276 in Blaine, head toward Blaine City Center. Turn left onto Peace Portal Dr. and just ahead, right onto Marine Dr. Follow for 0.3 mile into Blaine Marina Park. Park here.

This north-to-south state-crossing route scrolls through a mind-boggling array of Western Washington landscapes and terrains: from the glistening waters of the Strait of Georgia and Puget Sound to rural farmland and rolling prairies to one of the country's major metropolitan areas, and just about everything in between. The route takes advantage of some of the region's great paved trails too, including Snohomish County's Centennial Trail, King County's Interurban Trail, and the Yelm–Tenino. The only thing missing? Big mountains: the route runs parallel to (and not across) the Cascades. Still, it finds a way to serve up almost 11,000 feet of climbing.

Note: While certainly this route has some segments through low-population areas, unlike the Anacortes-to-Spokane cross-state route, this one has no truly remote stretches. Thus food, drink, and lodging/camping opportunities are never very far away.

Leave Blaine by heading south along Drayton Harbor and Birch Bay before cutting inland and making your way through rural flatlands into Bellingham. After a pleasant city- and bayside meander, hop on famed Chuckanut Drive for a 10-mile, cliff-hugging jaunt that snakes along the lower flanks of forested Chuckanut Mountain high above Samish Bay.

At 44 miles, pop out of the woods and onto the wide-open Skagit Flats, a popular

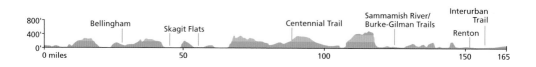

cycling destination that for the next 20-plus miles features almost no hills. Depending on the time of year, hawks, eagles, swans, snow geese, tulips, and daffodils are among this area's calling cards. Head inland on a couple state highways—534 and 9—and reach Arlington at the 83-mile mark. Here, you get to take advantage of the paved Centennial Trail and say good-bye to motorized traffic for the next 23 miles, until you arrive in Snohomish. (**Note:** Work on the Centennial Trail continues and in the future you will be able to substitute even more of State Route 9 with paved trail.)

From Snohomish, the route begins its approach to the Seattle metro area, the landscape gradually transforming from open forest and farmland to residential and eventually, urban. Reach Woodinville at mile 120, where, after a deft maneuver or two through a sprawly intersection, the route returns to paved trail—first the Sammamish River and then the granddaddy of them all, the Burke-Gilman.

Fifteen miles of paved pathway later, reach the University of Washington campus, where the route begins basically following that of the mega-popular Seattle to Portland Bicycle Classic (the STP). Following a network of connecting city streets and arterials through neighborhoods and along Lake Washington, the route serves up an urban riding experience that includes another paved trail: an 11-mile stretch of the Interurban through Kent and Auburn.

Back on road, skirt Sumner and Puyallup and soon enjoy what's known to STPers as "The Hill": a one-mile stretch of 72nd Street E. that climbs a hair over 300 feet and throws in a dastardly pitch at 15 percent. Continuing inland, the route trends in a southwest direction, bypassing Tacoma and Olympia, while following ever-more rural roads and highways through Spanaway, Roy, and eventually, at the 207-mile mark, Yelm. Here, the route hops back on paved trail, the lovely Yelm–Tenino Trail which 13 miles later, delivers to the small town of Tenino.

And thus begins the route's most extended stretch of rural, low-traffic riding: about 90 miles of country roads and low-traffic state highway through rolling prairie and the Newaukum and Cowlitz river valleys. Sure, there are a few towns and small cities along the way—Centralia, Chehalis, Kelso, Woodland, and so on—but after riding through the fifteenth biggest metro area in the United States, this part feels deserted. The above towns are welcome opportunities for food, drink, and lodging.

Just north of Woodland, on the Lewis River, you're treated to the route's toughest climb—Green Mountain Road, which gains 720 feet in just 1.4 miles and boasts a pitch at 18 percent. Yikes! Its descent is just as steep; be careful as you roll into Woodland at the route's 304-mile mark.

From here, the route's remaining 25 miles follow rural and suburban Clark County roadways, becoming progressively busier and more urban as you approach and enter Vancouver, the state's fourth largest city. Finish the ride at Fort Vancouver, a National Historic Site.

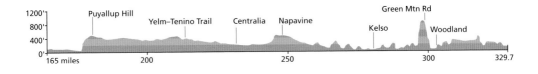

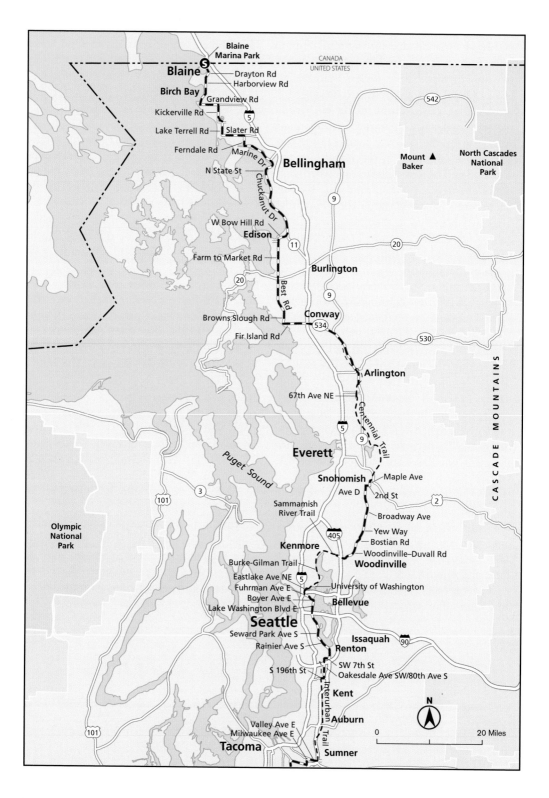

Blaine
Marina Park

CANADA
UNITED STATES

Blaine Ⓢ
—— Drayton Rd
—— Harborview Rd
Birch Bay
—— Grandview Rd
Kickerville Rd ——
Lake Terrell Rd —— Slater Rd
Ferndale Rd —— Marine Dr
N State St —— **Bellingham**

Mount ▲
Baker

North Cascades
National
Park

W Bow Hill Rd
Edison
Farm to Market Rd
Burlington

Browns Slough Rd
Fir Island Rd
Conway

Best Rd
Chuckanut Dr

Arlington

67th Ave NE

Centennial Trail

Puget Sound

Everett

Snohomish —— Maple Ave
Ave D
2nd St
Sammamish
River Trail —— Broadway Ave
Yew Way
Bostian Rd
Kenmore —— Woodinville–Duvall Rd
Burke-Gilman Trail —— **Woodinville**
Eastlake Ave NE
Fuhrman Ave E —— University of Washington
Boyer Ave E
Lake Washington Blvd E —— **Bellevue**
Seattle
Seward Park Ave S
Rainier Ave S —— **Issaquah**
Renton
SW 7th St
S 196th St —— Oakesdale Ave SW/80th Ave S

Interurban Trail

Kent

Auburn

Olympic
National
Park

Valley Ave E
Milwaukee Ave E

Tacoma —— **Sumner**

0   20 Miles

N

CASCADE MOUNTAINS

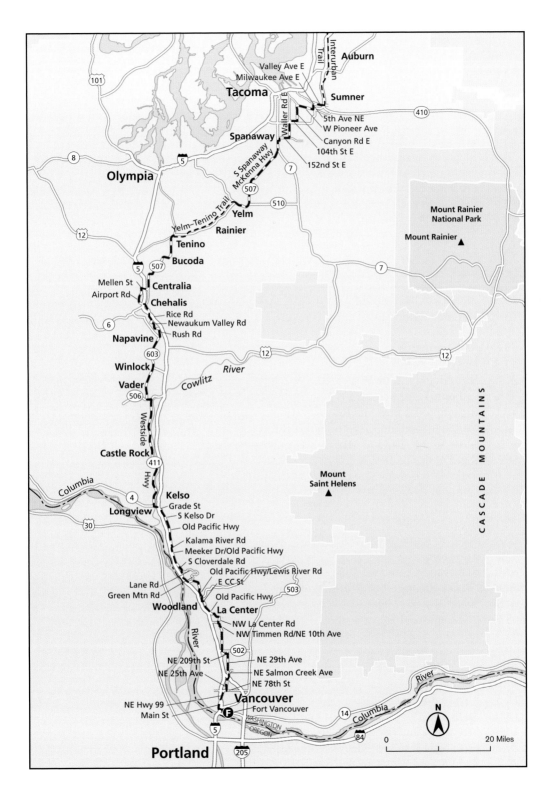

0.0	In Blaine, head northeast on Marine Dr.
0.2	Right onto Peace Portal Dr.
3.2	Right onto Drayton Rd.
4.1	Slight left onto Harborview Rd.
5.7	Left onto Birch Bay Dr. Birch Bay.
6.9	Right to stay on Birch Bay Dr.
8.8	Left onto Point Whitehorn Rd.
9.4	Left onto Grandview Rd.
12.4	Right onto Kickerville Rd.
14.4	Left onto Rainbow Rd.
16.1	Right onto Lake Terrell Rd.
18.1	Left onto Slater Rd.
22.1	Right onto Ferndale Rd.
24.0	Left onto Marine Dr.
25.5	Right onto Bancroft Rd.
26.1	Left onto Marine Dr.
28.3	Bellingham.
29.8	Right onto F St.
29.9	Left onto Roeder Ave.
30.6	Right onto N. State St.
33.2	Left onto Chuckanut Dr.
46.1	Right onto W. Bow Hill Rd.
47.4	Continue south on Farm to Market Rd.
55.2	Cross SR 20. (Farm to Market Rd. becomes Best Rd.)
60.3	Right to stay on Best Rd.
61.6	Right onto Browns Slough Rd./Fir Island Rd.
62.9	Left onto Fir Island Rd.
66.7	Left onto Pioneer Hwy. (SR 534). Conway.
72.3	Right onto SR 9 S.
72.4	Turn left to stay on SR 9 S.
82.5	Arlington.
82.6	Right onto Centennial Trail.
104.9	Sharp right onto Pine Ave. Snohomish.
104.9	Sharp left onto Maple Ave.
105.5	Right onto 2nd St.
105.9	Left onto Ave D. (Becomes Airport Wy., then Springhetti Rd.)
109.1	Left onto Broadway Ave.
113.8	Bear right onto Yew Wy.
114.3	Left onto Paradise Lake Rd.
114.5	Right onto Bostian Rd.
118.0	Right onto NE Woodinville–Duvall Rd.
118.6	Left to stay on NE Woodinville–Duvall Rd.
120.1	Left onto 131st Ave. NE. Woodinville.
120.2	Right toward Sammamish River Trail.

123.1	Right onto Burke-Gilman Trail. Kenmore.
136.5	Right onto Brooklyn Ave. NE. University of Washington.
136.6	Left onto NE Campus Pkwy.
136.8	Slight left toward Eastlake Ave. NE/University Bridge.
137.1	Left onto Fuhrman Ave. E.
138.1	Slight right onto Boyer Ave. E.
138.9	Right onto Lake Washington Blvd. E.
146.0	Right onto S. Juneau St.
146.0	Left onto Seward Park Ave. S.
146.5	Bear left to stay on Seward Park Ave. S.
148.3	Left onto Rainier Ave. S.
152.7	Right onto SW 7th St. Renton.
153.6	Left onto Oakesdale Ave. SW. (Becomes 80th Ave. S.)
156.9	Right onto S. 196th St.
157.4	Left at 72nd Ave. S. onto Interurban Trail.
160.5	Kent.
166.0	Auburn.
169.0	Right onto 3rd Ave. SW.
169.1	Left onto West Valley Hwy. S.
173.5	Left onto Sumner Heights Dr. E. Sumner.
173.6	Right onto Valley Ave. E.
175.2	Left onto Milwaukee Ave. E.
176.1	Right onto 5th Ave. NE. Puyallup.
176.5	Left onto 3rd St. NW.
176.6	Right onto W. Stewart Ave.
176.7	Left onto 5th St. NW.
176.9	Right onto W. Pioneer Ave.
178.7	Continue straight onto 72nd St E.
179.7	Left onto Canyon Rd. E.
181.8	Right onto 104th St. E.
183.3	Left onto Waller Rd. E.
186.7	Right onto 152nd St. E.
188.6	Left onto B St. E.
189.1	Right onto 159th St. E.
189.3	Left onto Pacific Ave. S./SR 7. Spanaway.
191.3	Slight right onto SR 507 S./Spanaway McKenna Hwy.
199.0	Left to stay on SR 507. Roy.
206.7	Left onto Railroad St. SW. Yelm.
206.8	Left onto Yelm–Tenino Trail.
220.5	Left onto W. Park Ave. Tenino.
220.9	Right onto W. 6th Ave.
221.1	Left onto SR 507 S./Bucoda Hwy. SE.
224.8	Bucoda.
232.0	Centralia.
233.5	Right onto W. Cherry St.
233.7	Left onto Alder St.

234.0	Right onto Mellen St.
234.5	Left onto Airport Rd.
238.4	Chehalis. Road becomes NW West St.
238.8	Right onto NW Front St.
238.9	Left onto NW Pacific Ave.
239.4	Left onto SW John St.
239.4	SW John St. turns right and becomes SW William Ave.
239.9	Right onto SW 9th St.
239.9	Left onto SW Pacific Ave.
240.3	Right onto 13th St. Interchange/SW Parkland Dr. (Becomes Rice Rd.)
243.0	Right onto La Bree Rd. (Becomes Newaukum Valley Rd.)
245.8	Right onto Rush Rd.
247.5	Right onto E. Washington St. Napavine.
247.6	Left onto SW Birch Ave./SR 603.
254.0	Winlock.
260.7	Left onto SR 506 E. Vader.
261.1	Right onto Main St.
261.2	Left onto 8th St.
261.9	Right onto Westside Hwy.
271.1	Castle Rock. Road becomes SR 411.
281.5	Longview. Left onto Allen St. Cross Cowlitz River into Kelso.
281.9	Right onto 4th Ave. S. Just ahead, bear left onto Oak St.
282.0	Slight right onto Grade St.
282.9	Right to stay on Grade St.
283.6	Right onto S. Kelso Dr.
285.3	S. Kelso Dr. turns left and becomes Old Pacific Hwy. S.
288.0	Slight left onto Old Hwy 99 S./Old Pacific Hwy. S.
290.2	Right onto Kalama River Rd.
290.3	Left onto Meeker Dr./Old Pacific Hwy.
296.0	Right onto S. Cloverdale Rd.
297.5	Right to stay on S. Cloverdale Rd.
298.2	Left onto Lane Rd. Big hill.
299.4	Slight right onto Green Mountain Rd.
302.8	Left onto Old Pacific Hwy. (Becomes Lewis River Rd.)
304.1	Left onto East CC St. Woodland.
304.3	Right onto NW Pacific Hwy.
309.2	La Center. Road becomes NW La Center Rd.
310.2	Left onto NW Timmen Rd. (Becomes NE 10th Ave.)
316.0	Left onto NE 209th St.
317.0	Right onto NE 29th Ave.
320.8	Left onto NE 134th St.
320.9	Right onto NE Salmon Creek Ave.
321.8	Right onto NE 119th St.
322.0	Left onto NE 26th Ave.
322.5	NE 26th Ave. turns left and becomes NE 109th St.

322.6	Right onto NE 28th Ave.
322.9	Right onto NE 104th St.
322.9	Left onto NE 27th Ave.
323.1	Right onto NE 100th St.
323.3	Left onto NE 23rd Ave.
323.4	Left onto NE 99th St.
323.4	Right onto NE 25th Ave.
324.4	Right onto NE 78th St.
325.2	Left onto NE Hwy 99. (Becomes Main St.) Vancouver.
328.4	Left onto E. 15th St.
328.9	Right onto Fort Vancouver Wy.
329.1	Left onto E. Evergreen Blvd.
329.7	Right into Fort Vancouver.

Riders cross the windswept flats of Western Whatcom County.

WASHINGTON BIKING

Here are some reources, offering valuable information on places to ride, people to ride with, and special events.

CYCLING CLUBS

Baddlands Cycling Club, Spokane; www.baddlands.org

B.I.K.E.S. Club of Snohomish County; www.bikesclub.org. Sponsor of the McClinchy Mile.

Boeing Employees' Bicycle Club, Seattle; www.bebc-seattle.org. You need to be associated with Boeing to be a member but not to participate in their rides.

Capital Bicycling Club, Olympia; www.capitalbicycleclub.org

Cascade Bicycle Club, Seattle; www.cascade.org. The area's largest club; sponsor of the Chilly Hilly, Seattle to Portland (STP), annual Bike Expo, and many other events.

Chinook Cycling Club, Yakima; www.chinookcycling.com

COGS (Cyclists of Greater Seattle), Seattle; www.cyclistsofgreaterseattle.org

Different Spokes, Seattle; www.differentspokes.org

Easy Riders Cycling Club, Seattle; www.seattleeasyriders.net

Evergreen Tandem Club, Puget Sound; www.evergreentandemclub.org

Marymoor Velodrome Association, Redmond; www.velodrome.org/mva

Methow Valley Sports Trail Association, Methow Valley; www.mvsta.com

Mountaineers; www.mountaineers.org. Some local chapters have cycling outings.

Mount Baker Bicycle Club, Bellingham; www.mtbakerbikeclub.org

Native Planet Cycling Social Group, Puget Sound region; www.facebook.com/groups /nativeplanetcycling

Port Townsend Bicycle Association, Port Townsend; www.ptbikes.org

Redmond Cycling Club, Redmond; www.redmondcyclingclub.org. Sponsor of Ride Around Mount Rainier in One Day (RAMROD); club slogan: "Where hill is not a four letter word."

Seattle Bicycle Club, Seattle; www.seattlebicycle.org. Sponsors social rides and a series of short tours around Washington State each summer.

Seattle International Randonneurs; www.seattlerandonneur.org. A club focused on randon-neuring—long-distance, unsupported, noncompetitive cycling.

Skagit Bicycle Club, Mount Vernon; www.skagitbicycleclub.org

Spokane Rocket Velo, Spokane; www.spokanerocketvelo.com

Squeaky Wheels, Bainbridge Island; www.sqeakywheels.org

< Stunning Mount Shuksan through the spokes

Tahoma Wheelmen's Bicycle Club, Tahoma; www.twbc.org. Sponsor of the Daffodil Classic.

Tri-City Bicycle Club, Richland; www.tricitybicycleclub.org

Vancouver Bicycle Club, Vancouver, www.vbc-usa.com

Walla Walla Valley Cycling, Walla Walla; www.wwvalleycycling.com

Wenatchee Valley Velo, Wenatchee; www.bikewenatchee.org

West Sound Cycling Club, Silverdale; www.westsoundcycling.com

Whidbey Island Bicycle Club, Whidbey Island; www.whidbeybicycleclub.org

ADVOCACY

Bicycle Alliance of Washington, Seattle; www.bicyclealliance.org. Among its many safety-related activities, BAW operates the Safe Routes to School program; offices co-located with Bikestation Seattle in Pioneer Square. (Many bike clubs also act as advocacy groups.)

BIKE MAPS

COUNTY

King: www.kingcounty.gov/transportation/kcdot/roads/bicycling.aspx
Kitsap: www.visitkitsap.com
Mason: www.co.mason.wa.us/forms/parks/rec_map.pdf
Pierce: www.co.pierce.wa.us/pc/abtus/ourorg/pwu/tpp/nonmotor/bicycle.htm
Skagit: www.beactiveskagit.org/uploads/Bike_Map.pdf
Snohomish: www.communitytransit.org/FAQs/BikeMaps.cfm
Thurston: www.trpcmaps.org/webmaps/bikemap/gbikemap.htm

CITY

Seattle: www.seattle.gov/transportation/bikemaps.htm

STATE

A Washington bicycle map showing the average daily traffic of major roads and highways across the state—and highways where bicycles are prohibited—can be ordered through the state Department of Transportation: www.wsdot.wa.gov/bike/statemap.htm.

CYCLING EVENTS

Here's a sampling of some organized annual cycling events throughout Washington.

FEBRUARY

Chilly Hilly, Bainbridge Island; www.cascade.org

MARCH
Gran Fondo Ephrata, Ephrata; www.beezleyburn.com
McClinchy Mile, Arlington; www.bikesclub.org

APRIL
Daffodil Classic, Orting; www.twbc.org
Northwest Crank, Wenatchee; www.northwestcrank.com
Tulip Pedal, La Connor; www.skagitems.com/safe-kids-skagit-county/annual-tulip-pedal

MAY
Camano Climb, Camano Island; www.stanwoodvelosport.com
Crime Stoppers Canyon for a Day, Yakima; www.crimestoppersyakco.org
Group Health Inland Empire Century, Richland; www.inlandempirecentury.org
Lilac Century and Family Ride, Spokane; www.northdivision.com
May Day Metric, Federal Way; www.maydaymetric.net
Ride Around Clark County (RACC), Vancouver; www.vbc-usa.com
Seattle Tour de Cure, Redmond; www.diabetes.org/tour
7 Hills of Kirkland, Kirkland; www.7hillskirkland.org
Skagit Spring Classic, Burlington; www.skagitspringclassic.org

JUNE
Ann Weatherill Cycling Classic, Walla Walla; www.wheatlandwheelers.com
Apple Century Ride, Wenatchee; www.applebikeride.com
Cannonball, Seattle; www.redmondcyclingclub.org
Chelan Century Challenge, Chelan; www.chelancenturychallenge.com
Flying Wheels Summer Century, Redmond; www.cascade.org
Mount Adams Country Bicycle Tour, Trout Lake; www.troutlake.org
Peninsula Metric Century, Southworth and Gig Harbor; www.twbc.org
Rock and Ride, Quincy; www.quincyvalley.org
Swan Century and Family Fun Riders, Sedro-Woolley; www.swancentury.com
Tour de Blast, Toutle; www.tourdeblast.com
Tour de Pierce, Puyallup; www.piercecountywa.org/parks
Two County Double Metric Century, Olympia; www.capitalbicycleclub.org

JULY
Group Health Seattle to Portland Bicycle Classic (STP), Seattle; www.cascade.org
Red Spoke, Redmond; www.redspoke.org
Ride Around Mount Rainier in One Day (RAMROD), Enumclaw; www.redmondcycling club.org
Seattle to Spokane (S2S), Lake City; www.redmondcyclingclub.org/index.html
Tour de Kitsap, Silverdale; www.westsoundcycling.com
Tour de Whatcom, Bellingham; www.tourdewhatcom.com

AUGUST

Ride Around Puget Sound (RAPSody), Tacoma; www.rapsodybikeride.com
Ride Around Washington (RAW), Raymond; www.cascade.org
RSVP, Seattle; www.cascade.org
Tour de Peaks, North Bend; www.tourdepeaks.com
TRYBR, Tenino; www.capitalbicycleclub.org

SEPTEMBER

Chuckanut Century, Bellingham; www.mtbakerbikeclub.org
Gran Fondo Walla Walla, Walla Walla; www.smmc.com
High Pass Challenge, Seattle; www.cascade.org
Kitsap Color Classic, Edmonds; www.cascade.org
Methow Valley Fall Bike Festival, Winthrop; www.mvsta.com
Mount Baker Hill Climb (Ride 542), Bellingham; www.festival542.com
Spoke Fest, Spokane; www.spokefest.com
Tour de Whidbey, Whidbey Island; www.whidbeygen.org/whidbeygeneralhospital
foundation/tourdewhidbey
Trek Tri-Island, Anacortes; www.cleanairadventures.org

OCTOBER

Manastash Metric Century, Ellensburg; www.rsvp-wa.org/ellensburg

INDEX

ABOUT THE AUTHOR

Mike McQuaide has written outdoor, travel, and lifestyle stories for everyone from *Adventure Cyclist* and *Runner's World* to *Sunset* and *Outside* as well as numerous other publications and websites. Currently, he writes and shoots photographs regularly for the *Seattle Times* and *Adventures NW*. McQuaide has written five books on outdoor recreation and travel including *Day Hike! Central Cascades* and *Insiders Guide to Bellingham and Mount Baker*. An avid road cyclist and mountain biker, McQuaide has finished Ironman triathlons in Arizona and Idaho, an eight-hour mountain bike race in California, Seattle-to-Portland (STP) in a day, the mega-hilly Mount Shasta Summit Century, and has twice completed the 154-mile Ride Around Mount Rainier in One Day (RAMROD). His bike-centric blog is www.mcqview.blogspot.com.

THE MOUNTAINEERS, founded in 1906, is a nonprofit outdoor activity and conservation organization whose mission is "to explore, study, preserve, and enjoy the natural beauty of the outdoors…" Based in Seattle, Washington, it is now one of the largest such organizations in the United States, with seven branches throughout Washington State.

The Mountaineers sponsors both classes and year-round outdoor activities in the Pacific Northwest, which include hiking, mountain climbing, ski-touring, snowshoeing, bicycling, camping, canoeing and kayaking, nature study, sailing, and adventure travel. The Mountaineers' conservation division supports environmental causes through educational activities, sponsoring legislation, and presenting informational programs.

All activities are led by skilled, experienced volunteers, who are dedicated to promoting safe and responsible enjoyment and preservation of the outdoors.

If you would like to participate in these organized outdoor activities or programs, consider a membership in The Mountaineers. For information and an application, write or call The Mountaineers Program Center, 7700 Sand Point Way NE, Seattle, WA 98115-3996; phone 206-521-6001; visit www.mountaineers.org; or email clubmail@mountaineers.org.

The Mountaineers Books, an active, nonprofit publishing program of The Mountaineers, produces guidebooks, instructional texts, historical works, natural history guides, and works on environmental conservation. All books produced by The Mountaineers Books fulfill the mission of The Mountaineers. Visit www.mountaineersbooks.org to find details about all our titles and the latest author events, as well as videos, web clips, links, and more!

The Mountaineers Books
1001 SW Klickitat Way, Suite 201
Seattle, WA 98134
800-553-4453
mbooks@mountaineersbooks.org

The Mountaineers Books is proud to be a corporate sponsor of The Leave No Trace Center for Outdoor Ethics, whose mission is to promote and inspire responsible outdoor recreation through education, research, and partnerships. The Leave No Trace program is focused specifically on human-powered (nonmotorized) recreation.

Leave No Trace strives to educate visitors about the nature of their recreational impacts and offers techniques to prevent and minimize such impacts. Leave No Trace is best understood as an educational and ethical program, not as a set of rules and regulations.

For more information, visit www.lnt.org, or call 800-332-4100.

OTHER TITLES YOU MIGHT ENJOY FROM THE MOUNTAINEERS BOOKS

75 Classic Rides: Oregon
The Best Road Biking Routes
Jim Moore
The "classic" routes for one of the nation's top cycling destinations—in full color

Biking Puget Sound
50 Rides from Olympia to the San Juans
Bill Thorness
The ultimate guide to exploring the Puget Sound region on two wheels

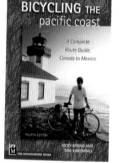

Bicycling the Pacific Coast
A Complete Route Guide, Canada to Mexico, 4th Edition
Tom Kirkendall & Vicky Spring
If you're ready for the Big Ride, this is your guide.

Cycling the Great Divide
From Canada to Mexico on America's Premier Long-Distance Mountain Bike Route
Michael McCoy
Get off the road and onto the rugged passes of the Continental Divide!

The Bar Mitzvah and the Beast
One Family's Cross-Country Ride of Passage by Bike
Matt Biers-Ariel
The light-hearted and hilarious story of an ordinary family's extraordinary journey

The Mountaineers Books has more than 500 outdoor recreation titles in print.
For more details, visit
www.mountaineersbooks.org